# Speaking Up for Animals

# Speaking Up for Animals

## An Anthology of Women's Voices

Edited by
Lisa Kemmerer

LONDON AND NEW YORK

First published 2012 by Paradigm Publishers

Published 2016 by Routledge
2 Park Square, Milton Park, Abingdon, Oxon OX14 4RN
711 Third Avenue, New York, NY 10017, USA

*Routledge is an imprint of the Taylor & Francis Group, an informa business*

Copyright © 2012 Lisa Kemmerer

All rights reserved. No part of this book may be reprinted or reproduced or utilised in any form or by any electronic, mechanical, or other means, now known or hereafter invented, including photocopying and recording, or in any information storage or retrieval system, without permission in writing from the publishers.

Notice:
Product or corporate names may be trademarks or registered trademarks, and are used only for identification and explanation without intent to infringe.

Library of Congress Cataloging-in-Publication Data
Speaking up for animals : an anthology of women's voices / edited by Lisa Kemmerer.
  p. cm.
 Includes index.
 ISBN 978-1-61205-087-4 (hardcover : alk. paper) — ISBN 978-1-61205-088-1 (pbk. : alk. paper)
 1. Animal rights movement. 2. Animal rights. 3. Animal welfare. I. Kemmerer, Lisa. II. Title.
 HV4708.S625 2011
 179'.3—dc23

                                                                             2011022818

Designed and Typeset by Straight Creek Bookmakers.

ISBN 13: 978-1-61205-087-4 (hbk)
ISBN 13: 978-1-61205-088-1 (pbk)

# Contents

| | | |
|---|---|---|
| *Dedication and Acknowledgments* | | *vii* |
| *Foreword*, Carol J. Adams | | *ix* |
| Introduction | | 1 |
| | Lisa Kemmerer | |

## Part I  Pondering What I Put in My Mouth

| | | |
|---|---|---|
| CHAPTER 1 | Weekends at the Mall with a Pig<br>*Dana Medoro* | 37 |
| CHAPTER 2 | On the Road with Open Rescue<br>*Patty Mark* | 45 |
| CHAPTER 3 | No One Left Behind<br>*Kymberlie Adams Matthews* | 55 |
| CHAPTER 4 | That's Some Sheep<br>*Lorri Houston* | 61 |
| CHAPTER 5 | Slaughtergate: Investigating Nonenforcement of Farmed Animal Laws<br>*Gail A. Eisnitz* | 71 |
| CHAPTER 6 | The Art of Love<br>*Sue Coe* | 79 |
| CHAPTER 7 | Here I Stand, by Faith<br>*Linda Elkin McDaniel* | 85 |
| CHAPTER 8 | The Fiercest Predators of the Sea<br>*Heather Moore* | 95 |

## Part II  Working for Wildlife

| | | |
|---|---|---|
| CHAPTER 9 | Pinnipeds in Peril: Marine Mammal Rescue<br>*Sue Pemberton* | 109 |
| CHAPTER 10 | The Pen Is Mightier Than the Sword<br>*Phaik Kee Lim* | 117 |
| CHAPTER 11 | The Meaning of Life<br>*Deborah D. Misotti* | 123 |
| CHAPTER 12 | Little Dog of Safety Bay<br>*Lynette Shanley* | 131 |
| CHAPTER 13 | A Whole New World: Rescue and Re-Education in Southeast Asia<br>*Amy Corrigan* | 139 |

## Part III  Potpourri—From Dancing Bears to Undercover Investigation

| | | |
|---|---|---|
| CHAPTER 14 | A Fight for Justice<br>*Anuradha Sawhney* | 151 |
| CHAPTER 15 | Using My Voice<br>*Kris "Risa" Candour* | 159 |
| CHAPTER 16 | Loving Life in Lebanon<br>*Joelle El-Massih* | 169 |
| CHAPTER 17 | Animal Ways<br>*Gay Bradshaw* | 177 |
| CHAPTER 18 | From the Files of Agent Nerd<br>*Michele Rokke* | 185 |

*Index*  197
*About the Editor*  201

# Dedication and Acknowledgments

I am grateful to the women in this anthology for their courageous commitment to animal advocacy, and for sharing their stories, experience, and expertise. The social justice work undertaken by these women—and by thousands of other animal advocates around the world—is among the most difficult of undertakings. But such work is essential if we are to move toward justice.

I dedicate this book to animal liberationists everywhere, and to the animals who anxiously await reprieve from their ongoing suffering.

Special thanks to my sister, Jan, for suggesting that I create this anthology, and for locating contributors. Also many thanks to a fellow activist and friend, Alex Bury.

# Foreword

## Action, Engagement, Remembering—
## All Together Now

*Carol J. Adams*

In her important book on violence and its consequences, *Trauma and Recovery*, Judith Herman writes, "All the perpetrator asks is that the bystander do nothing. He appeals to the universal desire to see, hear, and speak no evil. The victim on the contrary asks the bystander to share the burden of pain. The victim demands action, engagement, and remembering." I have lived with these powerful words for almost two decades now, and, to me, they underscore why individual activism matters; it matters because "the victim demands action, engagement, and remembering."

In this book you will encounter stories from the lives of women who understood at a deep, personal level just what this means. You will find eighteen individual stories of action, engagement, and remembering.

Lisa Kemmerer has done a magisterial job of identifying some of the different paths in which women have expressed their engagement, refined their activism, and remembered, always remembered, why they are doing this. Or rather, *for whom* they are doing this. They share the burden of pain: a thirsty pig, a thirsty downed cow, a goat with both of his ears cut off, a rescued turkey with an abscessed foot, a baby seal crying "ma." They work for the Taiping Four (illegally imprisoned gorillas), and Ruby the rust-colored ape. They sing with gibbons, and cradle a dying elephant. They spend years negotiating the release of two sun bears, Ompoom and Apec. They nurse a slow loris whose leg was amputated after being caught in a snare. They remember the dusky Brown Swiss cow who adopted two orphan calves. They remember the frightened pig who jumped from a pile of carcasses but was knived before they could reach her. They recognize that screaming parrots in pet-store cages, tigers roaring in zoos, swaying elephants in exhibits, lions howling in grief after their companion is killed by park rangers are not just unhappy animals but *souls in anguish from human-imposed suffering*. Even their attitude toward insects changes.

In these pages are the testimonies of eighteen women I deeply admire. Some are women whose work I know well, some I am meeting for the first time; but each of them, in their unique voice, has something to teach us. Yes, I hope you will feel inspired, as I have been, reading their stories. But their stories are more than inspiring. They expand our sense of what is possible and they affirm how much any individual can help to challenge evil. Because they have seen, heard, and engaged with evil, they show us not only that it can be done, but how to do it.

Along with the women whose voices are represented here, I do not believe it is the job of the human to be the voice of the animals; rather it is the job of the human to hear the wide variety of animals' voices, and to help us hear what the animals experience. I love the voices and the tone, and the subtle humor in these pages. In graphic, yet poetic descriptions, we experience beautiful lives in which engagement is the logical outcome of refusing to be a bystander. They refuse to accept the aroma of suffering.

I love the affirmation we can find in the writing itself against the depressing and overwhelming situations into which the authors have placed themselves. Watch for Patty Mark's comment "he had noticed our good work!" It's the kind of humor I find in a Jane Austen novel, and makes me appreciate all the more that she has retained her humor even when she is placing herself in dangerous situations.

## REFUSING TO BE A BYSTANDER

Why? Why did these women overthrow their lives and place themselves in the midst of incredible evil? Why did they stand up against the perpetrator? How did they learn to dismantle a duck bind; to feed an emaciated elephant or seal; to run a sanctuary; to oversee spaying and neutering of dogs and cats; to dress in such a way as to go undercover in oversized scrubs, big rubber boots, ridiculous safety glasses, and backpacks that hold essential gear for videoing in a vivisection lab?

If you don't know it yet, it is hard to discover you are a bystander. Many of the stories include memories of a time when the author failed to act. (Of course, the fact that many of these instances occurred when they were children or teens—times in our lives when we are incredibly disempowered—is an important factor.) They saw a dog being beaten; they saw hundreds of thousands of hens crowded together in small, decrepit wire cages, and ran out of the shed; they worried for a puppy left alone as the family went on an extended trip, a neighbor's dog outside on a short chain in all kinds of weather; they saw a cow shot in the throat bleed to death; they heard little lambs bleating as they died from slit throats; they saw a sheep being sacrificed to the president ("as a little kid, 'president' meant nothing to me, *but that sheep did.*")

And they recognized what it means to feel like a bystander and they knew ..., they knew that their failure to act had meaning.

Being a bystander burdens one with guilt. The question becomes "could I have stopped what I just witnessed?" They recognize how passivity protects the abuser, not the abused. And the answer becomes, "I might not have been able to stop that specific act of cruelty, but I will take from this encounter of my passivity a reminder: I have the ability to help. What must I do? What can I do?"

And they widen their information about nonhumans, and suddenly it isn't only one dog, one cow, but incredibly overwhelming information: What do you mean birds suffocating in manure pits? What do you mean sows in stalls for all their lives?

We didn't know it was *that* bad, and then suddenly we do.

When there is a moment of awareness, a shifting of the universe follows. Suddenly, the division of human and nonhuman is rendered illogical, unethical, and truly evil. After that moment of awareness, the question becomes: what do we do with the incredible power of the consciousness that animals, together with us, share the possibility of great joy and great suffering in their lives? What do we do with the moment of connection that affirms, "I am in relationship with nonhuman beings as well as human beings"?

When it comes to nonhumans, the line between being a perpetrator and a bystander is especially murky. Institutional oppression needs it that way.

## Restoring the Absent Referent

In *The Sexual Politics of Meat* I introduced the idea that nonhuman animals are the absent referent. In the production of flesh, dairy, and eggs, the animals disappear as individuals and become commodified. Behind every meal from animals is an absence: the death or exploitation of the animal whose place this food takes. The structure of the absent referent both insures and insulates violence. Someone who eats pieces of a dead animal or dairy or eggs not only benefits from this structure of the absent referent, they insure that it continues. They are not just bystanders. They are perpetrators. They don't have to personally hold the knife, operate the stun gun, or lock the pig into her farrowing crate. But they make sure that this happens. The absent referent creates entitlement to benefit from the abuse of others without having knowledge about the abuse. Through the structure of the absent referent, the abuse disappears and the consumed object is experienced without a past, without a biography, without individuality, without a history.

In a culture that moves away from the literal experiences of animals, one aspect of activism is trying to re-present and represent who has disappeared. A papier-mâché life-sized sow taken to malls to educate people about what pigs are experiencing. Writing about and drawing what happens in slaughterhouses. There are no bystanders: you are either restoring the absent referent or accepting and benefiting from the structure of the absent referent by eating nonhumans, using them for sport or entertainment, or "knowledge." It is so true: for every drop of milk there is blood.

As these contributors show, when you have restored the absent referent, you can imagine them dreaming, you can experience their songs, you can create a sanctuary so that a child can experience giving a belly rub to a pig.

## Traumatic Knowledge

The work of restoring the absent referent isn't intellectual work; it is activist work. And as activist work it is fraught with emotion. It exposes us to traumatic knowledge. Traumatic knowledge is the knowledge that a person has about the fate of the other animals. It is painful knowledge—knowledge about everyday practices and everyday sufferings. Traumatic knowledge makes us feel the suffering of animals acutely. It feels relentless. It does not provide relief but intensifies our emotional connections to animals.

Traumatic knowledge causes dissonance/disturbance/disjunction. It is a major challenge to any individual who experiences it and to any movement composed of individuals who bear its truths. It affects us personally, interpersonally, and strategically.

I have been thinking about traumatic knowledge for several years now, since I first encountered the term in Bonnie Smith's *The Gender of*

*History*. Smith describes how amateur history (the history associated with women) consists of "the writing of multiple traumas." She identifies the traumas that women historians of the early nineteenth century would have experienced: They were aware that their rights were eroding in the midst of a time when universal rights were being (supposedly) championed. They or their family members had survived revolutions and wars, and at a personal level had experienced the threat or actuality of rape, poverty, violence, abuse. Smith explains, "death, representing history's immanence, was always on hand."

In my introduction to the new printing of Howard Williams' magnificent nineteenth century historical survey of vegetarianism, *The Ethics of Diet*, I applied Bonnie Smith's idea of traumatic knowledge to the vegetarians who appear in Williams' volume. I explained that "The death of nonhumans, representing a violation of the nonhuman and a violation of the humane desire for the good and the just, is always on hand for vegetarians." I continued, "The knowledge that other animals are being butchered to feed humans, even though other foods are available that require no such Butchery, is also a form of traumatic knowledge."

For vegetarians and vegans, traumatic experiences are reencountered regularly. This adds to the trauma.

Through the structure of the absent referent, our culture protects consumers from the truth about the fate of animals in slaughtering, in zoos, in vivisection labs, in other forms of entertainment and production. We do not regularly encounter the barbarities of the slaughterhouse in our daily lives. Traumatic knowledge means that the referent is restored, and that responsibility to the referent is not only recognized but enacted.

One aspect of traumatic knowledge is that it asks to be heard, to be spoken about, to be named. Another aspect of traumatic knowledge is that it asks that the trauma-provoking experience be stopped.

Yes, it is painful to know what animals endure. It is very difficult to live with this information. But, the response to this is to say, "I would rather know, than not know, and I will find the inner strength to know and not collapse under the weight of knowing."

What these writers show so eloquently is that traumatic knowledge can be integrated within our lives. Yes, we do feel a wide variety of emotions in response to this knowledge about nonhumans. But it will not kill us. We can find ways to say, "Yes, here you are again, this feeling of pain and hurt and desperation. But I know I can live with it. I know it will not destroy me. I can take the time to acknowledge it, take a deep breath, regain my grounding, and then move forward."

The contributors tell us how they have dealt with traumatic knowledge. Patty Mark tells us, "We know *too much* about how animals suffer and die. Counterintuitively, my antidote to this grief, when it becomes too much to bear, is to go where the animals suffer, to be there at their side, and to help however I can."

Gail Eisnitz, after clambering into Dumpsters and documenting slaughterhouse abuses, is healed by a cat who lives with her, as well as supportive mentors and friends.

In these pages we encounter the difficult, heartbreaking work of mending Creation.

Sometimes keeping the big picture in mind helps, and sometimes experiencing the life-saving intervention for an individual animal helps.

Sometimes just knowing that you are working to change these practices, to challenge the perpetration of evil, helps.

Sometimes knowing ahead of time that *there is no such thing as a "worst case of cruelty"—they are all the worst* helps.

Our hearts are marked by memories. They are enlarged, not shrunken. We are taught by these contributors to experience gratitude where we can, to find hope from small changes: yes, a truck filled with chickens and ducks crammed in their crates on their way to slaughter has just driven by, but perhaps you have touched someone to become a vegan.

You live with the knowledge that if you are too depressed you can't help change the world. Keeping up your spirits helps your activism.

Let's say now what is heroic, what is courageous.

It's sitting in a mall in a meat-packing district of a city with a full-size replica of a pig.

It's realizing that four women cannot carry a dying, 300-pound pig across four paddocks and barbed wire fences.

It's watching a free-range pig being killed.

It's trying to save some of the millions of birds trapped in the rubble after tornadoes destroy the warehouses where they "lived," and knowing you can only save proportionally few.

It's hearing squawks and screeches and fading peeps, and digging through to find the broken, bruised, thirsty, hungry chickens.

It's finding debilitated horses being sold to buyers who will kill them.

It's climbing into Dumpsters to retrieve pig carcasses, and documenting the routine dragging, strangling, scalding, and dismembering of fully conscious beings at every single slaughterhouse.

It's helping a premature harbor seal baby grow and get healthy and then saying goodbye as he is released into the water.

It's entering a primate breeding colony without permission.

It's futilely trying to keep alive an emaciated, hypoglycemic, cold Guadalupe fur seal, feeding her hourly. It's living with the risk of grief as you try to help each individual sea animal.

It's exposing yourself, repeatedly, to unabashed cruelty and unfairness. It's learning how to become more cunning and strategic.

I once heard my father telling someone about his World War II experience as a submariner. His captain had said, "Anyone can be brave during a depth charge; there's nothing else you can do but survive it." What is really courageous is to get back into a submarine knowing that at some point you are *going to be* depth charged.

The courage isn't just entering the slaughterhouse. Sure that is courage. But the courage is to go home and know that the next day you will again enter the slaughterhouse, again comb the streets of a war-torn city looking for strays, again enter a factory farm to do an Open Rescue, again face a manure mountain trying to save a few of the animals trying not to drown there.

In activism, no guarantee of outcome exists. You take the stance because you know the absent referent is not absent at all but is instead awaiting acts of solidarity that transform the structures creating the absence.

What these contributors show us is that courage is not so much *an act* as a *commitment to a process*. Each step becomes the self-evident one because of the previous step. They didn't have maps for what they would do; they had conviction. Courage was their commitment to meet whatever happened as they took the next step. And each essay reminds us: you only have to have the courage to take the next step.

There is knowledge of evil but there is the blessing of siding with the victims. Those blessings reveal themselves in many strange and wonderful ways. They are the gifts of activism, and you only know them when you stop being a bystander. As Lynette Shanley writes, "Animals give life meaning and hope. They can help us face pain, and to understand that life is a gift to be cherished."

## All Together Now

All around the world, people are working in quiet, consistent, visionary ways to change the way we humans relate to (read: destroy) nonhuman animals. Take these eighteen essays and imagine that for every voice represented here, there are hundreds, thousands of individuals, showing the life-changing work of action, engagement, and remembrance. Sure it changes the lives of the animals who they are able to help. But as any activist will tell you, it changes us, changes how we live in the world. To be released from the terrible defeat of being a bystander, to be freed from being hooked into dominance and perpetrating violence, gives us new lives, too. Lives that recognize how truly interconnected we all are. As Gay Bradshaw observes, "Whatever we imagined made us different from all other creatures is a fantasy."

What is asked of us as we stop being bystanders? That we do what we can. We can't do everything. But we can do something. We stop being bystanders when we recognize that doing nothing is *not* acceptable. A vegan potluck, a leaflet, giving a book that matters, speaking up and speaking out, contributing money, volunteering, writing letters. The thing is to start. As these stories show, you might not know the path your activism will lead you on, but stepping onto it is a very exciting and important start. We sing, we draw, we work for legislation, we create sanctuaries, we heal sea mammals one at a time, we know that we can do something.

Will those with dominance, those who benefit from dominance, those who adhere to dominant values listen to the voices in these pages—voices who challenge that dominance? Dominance doesn't like to be disturbed. Complacency wants itself undisturbed; complacency wants complacency. It doesn't want words about bystanders, about evil, about perpetrators, about victims. It doesn't want action, engagement, remembering. Complacency just wants to be.

But, here's the most important thing that is affirmed in these pages: these women understand we all can change, they believe in our adaptability. They believe that when you understand what is happening to pigs, or gorillas, or chickens, or dogs and cats, you find that you can change. They believe that everyone can stop being bystanders and perpetrators.

They—who have the reason to lose hope—are the ones who believe in all of us. Now that is earth-shaking news.

A story is told of some willful young people. One of them intensely disliked an elderly woman, who everyone else judged to be very wise. "We'll show her," the young person said. And grabbing a small bird within his two hands, he accosted the old woman.

"Old woman!" he called brusquely.

The old woman approached him.

"Tell me, old woman, is the bird in my hand living or dead?" The young man had decided that if the old woman said the bird was alive, he would crush the bird in his hands and show her to be dead. If the old woman said the bird was dead, the young man would release the bird into the air. Either way, the young man would show that the old woman was wrong.

The old woman appraised the young person as she stood before him. She could see the tension in the young man's arms, the hands cupped together. She watched as the young man defiantly repeated the question, "Is the bird in my hand living or dead?" The old woman paused a moment and then replied:

"It's in your hands."

In these pages, we find diverse experiences united in one anthology; diverse activisms represented together; women's activism for animals, all together now. And the incredible thing is that after all they have seen, they still believe in you, the reader.

When it comes to nonhumans, there are no bystanders. When it comes to the fate of nonhumans, it truly is in your hands.

# Introduction

*Lisa Kemmerer*

> Women should be protected from anyone's exercise of unrighteous power ... but then, so should every other living creature.
> —Mary Ann (Marian) Evans (George Eliot), 1819–1880,
> from a letter ("George")

Abundantly pierced punk teens and older women with simple silver hair filled the large greeting room—females outnumbered males by about ninety-eight to one. Still, the single person in charge, the one who welcomed us from the front pedestal, was a man. I thumbed through the conference program, focusing on keynote speakers: Paul, John, Ken—suspiciously masculine-sounding names. As the weekend wore on, I mingled overwhelmingly with women while listening to a battery of male speakers, most of whom took the time to thank a handful of women for their unwavering dedication—their unpaid, behind-the-scenes work both for animals and to support the men behind the podium.

I had just arrived at my first animal rights conference, but it was clear that I had not arrived at a socially progressive gathering. Here, as elsewhere, men held leading roles while women filled supporting roles. Men spoke while women listened. Men founded organizations, and women joined those organizations. What I did not understand at that time were the many powerful links between patriarchy and factory farming—between the exploitation of women (their lack of voice and power, and their tendency to be exploited by men), and the exploitation of nonhuman animals (their lack of voice and power, and their tendency to be exploited by men). Clearly, neither did the people who had put on the conference.

For those inclined to notice, the similarities between the exploitation and subjugation of women and nonhuman animals are difficult to ignore. For example, Wyeth-Ayerst Laboratories, Inc., produces estrogen replacement called Premarin (also sold under the name Prempro). Premarin is made from the urine of pregnant mares, who are, specifically for this purpose, tethered in small stalls for four or five months out of each year. Their foals—some 40,000 strong—are shipped off to be fattened and slaughtered after a mere four months, when they would normally still be nursing.

The Premarin market exists because of the archaic assumption that a woman's body is problematic, that there is something inherently not-quite-right about female biology, and that women therefore require the care of medical professionals—traditionally males (Ehrenreich and English 6). Premarin is on the market because people have been led to believe that a woman's natural ways of aging are a sickness in need of a cure. This attitude toward aging is indubitably linked with the patriarchal, exploitative view of females as childbearers, a view which makes a woman's aging and menopause appear to be problematic and undesirable. "Marketed as a cure for menopause, Premarin hurts both female horses and female humans in order to provide profits for a pharmaceutical corporation" ("Sexism"). Needless to say, most corporations are owned and managed by males.

Hunting provides another apt example. In Euro-American cultures (and many other human communities), both hunting and heterosexual sex are assumed to be fundamental to manliness. This ridiculous link between sex with women and killing "wild" animals is made explicit in the language of the hunt: Bullets are called "balls," firing is referred to as "discharge," hitting a body with a bullet is called "penetration," and firing prematurely is called "premature discharge" (Kheel, "License" 91–92).

Other forms of animal exploitation show similar linguistic evidence of an exploitative patriarchal viewpoint. For example, the terms "livestock" and "cunt" similarly present individuals as means to others' ends, "Live stock" presents a living, thinking, feeling, individual as disembodied merchandise awaiting sale, while "cunt" presents a living, thinking, feeling, individual as a disembodied vagina awaiting sex. Similarly, elk and moose are often called "game" and are shot for sport; incidentally female elk and moose are also labeled as "cows"—like those we exploit for their nursing milk and flesh. And, of course, "cow" is also a derogatory term for human females.

Hunting "ethics" are also a product of patriarchy. They are "predicated on the need to harness an aggressive, sexual energy and to channel [this energy] in appropriate ways," in order to foster "the continuation of man's aggressive drive" (Kheel, "License" 92, 95). This aggressive drive is not questioned, but merely channeled.

When pressed, hunters who claim that they just want "to be out in the wilderness," will admit that the kill is essential—or at least the hope of a kill. As it turns out, there is no correlation between hunting and hiking, climbing, backpacking, kayaking, or any other outdoor activity. Hunters do not purposefully linger in the woods after a kill, but quickly begin the process of preparing to head home with the corpse. For hunters, the kill is the climax—the most important moment. They are not driving into the woods (or sometimes actually walking) for the sake of beauty, but in the hope of a kill. The kill can be likened to male orgasm. Sex is traditionally thought to be over when the man has an orgasm, and the hunt is never so decisively over as it is after a successful kill. "Without the pursuit of orgasm, sex typically is thought to have no meaning or narrative structure; without the intent to kill, the hunt, we are told, has none as well" (Kheel, "License" 91). As a teacher, I impatiently listened to a young man matter-of-factly defend the importance of hunting because he found the experience "orgasmic." From his point of view, all that mattered was how exciting and wonderful the experience was for him. The "side effects" of the man's preferred action—the experience of the deer and the woman—are deemed to be so irrelevant that they are not even mentioned.

In patriarchal cultures men hold the lion's share of power, and therefore tend to control sex. In the United States, for example, sexual assault—including rape—is common. Nearly 20 percent of the U.S. female population has suffered rape or attempted rape ("Facts"). Rape is generally about power, not sex. Rapists simply enact, albeit in an illegal manner that is shunned by the majority, a general cultural tendency to view females as "objects that can be used for pleasure without regard for [a woman's] wishes or subjective experiences" ("Sexism"). The sex trade is also flourishing under the patriarchal objectification of women, paid for by men who are willing and able to own or rent a girl (or sometimes a woman) for sex. Those who are exploited are comparatively powerless, and cannot refuse sexual advances or deny the wishes of those who pay (someone else) for their services.

In these situations and many others, men own and control the bodies of women as they own and control the bodies of sows and cows and hens. Sexual exploitation of human females for the benefit of males is mirrored in contemporary animal industries. Men who control animal industries exploit females for their reproductive abilities as if nonhuman animals were objects devoid of will and sensation. Sows are treated as if they were bacon factories and cows are treated as if they were milk machines. Sows, cows, hens, turkeys, and horses are artificially inseminated to bring profits to the men who control their bodies and their lives. Women in the sex trade are similar to factory farmed females, "Locked up and raped daily, these women and children suffer unspeakable physical and emotional trauma. Like the hens in egg factories, many are murdered when their bodies have become so exhausted by the abuse that [they are] no longer profitable to maintain" ("Sexism").

Even comparatively privileged women in relatively fortunate marriages can readily be likened to sows and cows: Marriage grants a man "legal license to his wife's sexual and reproductive services, [while] the model of animal husbandry grants agribusiness and wildlife managers access to the bodies and reproductive services of other-than-human animals" (Kheel, *Nature* 231). The reproductive abilities of women and other female animals are controlled and exploited by those in power (usually men) and both are devalued as they age and wear out—when they no longer reproduce. Cows, hens, and women are routinely treated as if they were objects to be manipulated in order to satisfy the desires of powerful men, without regard to females' wishes or feelings.

While feminists and animal advocates both struggle against patriarchal exploitation, overtly associating women with nonhuman animals (as I have just done) unsettles many—if not most—feminists (as well as the vast majority of nonfeminists). Such an association is viewed as demeaning, just as it is viewed as demeaning in patriarchal societies to associate men with anything that is feminine—such associations are damaging to men. Similarly, comparing the lowly cow to a woman is viewed as further endangering the already diminished status of women: Overtly associating women with turkeys and pigs is viewed as a "substantial threat" to women (Scholtmeijer 233), because farmed animals are "property"—dumb, despicable, and expendable—and are cruelly exploited as a matter of economic habit. Women, who have tended to be treated similarly, must be extricated from such situations and from any such associations. "The suggestion that the otherness of nonhuman animals can inform the otherness of women, therefore, appears to be counterproductive, to pull women down into a condition of defeat along with the animals" (Scholtmeijer 234).

Consequently, feminists have often highlighted the "otherness" of nonhuman animals while highlighting similarities between women and the men who hold power. Biologically speaking, any two humans will be more similar than a human and any other species. But the position of most women in patriarchal societies is closer to that of chickens and cows than it is to that of men who hold power. Consider, for example, the labels given to human females: bitch, bitch in heat, cow, heifer, sow, pussy, kitten, hen, biddy, chick. When I type "bitch" in Google, and click on "images," I do not find pictures of dogs, as I would expect. Instead, I find pictures of women. Women are also verbally associated with nondomesticated species, like foxes and the cougars. Language tells us much about the place of women in society in relation to men and nonhuman animals.

There is an ugly, unmentioned truth behind a feminist's tendency to associate women with men, rather than with similarly exploited pigs or cattle: Those who purposefully distance women from other female animals hope to liberate female humans *while leaving nonhuman animals in the category of exploitable "other"* (Scholtmeijer 257; Adams, "Feminist" 204). But it is reprehensible for individuals who are seeking release from oppression to purposefully leave others in the dungeons of exploitation—even to condemn others to such exploitation—in the process of working to extricate themselves.

In any event, this selfish approach has not worked, and the reason for this seems somewhat obvious: As long as we foster power-over—whether over pigs or turkeys or women—most human females will remain under the control of men, along with pigs and cows and chickens (who will generally remain yet lower on the rungs of power). In seeking to stand above nonhuman females, women help to maintain a hierarchy through which they are held below men. As long as we support a hierarchy, as long as we support a system which grants some individuals power over other individuals, men will dominate over women. Hierarchies entail power-over, and the power of one individual over another inevitably supports oppression. Those who seek to pass "exploitation 'down' the ladder" (Kappeler 335) will never eradicate oppression, they will simply continue to "mirror patriarchal oppressors" (Dunayer 19). Feminists who "engage in this kind of denial, [who] support and participate in the oppression of the less powerful" in the hope of elevating themselves, are "not only hypocritical" but also engage in a "profound betrayal of [feminism's] deepest commitments" (Adams and Donovan 8).

Women who seek equality must not support the oppression of nonhuman animals. To oppress others while seeking your own autonomy and freedom is selfish and inconsistent. In any event, if women are ever to achieve equality, we must topple hierarchy *en total*. Activists and theorists who fail in this regard adopt the same sort of "exclusionary theorizing" that they ostensibly reject (Gruen 61). Feminists who refuse to acknowledge that they are animals are similar to "men who prefer to ignore that women are human" (Dunayer 19). For those who seek freedom "from violation by the powerful—power and privilege must not be more widely shared, they must be radically dismantled" (Kappeler 335).

## Factory Farming Females[1]

For most women (as for most men) links between sexism and speciesism are not readily apparent. We have been conditioned *not* to see exploitation. For example, men generally have no idea how patriarchy affects women—unless they go out of their way to learn. The same is true for women with regard to cows and pigs and chickens and turkeys. Therefore, this section exposes the realities of speciesist exploitation, more specifically animal agriculture—realities that are purposefully hidden behind closed doors and false advertising.

Both women and nonhuman animals have traditionally been viewed as property—"things" to be owned and controlled by those in power. While the plight of women is linked with that of nonhuman animals through a single system of oppression, through their comparative powerlessness and invisibility, and through sexual exploitation, it is important to elucidate these similarities through concrete examples. Links between women and nonhuman animals are nowhere more apparent than through the vulnerabilities of mothers and their young, and the control of pregnancies and offspring; this particular form of oppression is nowhere more blatant than on factory farms.

### *Reproductive Commodities*

#### Cows
Cows, like humans and other mammals, only lactate when they have given birth. In order to produce milk, cows must be repeatedly, forcibly, artificially impregnated. Each time they are impregnated, cows carry their young for nine months, then their calves are stolen shortly after birth (though they try desperately to defend and protect their young). Cows have a strong mothering instinct (as do most mammals), but how can they protect their newborns against exploitative human oppressors? They invariably lose their babies, and then bawl for days.

The motherless calves are then sold for veal: The veal industry exists because people buy yogurt and ice cream, cheese and milk. The veal industry was created to take advantage of an abundant supply of calves who are merely byproducts of the dairy industry. "Dairy" calves are either killed shortly after birth, and sold as "bob" veal for low-quality dishes (like frozen TV dinners), or they are chained by the neck in a two-by-five-foot wooden crate, where they are unable to turn, and where they can neither stretch nor lie down comfortably. While we drink their mothers' milk, these miserable little beings are given a milk substitute that is deficient in iron and fiber. This creates an anemic, light-colored flesh that is prized by those who purchase veal.

These unfortunate calves are usually slaughtered when they are four months old. The veal industry confines and kills one million calves every year.

Life is no better for those calves who are kept to produce dairy products. "Dairy" calves' tails are "docked" to prevent swishing around udders and equipment. But tails are a cow's best defense against annoying insects in all of the areas they can't otherwise reach. Nonetheless, their tails are docked. During tail docking, "bladed clamps" are secured to a one-month-old calf's tail, then blades cut through flesh, vertebrae, and tendons. These calves are also "disbudded"—the buds from which their horns would normally grow are seared from their skulls. An undercover investigator (Mercy for Animals) who witnessed this procedure noted that the calves were muzzled with cable and their heads were tied to steel fencing. Once the calves were immobilized "workers used a smoking iron to burn out their nascent horns, searing through flesh and bone and leaving behind molten, bloody cavities" ("Dairy's" 11). Despite their bound mouths, the calves bellowed, "wheezed, frothed and strained" ("Dairy's" 11).

When they are old enough to be impregnated and to bear young (only to have both their calf and their milk stolen), they endure mechanized milking for ten out of twelve months per year (including seven months of their nine-month pregnancies). To be milked, cows are herded into a milking parlor with the help of electrified gates, which presumably keep the herd moving, but which can only shock the cattle who are at the back of the herd. These unfortunate cows are perpetually shocked if they are trapped behind other cattle in clogged passageways.

Once in the parlor (a name that elicits images of soft chairs, tea, and books), a cow is locked into place via metal bars on each side of her neck. Milking machines are roughly and hurriedly attached to the cow's teats, and she stands there while her nursing milk, which she generated to feed her calf, is extracted. This process is repeated two or three times each day.

Genetic manipulation and dietary controls cause extraordinary and unnatural milk output—fifty pounds of milk per day. Cows naturally produce just over two tons of milk per year, but recombinant bovine growth hormone (rBGH) and recombinant bovine somatotropin (rBST)—synthetic human-created hormones—have increased milk flow so that cows now provide as much as thirty tons of milk annually, enough for *ten* calves. In this unhealthy and unhappy existence, one in five factory farmed "dairy" cows secretes pus from her udder (which invariably mixes with her milk).

Most cows coming from the dairy industry are pregnant when they are slaughtered. Cows are so exhausted by the dairy process that they are "spent" and sent to slaughter after just four or five years of repeated impregnation, birth, hormone doses, and machine milking. (Those few cows who find their way to sanctuaries can live upwards of twenty years.) "Dairy" cattle are much older than cattle who are slaughtered to produce beef, so their flesh is considered low quality, and is used for soup, burgers, or processed foods.

Many people become vegetarians to avoid supporting cruelty and premature death, but purchasing dairy products causes the slaughter of cattle just as surely as does eating a hamburger: When we buy the nursing milk of mother cows in our local supermarkets, we support the oppression and premature deaths of both "dairy" cows and "veal" calves. It is not financially feasible to keep so many millions of calves and cows—cows who are too young to produce milk, who are males, or who can no longer continue to produce extraordinary quantities of nursing milk. *Both "dairy" cows and their unfortunate young are slaughtered for human consumption while yet young.* Additionally, vegetarians who avoid flesh for moral reasons must remember that "dairy" cows are invasively impregnated, their young are stolen, and then their nursing milk is stolen, and all of this is done because people buy dairy products. While most calves born into the dairy industry live a short and horrific life, mother cows endure prolonged suffering—year after year. Those who are willing to adapt their diet to avoid supporting extreme cruelty and premature death must not shift to a vegetarian diet that increases dairy products. To reduce extreme suffering and premature death, we must cut back on *all* animal products.

Dairy farmers control, manipulate, and capitalize on a cow's reproductive abilities—her nursing milk and her calf—and finally her flesh. To add insult to injury, the dairy industry has convinced consumers that cows' nursing milk is essential for good health. If milk is essential to human health, how have people in China lived so long without dairy products—and with comparatively much less osteoporosis?

Like Premarin, dairy products are completely unnecessary. Like those who produce Premarin, those who produce dairy products have gone to great lengths to make people believe that their product is essential. This is not the case. In truth, the "mammary glands of cows are exploited in order to produce a product that harms the mammary glands of women" ("Sexism"). Milk products have been linked with ovarian and breast cancer ("Cancer") as well as early onset of menses (Cohen). If we aren't willing to quit dairy for the sake of suffering, exploited cows, we ought to quit for our own sake.

**Sows**

Because cows are exploited specially for their female biology—for their nursing milk—it is perhaps easier to grasp the link between sexism and speciesism with regard to cows, and perhaps more difficult for feminists to see the link between the oppression of women and the oppression of sows. A brief visit to a pig farm would quickly put any uncertainty to rest. In lieu of a pig farm tour, an explanation will have to suffice.

Pigs are intelligent and social, in many ways similar to dogs. They are also very tidy: When pigs have sufficient space, they do not defecate in areas where they sleep or eat. More than 95 percent of today's pigs are factory farmed, spending their entire lives crowded in small, concrete, indoor pens. On factory farms, where a few extra feet of cage space reduces profit margins, pigs must live in their own feces, urine, vomit—even amid the corpses of other pigs (as discovered by many undercover agents).

One hundred million pigs are raised and slaughtered every year. Among these unfortunate pigs, breeding sows are the most unfortunate. Like cattle in the dairy industry, sows suffer a continuous cycle of artificial impregnation, controlled birth, and the stealing of their young. During four months of pregnancy, breeding sows are isolated in gestation crates—small metal pens just two feet wide—where they stand on cement floors. Lack of space prevents them from turning, or even lying down comfortably, and the sides of larger sows perpetually rub on surrounding bars.

When it is time to give birth, sows are transferred to similarly cramped farrowing crates, with concrete or metal floors, and bars that prevent mothers from reaching their piglets—while allowing the young to reach the mother's teats. Short chains or rubber straps are sometimes used to immobilize the mother, allowing for perpetual nursing (in order to fatten the piglets for slaughter). This intense, unlimited nursing frequently causes lacerations and painful infections on sows' udders, but they have no choice—they are unable to move.

Normally piglets nurse for about fifteen weeks, but factory farmed piglets are taken from their mothers at just two or three weeks of age. These piglets are weaned in crowded, concrete "nursery" pens surrounded by metal bars, with little more than one square yard of floor space per pig. They are slaughtered at about six months of age, though pigs lucky enough to find a home in a sanctuary can easily live beyond fifteen years.

Five days after her piglets have been taken, a sow is again forcibly, artificially impregnated. Sows endure at least two pregnancies, births, and nursing stints per year, generally giving birth to more than twenty piglets annually. When a sow is no longer considered productive (after birthing four to seven times), she is sent to slaughter, usually at about four years of age.

As with cattle, in a system as cruel as factory farming the lucky ones are slaughtered young. Factory farmed sows, who are repeatedly impregnated and perpetually confined, have weak bones and muscles, heart problems, and frequent urinary tract infections. The concrete that they stand on causes crippling leg disorders, which leads to arthritis, and a lack of exercise causes obesity—which farmers *strive* to create, breeding and feeding pigs so that they will grow as quickly as possible. (Transgenic pigs have recently been bred to grow even faster.) With barely enough room to stand or lie down, and no bedding to speak of, many sows have chronic sores on their shoulders and knees. Respiratory diseases are also common: 70 percent of factory farmed pigs suffer from pneumonia. Despite these common problems, throughout the course of a year one in four commercial pig operations never summons a veterinarian.

Deprivation, chronic pain, and frustration cause sows to adopt neurotic coping behaviors. Sows would normally build a nest of leaves or straw before giving birth. In their barren cells, sows repeatedly and desperately try to build a nest, moving their heads backwards and forwards pointlessly in a rhythmic fashion, gnawing on metal bars that surround them. Overcrowding and boredom also cause aggression, which is why pigs' tails are chopped off and their teeth cut at birth (without anesthesia). Giving pigs more space would allow them to create nests, root, and wallow—normal pig behaviors—which would also prevent neurotic behaviors and aggression. But from an economic point of view, it is cheaper to dock tails and cut teeth than it is to provide pigs with adequate space; a pig's psychosis does not affect a pig farmer's bottom line.

## "Laying" hens

Battery hens are also exploited because of their female biology—because they lay eggs. Factory farmers exploit 300 million "laying" hens each year.

Shortly after hatching, without anesthesia, female chicks are "debeaked"—the tips of their sensitive beaks are sliced off with a hot blade, cutting through bone, cartilage, and soft tissue. This procedure is intended to reduce injuries caused by stressed birds in overcrowded conditions, but it comes with a price: Debeaking causes many fragile little chicks to bleed to death or die of shock, but newly hatched chickens are considered expendable in the poultry industry.

When they are just eighteen weeks old, four or more young hens are placed in crowded 1.5 square foot cages (slightly bigger than your average microwave oven) even though one hen's wing span is roughly 2.5 feet. In these crowded conditions, their wings constantly rub against wire, causing featherless sore spots. Nonetheless, these cages are piled one on top of the other in giant sheds, where the hens remain until they are sent to slaughter.

Hens lay eggs (and cows produce milk) as part of their basic, biological functioning, and they do so in excessive quantities due to biological manipulation—not because they are well cared for or contented. Even the most miserable human, if provided with adequate food, is likely to menstruate (pass eggs) and lactate (produce milk) after birth. Common sense tells us that the same is true for chickens (and cattle). Though these hens are miserable, they ovulate, and when they ovulate they feel a strong nesting urge, which they cannot satisfy in their cramped wire cages. Hens are forced to lay their eggs under their crowded feet, on wire, and their eggs simply roll onto a conveyor belt to be taken away and boxed. Though each hen annually produces upwards of 250 eggs (while their wild counterparts lay roughly twenty eggs per year), factory farmed hens are never permitted to build a nest, sit on their eggs, or tend young—or even step out into the sun or onto dust or grass.

When a hen's egg production goes into a natural decline (after a few months), they are put through "forced molt," in which they are starved and kept in total darkness for as long as eighteen days. This shocks the hens' exhausted bodies into yet another egg-cycle, and simultaneously causes hens to lose a great deal of weight. Some lose more than 25 percent of their body weight, and 5 to 10 percent of the hens die in the course of forced molt—all of the hens suffer terribly. But this cruel practice increases profits by bringing on another cycle of ovulation. Hens who die during forced molt are considered no loss whatsoever to the industry because their egg production has already declined, and factory farmers quickly rid themselves of such birds if they cannot shock them into another laying cycle.

Due to their abnormal rate of ovulation, factory farmed hens sometimes suffer from "cage layer fatigue," a condition in which they become "egg bound," and die because they are too weak to expel yet one more egg. Factory farmed hens also suffer from prolapse (the uterus is expelled along with an egg), egg peritonitis (an inflammation), cancers, severe liver and kidney disease, and infectious bronchitis (caused by living in their own excrement). Because it requires a tremendous amount of calcium to produce egg shells, hens also commonly suffer from calcium deficiencies, and often suffer from broken bones and paralysis.

Chickens at sanctuaries can live up to fifteen years, but factory farmed hens are destroyed roughly one year after they hatch. "Egg-laying" chickens are bred for egg production; they don't grow fast or large enough to bring a profit in the flesh market, so it is not cost-effective to send these birds to slaughter. Millions of spent hens are therefore thrown into wood chippers, alive. Undercover investigators documented Ward Egg Ranch (California) throwing more than 15,000 live, "spent" laying hens into a wood-chipping machine. Despite tremendous outcry from a newly informed and horrified public, the district attorney declined to prosecute, noting that disposing of live hens in a wood-chipper is legal, and is a "common industry practice" ("Factory").

Roughly half of a hen's offspring are males. Like calves exploited for veal in the dairy industry, male chicks are an unwanted byproduct of factory farming. Two hundred million newly hatched male chicks are discarded every year. These chicks are of no economic value to the egg industry (or to the flesh industry, because roosters are too aggressive to be kept in cramped factory-farming conditions); these little fellows are gassed, crushed, or simply thrown into garbage bins, where they dehydrate or asphyxiate, or they are tossed into a grinder or chipper (like their spent mothers). Eyewitness accounts describe struggling, peeping chicks dismembered by metal blades. Their little fluffy bodies, when ground to oblivion, can be sold as fertilizer, or as feed for other farmed animals—who would naturally eat only grass and grains.

When laying hens are sent to slaughter, though just beyond adolescence, they are much older than "broilers," who are raised for flesh. The flesh of "laying" hens is therefore of less value, and is used for soups, baby food, stock cubes, school dinners, pot pies, the restaurant trade, animal food, or other low-grade products, for which their "spent" bodies are shredded.

Please know that you cause extreme suffering if you purchase dairy products or eggs from your local stores. Both of these industries cause extreme, prolonged suffering and premature death. If there was not a market for products like skim milk, omelets, peach yogurt, mozzarella cheese, egg salad sandwiches, and strawberry ice cream, all of the aforementioned suffering would cease. No one person can shut down the entire industry, but every dollar spent on dairy and eggs is a vote for these cruel industries. Every dollar spent on dairy and eggs is a vote in favor of this ongoing exploitation and premature slaughter that targets females: pregnancy, birth, and tending young offspring are central both to female biology and to factory farming.

## "Broiler" hens

Hens are not only exploited for their reproductive abilities, but also for their flesh. Hens in the broiler industry are crowded by the thousands into warehouses that hold up to 100,000 birds. Roosters are far too aggressive to live in these unbearably crowded conditions. Consequently, like hens who are exploited for their eggs, "broilers" are sexed, and females are debeaked just after they hatch, while males are cast into a bin to suffocate, or into a chopper to be ground to bits.

Chickens have natural sleep rhythms that are determined by daylight and darkness. Light deters hens from sleeping, which encourages them to eat too much, which causes them to gain weight rapidly. Most of the windowless sheds that are typical of the battery hen business are therefore equipped with artificial lighting that remains on for most of a twenty-four hour period, perpetually disturbing and manipulating the hens' sleep patterns. Can you imagine being kept awake most of your life—rarely being allowed to sleep soundly, comfortably, or for a full night?

Not only is the lighting manipulated to help fatten hens, but they are also given high-protein feed and growth-promoting antibiotics, and they are genetically altered to make them grow twice as fast, and twice as large, as their recent ancestors. "Broiler" hens reach four pounds—slaughter weight—in just six weeks. But their immature bones cannot possibly support such unnatural weight gain, and these hens live in chronic pain for the last weeks of their short lives. Consequently, factory farmed hens do not move much "because it hurts" (John Webster, *The Guardian* [October 14, 1991] in "An HSUS"). But those who are interested in profits see this as a benefit—a hen who does not attempt to move about freely is likely to gain yet more weight.

Hens trapped in the broiler industry are handled with the expectation that their lives will be very short, and significant losses are expected—individual hens do not matter. The floors of these giant, crowded sheds are quickly covered with excrement, creating lung-damaging air. Broilers stand and lie in their own heaped droppings, developing blisters, ulcers, and burns on their feet, legs, and breasts from living in their own nutrient-rich manure. Because hens in broiler sheds are confined in crowded, unsanitary conditions, thousands succumb to heat prostration, infectious disease, and cancers. Hens that humans manipulate for their flesh also die frequently of heart failure because their hearts and lungs cannot sustain such fast and excessive growth (*Feedstuffs* in "Viva!USA").

"Broiler" hens reach "market weight" just forty-five days after they hatch, at which time workers enter the dismal sheds, grabbing the frightened, overweight birds by a wing, leg, or head—whatever they can grab—then cramming them into crates stacked on trucks. The terror-stricken, plump birds, with weak hearts and fragile bones, dislocate and break hips, legs, and wings; hemorrhage internally; and suffer heart attacks as they try desperately to escape. The end, like their lives in general, is a testament to human cruelty and indifference.

More and more people are moving from "red" flesh to poultry flesh in the hope of staving off heart attacks, strokes, and cancers linked with the consumption of these animal products. This change in demand has bolstered the "broiler" industry.

## Slaughter

Transport and slaughter are as miserable as the lives of factory farmed animals. Mammals are supposed to be "stunned" (rendered unconscious) before they are killed (federal Humane Slaughter Act, 1958), but slaughter (like most contemporary businesses) is shaped and driven by economic factors: In the slaughterhouse, the quicker each animal is killed, the higher the profit margin. Time is money. Workers must be paid for their time, and while one animal's body is on the dismemberment line, no other corpse can be processed. Consequently, speed is essential, which works against our government's extremely minimal attempt to reduce suffering. A USDA survey concluded that stunning was either "unacceptable" or a "serious problem" in 36 percent of sheep and pig slaughterhouses, and 64 percent of cattle slaughterhouses. Even more remarkable, chickens, turkeys, ducks—all poultry—are exempt from the Humane Slaughter Act, *even though 90 percent of those killed in U.S. slaughterhouses are birds*. While slaughter is inherently ugly, contemporary assembly-line slaughter is unconscionable.

Economic considerations also make transport horrific for factory farmed animals. It is cheaper to absorb high transportation mortality rates than it is to pay for enclosed transport trucks. Consequently, though factory farmed animals must travel as much as eighty miles per hour in all weather conditions, they are transported in open trucks, without food, water, or protection from rain, snow, or intense heat. Some farmed animals inevitably freeze to death during transport, while others die of heat stress or suffocation.

When they reach the slaughterhouse, misery is extended and enhanced by a system in which the suffering of nonhuman animals counts for nothing.

Roughly one million factory farmed hens are killed each hour for human consumption. (Turkeys, who are raised and slaughtered in the same way that "broiler" hens are raised and slaughtered, are also killed in large numbers.) On arrival at the slaughter house, hens are dumped onto a fast-moving conveyor belt, but some of the flapping and frightened birds inevitably miss the belt and fall onto the ground. Once on the ground, they are either crushed by machinery or they die of starvation or exposure.

Hens who land on the conveyor belt are hastily hung upside down by their legs in metal shackles. For the sake of efficiency, most slaughterhouses attempt to immobilize birds before slaughter—it is much easier to kill a bird when she is not struggling, so the birds soon pass an electrified basin of water. As the hens move along the assembly line, turning their upside-down heads to see what might befall them next, they are supposed to touch the electrified water. Needless to say, many hens, particularly smaller ones, miss the water. Even if their heads touch the water, the shock does nothing to help the suffering of the hens. A strong shock would damage the flesh and reduce profits, so managers tend to err on the side of less current. As a result, birds are usually immobilized by the electric basin, but remain sentient—they are aware of and can feel everything that happens to them.

After they pass the electric water basin, a hen's throat is supposedly cut either by hand or with a mechanical blade. Slaughter lines run up to 8,400 chickens *per hour*, so accuracy is the exception rather than the rule—the Livingston plant (California) kills nearly 600,000 chickens daily (Morrissey 12). Afterward, whether or not their throats have actually been slit, birds are submerged in scalding water (to loosen their feathers). If a hen's throat is not slit, or was not slit properly—which includes millions of birds annually—she is boiled alive.

Cattle also suffer enormously between feedlots and their untimely deaths. Four corporations slaughter more than 80 percent of the 35 million cattle killed annually in the United States. A standard slaughterhouse kills 250 cattle *every hour*, a rate at which it is impossible for workers to assure a quick or relatively painless death. In any event, killing cattle all day at high speeds does not create an attitude of caring or compassion. Hidden videos testify to the many animals who are hoisted onto the slaughter assembly line kicking, struggling, and fully conscious. The *Washington Post* (April 2001) related the words of a slaughterhouse employee and his friend, Moreno:

> The cattle were supposed to be dead before they got to Moreno. But too often they weren't. "They blink. They make noises," he said softly. "The head moves, the eyes are wide and looking around." Still Moreno would

cut. On bad days, he says, dozens of animals reached his station clearly alive and conscious. Some would survive as far as the tail cutter, the belly ripper, the hide puller. "They die," said Moreno, "piece by piece." (*Washington Post* [April 2001] in "Factory Beef")

As noted, animals arrive at slaughter exhausted, thirsty, hungry, and terrified. Every year 100,000 factory farmed cattle arrive at slaughter injured, or too dispirited to walk (Kirchheimer); undercover investigators have repeatedly documented downed animals who are kicked, beaten, pushed with bulldozers, and dragged from transport trucks with ropes or chains, though they are fully conscious, in pain, and bellowing pitifully. Cows exploited in the dairy industry, because they are older and their bodies have been exhausted by perpetual pregnancy, birthing, and milking, are among the most pitiable during transport and when they arrive at slaughter.

### *"Free Range," "Cruelty Free," "Organic," and "Natural" Labels*

Some people seek to avoid supporting the excessive cruelty of factory farms by purchasing products with special labels, *but these labels do not satisfy even the most basic requirements for a compassionate consumer.* "Free range," "cruelty free," "organic," and "natural foods" industries exploit farmed animals for flesh, nursing milk, and reproductive eggs almost exactly as do other factory farms.

"Organic" labels protect farmed animals in only one, meager way: Organic labels indicate that farmers only feed organic foods to their victims—no hormones. Organic guidelines provide no further protections for farmed animals. Therefore animals who are exploited for "organic" foods are raised, maintained, transported, and slaughtered *just like their "non-organic" counterparts*: They are debeaked, dehorned, detoed, castrated, and/or branded, and they are kept, transported, and slaughtered in the same deplorable conditions.

"Organic" labels do *nothing* for a cow who is still perpetually impregnated and milked, who still loses her calf to the veal industry—or to protect her calf, who is still sold at birth to the veal industry to be slaughtered. "Organic" products are designed to optimize human health and reduce environmental degradation. Those who invest in organic products are not making a choice that promotes the well-being of farmed animals.

Despite the ugly truth of organic products, it is increasingly common for those touting "organic" products to claim that their label includes "rules about the humane treatment of animals" ("What Do"). (I suppose organic industries justify this because they have one inconsequential rule that ostensibly benefits their imprisoned, exploited farmed animals—they receive organic feed.) One need only look up the Organic Foods Production Act of 1990—today's organic guidelines (http://www.ams.usda.gov/AMSv1.0/getfile?dDocName=STELPRDC5060370&acct= nopgeninf) to see that organic regulations are not designed to alleviate the prolonged, extreme suffering of factory farmed animals—and they certainly do not do so. Neither do we vote against cruel animal exploitation if we buy "natural" or "all natural" products. In fact, these labels don't even protect consumers, because they don't indicate products that provide all-natural ingredients.

"Natural" labels merely indicate that a product has no "artificial flavors, colors, or chemical preservatives" ("What Do"). There is no requirement that cows, pigs, or hens who were exploited to create "natural" products be treated any differently from how other factory farmed animals are treated. Farmed animals who are exploited for "natural" products are not allowed to live in natural conditions—they are not even allowed to satisfy their most basic natural behaviors. Despite consumer assumptions about what "natural" means with regard to animal products holding this label, the USDA's "natural" food labels *only* regulate "the presence of artificial additives and the degree of processing" ("Farm").

"Free range," "cage free," and "certified humane" labels are just as meaningless for farmed animals as are "all natural" labels. Just like farmed animals enslaved by organic industries, farmed animals exploited by "free range," "cage free," and "certified humane" producers are routinely debeaked, disbudded, detoed, castrated, their tails are docked, and/or they are branded (depending on their species). Neither do "free range" and "certified humane" labels protect cows from perpetual impregnation, pregnancy, birth, calf-snatching, transport, or dismemberment (slaughter) at a very young age. Finally, "free range," "cage free," and "certified humane" labels fail to help "spent" hens, who are sent to slaughter at the same youthful age.

Eggs and chicken flesh marketed as "free range" very rarely have more space than hens crowded into battery cages, and they may or may not be able to step outside. *If* they can step outside, their outdoor pen is likely tiny, crowded, and barren—it is simply not profitable to keep fewer hens on more land; it *is* profitable to keep more hens on less land. It is perfectly legal to keep twenty thousand or more "free range" hens in captivity such that each hen is allotted no more space than is encompassed in an average-size sheet of paper, "with little or no access to the outdoors. If the hens can go outside, the exit is often very small, allowing only the closest hens to get out" ("Free-Range"). For those few who might be able to access the small doorway that leads to the outside world, much-touted "free range" may be "nothing more than a mudyard saturated with manure" ("Free-Range").

Facilities that bill their eggs as "cage free" are equally uninspiring:

> "Cage-free" means that, while the hens are not squeezed into small wire cages, they never go outside. "Cage-free" hens are typically confined in dark, crowded buildings filled with toxic gases and disease microbes the same as their battery-caged sisters. And like their battery-caged sisters, they are painfully debeaked at the hatchery. ("Cage-Free")

Uninformed visitors arriving at an organic egg farm were surprised to find that, despite "certified humane" and "free range" logos,

> 100,000 debeaked hens [were] crowded into five 400 foot long sheds, each holding "a sea of 20,000 brown hens," so densely crowded the floor was invisible.... The "range," even if the hens had been outside, was just "a bare patch of dirt between the sheds." ("Organic")

In our capitalistic system, farmed animals are merely units of production—"live stock." It is therefore inevitable that millions of farmed animals raised for profit will be viewed—and treated—as if they were expendable, especially in the poultry and dairy industries. Male "dairy" calves have no reason to exist on dairy farms, and male chicks have no reason to exist on egg-producing farms, or in poultry flesh industries. Yet male calves and male chicks are inevitably produced by these industries. How might "free range," "certified humane," or "organic" labels protect male calves in the dairy industry, when these calves have no economic value except through a veal industry that emerged to capitalize on a plethora of unwanted "dairy" calves? Similarly, "free range," "cage free," and "certified humane" labels do nothing to protect male chicks, who are a natural and constant byproduct of poultry industries, yet are economically useless. In our capitalistic system, what is to keep these newly-hatched chicks from being tossed into garbage bags and chippers? What do concerned consumers imagine a business might do with millions of animals who are born/hatched every year on their premises, who must be fed, watered, and housed, but who are useless to their economic enterprise?

Farmed animals who are exploited for "free range," "cage free," "certified humane," and "organic" products are also sent through an identical transport and slaughterhouse process as other factory farmed animals, at the same youthful age. "Free range," "cage free," "certified humane," and "organic" labels cannot satisfy the compassionate (or ethical) consumer.

For the sake of farmed animals, who suffer terribly in their artificially short lives, please do not reject red flesh in preference for poultry flesh. Please do not replace flesh with eggs or dairy products. Please do not buy animal products that try to disguise cruel exploitation behind meaningless feel-good labels such as "free range," "cruelty free," "organic," and "natural." For the sake of your own health, and for the sake of farmed animals, please eliminate (or at least reduce) your consumption of animal products.

## FEMINISM AND ANIMAL LIBERATION

Cows, sows, and hens are exploited in our food industry *because* they are females—because they produce young, provide nursing milk, and ovulate. Because of their female biology, cows, sows, chickens, and turkeys endure longer periods of time in more rigid confinement than other factory farmed animals. Because of their sex, cows, sows, chickens, and turkeys are manipulated and exploited from motherless infancy to premature death, through a host of forced pregnancies and stolen offspring.

Controlling reproduction is central to patriarchy. Just as cows, sows, and hens "are oppressed specifically so that their reproductive organs can be exploited," many people recognize "that the original point of patriarchy was to control the reproductive systems of women" ("Sexism"). Females—sows, cows, hens, women, and girls—suffer under patriarchy. We suffer because of our sex; our female bodies are exploited by and for men who hold power. If *we* detest and try to prevent male control over *our* bodies—how can we turn away from these much more helpless, and much more cruelly exploited fellow females, let alone contribute to their suffering and premature deaths?

Perhaps these domesticated, servile cows, sows, and hens are far too much like women and girls to be worthy of respect or concern in our patriarchal society: Cows, sows, chickens, and turkeys provide men with what they desire, are never as intelligent or strong as their oppressors, and are completely unable to bring about their own liberation. Men and women alike—even some animal activists—exhibit "culturally conditioned indifference toward, and prejudice against, creatures whose lives appear too slavishly, too boringly, too stupidly female, too 'cowlike'" to be worthy of our concern (Davis 197). Human beings are much more likely to speak up on behalf of killer whales and tigers—animals associated with freedom, strength, independence (manly attributes)—than for the billions of females whom *we* exploit when we buy dairy, eggs, and flesh. What will bring us to care about the much maligned and neglected individuals who have been "bred to docility, tractability, stupidity, and dependency" to provide us with milk, eggs, and flesh (Davis 201)?

Not only do we harbor patriarchal indifference to uniquely female suffering, but additionally, most of us are ignorant of the horrible cruelty inherent in factory farming. It is easy to buy a bucket of chicken or a carton of vanilla yogurt *without even knowing* about the females whose sad lives lie behind these unnecessary products. It is easy to forget that mozzarella and cream come from a mother's munificence—mothers who would have desperately preferred to tend their young, and to live out their lives with a measure of freedom and comfort—or not to be born at all. Most consumers are unaware of the ongoing, intense suffering and billions of premature deaths that lurk behind mayonnaise and cream, cold cuts and egg sandwiches.

Even with the onset of contemporary animal advocacy, and the unavoidability of at least some knowledge of what goes on in slaughterhouses and on factory farms, most of us choose to look away—even feminists. Collectively, feminists remain largely unaware of the well-documented links between the exploitation of women and girls, and the exploitation of cows, sows, and hens. Similarly, few people are aware of disturbing national and international rape statistics—especially statistics on domestic rape and our high incidences of wife battery. The abuse of women and girls is not of much concern or interest in patriarchal societies, where "female" problems are systematic.

Similarly, many feminists don't care about the females whom *they* exploit—at least not enough to alter their diet. Most of us have grown accustomed to consuming nursing milk, reproductive eggs, and flesh; who wants to give up macaroni and cheese, or that heaping bowl of chocolate ice cream, when pretty much everyone else continues to indulge? Anyway, it is much more glamorous to protest the cruelties of Japanese whalers (cruelties caused by *other* people), or lament the suffering of the poor in Darfur (problems that exist in *other* nations)—than it is to reconsider one's own consumption of cheddar or hamburger.

Those who *are* willing to work for change, and make changes, too often do so only for the sake of their own liberation, without much thought to the oppression of others—especially other species. Feminists lobby against sex wage discrepancies, gays fight homophobic laws, and the physically challenged demand greater access—each fighting for injustices that affect *their* lives, and/or the lives of *their* loved ones. Yet these dedicated activists usually fail to make even a slight change in their consumer choices for the sake of much more egregiously oppressed and exploited individuals. While it is important to fight for one's own liberation, it is counterproductive (not to mention selfish and small-minded) to fight for one's own liberation while willfully continuing to oppress others who are yet lower on the rungs of hierarchy. While fighting for liberation, it makes no sense for feminists to trample on gays, for gays to trample on the physically challenged, or for the physically challenged to trample on feminists. It also makes no sense for any of these social justice activists to willfully exploit factory farmed animals. Can we not *at least* avoid exploiting and dominating others while working for our personal liberation? Those who seek greater justice—whatever their cause—must make consumer choices that diminish the cruel exploitation of others. As a matter of consistency and solidarity, social justice activists must reject dairy products, eggs, and flesh.

There is no other industry as cruel and oppressive as factory farming. With regard to numbers affected, extent and length of suffering, and numbers of premature deaths, no other industry can even approach factory farming. Billions of individuals are exploited from genetically engineered birth, through excruciating confinement, to conveyor belt dismemberment. Consequently, there is no industry more appropriate for social justice activists to boycott. Even if we aren't prepared to take a public stand, or take on another cause, we must at least make a private commitment on behalf of cows, pigs, and hens by leaving animal products on the shelf at the grocery store.

## Women and Animal Advocacy

While it is one thing to strive for a cause that fundamentally and primarily benefits *you*—your freedom and equality (or the freedom and equality of those you know and care about), or for your environment (on which you depend for survival)—it is quite another matter to struggle on behalf of a cause that does *not* benefit you directly. As social justice activists, we must remember how ardently we wish that those in power would help bring change. The oppressed wish that those in power could empathize enough to understand the wrongness of what is happening, and how much *they* would need and appreciate the active participation of those in power to bring about a measure of justice. With regard to farmed animals, we are the ones who are in power. We are the ones who have the power to change our consumer habits. We are the ones who either put our money down for their lives, or boycott animal products.

Historically, feminists have set the stage for a more expansive activism, for an ethic that reaches beyond one's immediate, personal gains. Feminists have often taken on other social justice causes. For example, Irish-born

Francis Cobbe (1822–1904), an early British suffragette who was denied a formal education, worked for social justice on many fronts. She struggled to curb violence against women, especially domestic violence, and advocated for improved education for girls. Cobbe identified financial dependence as a primary cause of domestic violence, and noted that transferring a woman's property rights to a man in marriage doomed her to dependence, thereby placing women in a vulnerable position. With such unjust laws ruling marriage, Cobbe advocated for the single life. She

> was obviously not concerned with men's evaluation of her suitability as a servant for them. She was far more concerned with their unsuitability as leaders and lawmakers, and made many caustic and challenging comments about the limitations of male logic, the tyranny and injustice of male rules, and the flagrantly self-interested way men had organized society to make women available to them. ("Francis")

Cobbe was outspoken, thoughtful, and determined—she exposed patriarchy for what it is—rule by and for men.

Inasmuch as Cobbe did not enjoy the denigration and powerlessness that came with her sex, she perhaps intuited that other individuals also preferred at least some measure of control over *their* lives. In addition to working on behalf of women and girls, Cobbe worked to reform poor laws, and to change animal experimentation. In her meticulous book, *Vivisection in America* (1890), Cobbe detailed the realities of animal experimentation in the United States, advocating for an end to vivisection. She catalogued species used for experimentation, the numbers of creatures involved, and noted how these victims of science were exploited. After informing readers of the horrors performed behind closed doors in the name of science, she challenged people to reflect on their understanding of morality, and asked that readers help abolish such injustice:

> [W]hether the practice be useful or useless, we ask you to reflect whether it be morally lawful—(not to speak of humane, or generous, or manly)—to seek to relieve our own pains at the cost of such unutterable anguish as has been already inflicted on unoffending creatures in the name of Science? You now know, to a certain extent, what it is that the advocates of vivisection really mean when they ask you to endow "Research." Will you—bearing their experiments in mind—pay them to repeat such cruelties? (Cobbe)

Francis Cobbe stands out amid social activists of her day because she not only worked for her own liberation, but also for the liberation of the poor and for the liberation of nonhuman animals. She was sensitive to those who were yet more devalued than women and girls; she noticed that nonhuman animals were among the most needy and downtrodden. In 1875, she founded the world's first organization fighting animal experimentation, the Society for the Protection of Animals Liable to Vivisection (SPALV); in 1898 she founded the British Union for the Abolition of Vivisection (BUAV). More than a century later, both groups continue to fight vivisection.

Similarly, Caroline White (1833–1916) advocated for an array of social justice causes. She objected to slavery, was an advocate for children, and in 1883 founded the American Anti-Vivisection Society (AAVS) to fight the exploitation of nonhuman animals in education, research, and product testing. AAVS was the first organization to challenge powerful, privileged U.S. animal experimenters in a court of law on cruelty charges. White also started a congressional investigation of "livestock" transportation in railroad cars. Her efforts led to legislation requiring railroad workers to feed and water farmed animals in transport at least every twenty-eight hours.

Francis Cobbe and Caroline White were forerunners in a long line of contemporary women working on behalf of nonhuman animals, many of whom simultaneously took on other social justice causes. Increasingly, women have turned their energy toward the selfless but desperate cause of nonhuman animals in disproportionate numbers. Animal advocates are *overwhelmingly* female (in contrast with the environmental movement, for example, which is overwhelmingly male).

Given this demography, it is surprising how few contemporary feminists understand the many ways in which patriarchy undergirds both the oppression of women and the oppression of nonhuman animals. While contemporary authors such as Carol Adams, Greta Gaard, and Marti Kheel continue to expose these oppressions as interlocking, feminists and animal advocates rarely recognize one another as essential allies. When feminists and animal advocates recognize that they are on the same side, they will each markedly increase their strength, their power, and their chances of bringing about meaningful and lasting change.

## Authors and Essays

This anthology of essays written by women highlights diversity within a vibrant and growing animal advocacy movement. Authors in this anthology come from different nations, different races, different age groups, and different focuses; they are educators, writers, researchers, musicians, undercover investigators, artists, scholars, lawyers, and ministers working on behalf of wild animals, animals confined in laboratories, farmed animals, or homeless companion animals. They speak of the beauty and suffering of pigs, dogs, fish, cats, cattle, chickens, primates, seals, lobsters, and bears. They live and work in Malaysia, Singapore, the United States, Lebanon, India, Canada, and Australia—including Indian, Lebanese, Malaysian, American, African-American, and Latino activists—and they each share a strong commitment to animal activism.

It is interesting to note that only a few authors in this anthology mention partners or families, and when they do, mention is made only in passing. Such references are buried somewhere in the middle of a narrative that is focused on the lives of pigs on factory farms, stray dogs, or chimpanzees. In more than one instance, I needed to ask authors to "say a little more" about a partner or child who seemed to drop out of the sky between rallies and rescues, three quarters of the way through a narrative—a side-issue in their central story of suffering and need and activism. Contributors were invariably focused beyond their immediate family—on the bigger picture, rather than the insular life of the home. On reflection, this seems profoundly healthy. For these women, their greatest contribution to the next generation is working toward greater justice.

Most authors in *Speaking Up for Animals* are activists; they are not accustomed to writing essays for anthologies. They graciously squeezed in a little writing between rescuing a flock of hens, investigating a new tip from an informant, or traveling abroad for an extended tour of education and outreach. Some authors know English only as a second (or third) language. Consequently, authors frequently submitted a rough draft and allowed me to finish their work while they flew across continents to plead on behalf of cattle, or rushed to the defense of circus elephants. Using e-mail and Track Changes, working together, we turned their understanding, experience, and knowledge into the chapters of this anthology.

## Part I: Pondering What I Put in My Mouth

**Dana Medoro** admits that she came to animal liberation "in a rather slow and awkward way." She remembers learning how factory farmers trap sows in gestation crates, and how, in response to this new information, she "wailed inarticulately all the way home." She writes, "I knew the industry was bad, but I didn't know it was *that* bad." Ultimately, Medoro took up action on behalf of factory farmed pigs, joining a weekend protest that revolved around a life-sized, papier-mâché sow. Her journey through ignorance and lamentation to outreach led her into unexplored areas of communication that are foundational to advocacy, and Medoro ponders which methods of activism worked, which didn't, and why. As an animal activist explaining the truths of animal exploitation, she notes that it is "important to be dexterous when advocating for animals because it's difficult for people to absorb the shock." She adds, "I understand the resistance—as someone who really did shuffle, all stiffly and sideways, sort of like a crab, toward the cause of helping animals, and I would hate to be told that I arrived too late or that I didn't do enough."

Pioneer of "Open Rescue," **Patty Mark** risks personal safety and freedom on behalf of nonhuman animals. She and a handful of fellow activists enter a factory farm in the wee hours of the morning and "steal" some gravely ill and dying hens—and they videotape their crime. They hand the evidence over to the media, and their illegal rescue is broadcast to the general public, exposing the horrors of factory farming to citizens relaxing in soft chairs after a hard day at work ... and simultaneously exposing their own "illegal" acts. Activism is often risky business—as it always is to expose the truths of economic powers—but Mark is compelled to carry on, "Chickens have captured the minds and hearts of our rescue teams," she notes. "Their intelligent and amiable personalities are largely unknown among humans. Chickens are wonderful beings."

Dressed in black and armed with flashlights, thirteen-year-old **Kymberlie Adams Matthews** and her sister crept out of their house in rural New York under cover of darkness to see what lurked in their neighbor's long sheds. That dark night, Adams Matthews unwittingly gained her first glimpse of a poultry farm, "Hundreds of thousands of hens were crowded together in small, decrepit wire cages. Dead hens scattered the floor." Leaving the hens to their fate, the girls fled in terror. But Adams Matthews returned as an adult, and her essay carries us to twelve tornado-damaged battery sheds in Ohio Valley, "Topsy-turvy cages, mangled limbs, loose feathers everywhere. Squacks and screeches and fading peeps told of the suffering." Adams Matthews shares a fundamental truth of animal advocacy, "It's brutal. It's unfair. But it's true: There will always be those I cannot save."

In 2005, **Lorri Houston** (previously Bauston, cofounder of Farm Sanctuary in 1986), founded Animal Acres, a 26-acre farm outside of Los Angeles. At her new sanctuary, Houston continues the same work she has done for the past twenty-five years—lobbying for change and rescuing farmed animals, and exposing the grizzly, hidden realities of factory farming. Rescued residents of Animal Acres—like Henny the hen and Colin the goat—speak for themselves, touching the lives of thousands of visitors each year. Houston comments that "sanctuaries provide a positive way for the public to learn that farmed animals are friends, not food." With their winsome personalities, residents at Animal Acres remind visitors of what they were told when they were children: Be careful what you put in your mouth.

**Gail A. Eisnitz** wanted to help nonhuman animals, but no one would hire her. She took whatever animal advocacy job she could find, and created jobs where there weren't any. When she landed a job as an investigator for the Humane Farming Association, Eisnitz "traveled from slaughterhouse to slaughterhouse collecting eyeballs and bladders from veal calves," exposing toxic drugs sold to unsuspecting citizens in supermarkets. She also spent "five years crisscrossing the country documenting the routine dragging, strangling, skinning, scalding, and dismembering of fully conscious animals at essentially every slaughterhouse" she visited. Her work ultimately gained national attention, and she is now widely known and highly esteemed for her courageous, hard-hitting publication, *Slaughterhouse*.

Artist **Sue Coe** remembers raiding school laboratories to rescue mice and guinea pigs with a gang of other young activists. She also remembers the screaming that came from inside a slaughterhouse near her childhood home. Coe, now an internationally acclaimed artist, still sees and hears sorrow in her community; she describes the sad lives of cows and calves on the dairy farm next to her home, "Profit over life. The crime is economics," and we are "trained to keep quiet." Coe has no intention of keeping quiet—though she may not utter a word. The "apex of Western civilization is the art of denial," Coe writes. She has fostered the art of exposing truth. Coe records and documents the atrocities of factory farms on canvas, re-representing "to the viewer's eye" that which has too long been hidden.

At 35, **Linda McDaniel** "felt God's call to the ordained ministry." Gifted with "a special sensitivity for all life forms," McDaniel brought fresh eyes to the Bible, critically exploring scriptural accounts of God's relationship with nonhumans, visions of the Peaceable Kingdom, the concept of "soul," and writings on salvation. McDaniel brings scripture to bear on the problems of factory farming: Environmental destruction, exploitation of poor farmers, harm to human health, and the ungodly exploitation of sentient beings. She writes, "Christ intends the Church, led by the Spirit, to work to bring people and animals into one community. God is reshaping me in this new and different ministry to lead a skeptical Church to a broader understanding of God's plan for creation."

**Heather Moore** is a freelance writer, working on a home computer with one firm goal: helping nonhuman animals. Moore's essay "The Fiercest

Predators of the Sea," exemplifies freelance activism. Her essay highlights the sentience, social structure, and individual personalities of lobsters and octopuses—as well as the cruelty that is inherent in both our fisheries and our kitchens. Her entertaining and informative essay stands as testimony to the effectiveness of writing as a form of animal advocacy.

## PART II: WORKING FOR WILDLIFE

**Sue Pemberton** rescues and rehabilitates pinnipeds. She introduces us to Coneely, a premature harbor seal who was born six weeks before due date; Anniversary, a bulbous sea lion who arrived comatose at the rescue center; and D-Day, a teenaged California sea lion who showed up on Pier 39 weighing a whopping 400 pounds and sporting a twelve-inch fishing flasher. When 58,000 gallons of bunker fuel spilled into San Francisco Bay, Pemberton rescued gooey birds who were visibly "stunned and in shock." Despite the obvious importance of her rescue efforts, she was told to "stop or face arrest" for working around bunker fuel, labeled a hazardous substance. "That was quite possibly the dumbest reason I had ever heard, in a life or death situation, to stop rescue efforts," she comments. Pemberton, prepared to "ruffle some feathers" and face arrest, notes that advocacy is the least we can do "to reverse a little bit of our careless damage."

Like many authors in this anthology, **Phaik Kee Lim** vividly remembers commonplace animal abuse from her childhood, and her helplessness in the face of ongoing animal suffering. She turned these bleak memories to good cause, and has worked with Friends of the Earth Malaysia for more than twenty-five years, working behind the scenes with pen in hand to improve the plight of nonhuman animals. Lim explains how a few skillfully placed strokes of ink, when combined with a will to bring change, can push powerful officials to enforce laws on behalf of critically endangered animals such as African chimpanzees and Indonesian orangutans. Lim notes that even those with few resources "can speak up or write letters to encourage change."

**Deborah D. Misotti** was lost after the death of her sons...then she sang with a gibbon. Founder of a Florida primate sanctuary (Talkin' Monkeys Project, Inc.), Misotti is painfully aware that gibbons in captivity are denied the most simple and seemingly inalienable rights, such as the right to travel across a forest canopy by swinging from their long arms, and the right to communicate with others of their kind by lifting their beautiful voices in song. At Talkin' Monkeys, Misotti provides life-long care for nonhuman primates who have been rescued from unfortunate situations under the grip of capitalistic human exploitation, whether through trade in "exotic pets," research laboratories, or breeding facilities. By reaching out to others in need—in this case a gibbon named Webster—Misotti heals alongside other primates at the Talkin' Monkeys sanctuary.

**Lynette Shanley** abandoned a well-paying, mainstream job in order to search for a more meaningful life. She volunteered at a local hospital and soon brought home Marcus, a cat who taught her something of the world beyond humanity. She began rescuing cats and joined various animal advocacy groups, but Shanley found that she worked best alone and subsequently founded two nonprofits, one for wildcats and one for primates. Over the course of her work, Shanley illegally enters primate quarters, exposes and shuts down zoos, lobbies to change public school practices, and pushes for stronger laws regulating trade in "exotic pets." She reminds advocates that patience is critical to success, and demonstrates how saving nonhuman animals is a healing experience that can simultaneously save one's own life.

As a child, **Amy Corrigan** saved worms from the sidewalk, nurtured a passel of soft and fluffy toy animals ... and chewed on cow flesh for dinner. But when she came upon vivid posters depicting animal exploitation—cats "with electrodes screwed into their brains, ... a live fox being torn limb from limb by hounds; a sheep having her throat cut with a look of absolute terror in her eyes"—her fate was sealed. As a young adult Corrigan headed for Thailand, where she rehabilitated a slow loris, shared an elephant's final moments, rescued sun bears, and raised baby gibbons. These experiences, and her determination to bring change, have led her to continue the tradition of educating passersby with posters and leaflets, with one major difference—she hands her literature to people in Singapore. She writes, "The most important decision I have made in my work with nonhuman animals was the decision to move to Southeast Asia, to be part of an animal welfare movement still in its infancy."

## PART III: POTPOURRI—FROM DANCING BEARS TO UNDERCOVER INVESTIGATION

"Sometimes in life, you cross paths with people who inspire you, touch your soul, and leave you changed forever. This happened to me when I met Ingrid Newkirk, the founder of PETA." In her work for PETA India, **Anuradha Sawhney** apprehends aggressive *madaris* who illegally force bears to dance in the streets, and when possible, relocates these beleaguered bears to sanctuaries. She also rescues animals who have been exploited and damaged by scientists, transporting these unfortunate victims to a life of peace and well-being in one of India's animal sanctuaries. Sawhney also educates the public about animal suffering and human health concerns associated with a diet rich in animal products. Sawhney reflects on years of activism, "this was the job I had always wanted, but until I joined PETA India I had not known that it was possible to work for animals as a career."

**Kris "Risa" Candour** was a vegetarian at sixteen and a vegan two years later, and she turned school presentations and paper assignments into activism and into educational activities for teachers and classmates. In college, she protested circuses, fur shops, vivisection, rodeos, joined the Primate Freedom Tour, and protested with "die-hard" British activists during a semester abroad. As an African American, Candour is intimately "aware of racism and its subtle manifestations as prejudice." Her mother taught her to handle race oppression with "refined defiance," an approach that also came in handy for animal advocacy. As a graduate student, she was ready to cofound her own organization, Justice for All Species (JAS), connecting animal advocacy with other social justice movements—most notably racial equality. As "a minority in a minority movement" Candour advises animal advocates to "recognize ways that we might improve, especially concerning how we relate to and take care of one another."

Animal advocacy is never easy, but it is even more difficult in the midst of war. **Joelle El-Massih**, a founding member of Lebanon's Beirut for the Ethical Treatment of Animals (BETA), stresses the close bonds she formed with other activists, and writes with tenderness of the dogs she protects from a world saturated with violence, indifference, and unending need. Despite the challenges that lie before her, El-Massih faces down Hezbollah to feed, water, and transport some of war's most innocent victims and works to educate locals on the subject of spay-neuter and heightened compassion. But animal advocacy is a hard sell in a land so long torn by violence, a nation where food is sometimes scarce among human beings.

Psychologist and ecologist **Gay Bradshaw** remembers when she struggled to balance her "personal life of feeling" with "the professional world of the mind." As a scientist she tiptoed around affection and caring for the sake of reason and research until she came to see that life as a conventional scientist was stifling vital aspects of her humanity. She simultaneously came to understand that this stunted approach "was not serving animals." A pioneer in interspecies trauma studies, Bradshaw's research explores symptoms of trauma shared by children, women, political prisoners, elephants, chimpanzees, and parrots. She writes, the "animal rights movement is about coming to our senses, about understanding the subtle connections that link the horror of dolphin hunts with the sensation of Sea World and a seafood dinner." Her essay—and her research—expose crucial connections between nonhuman animals and the human animal that continue to help a reluctant humanity to come to its senses.

The final essay, written by **Michele Rokke**, carries us from a Minnesota farming community to the mysterious world of undercover investigations. Working for People for the Ethical Treatment of Animals (PETA), Rokke spent nine months undercover in a notorious research facility, Huntingdon Life Sciences (HLS). As a result, Rokke attests "unequivocally that animal testing is a fraudulent system, designed to garner profits." She describes forays into enemy territory—HLS—as "Agent Nerd," disguised behind ridiculous glasses and large hats that concealed a hidden camera and recorder, wearing "an enormous bra, loaded with equipment packed in a lot of socks." She quips, "I never had so many people, men and women, check me out." While Rokke reveals an indomitable sense of humor, she admits to having "untold scenes of suffering freeze-framed in my mind.... There is no such thing as a 'worst case of cruelty'—they are all the worst."

## Taking Action

Unlike most of us, activists who submitted essays for this anthology have seen farmed animals in unconscionable confinement. They have stood amid the unbearable pain of animal experimentation, tried to catch companion animals abandoned in war zones, and worked with demoralized animal individuals who have been kidnapped from their homes to entertain an easily bored humanity. They have seen firsthand how human ignorance, indifference, and corporate greed affect nonhuman animals. As a consequence, they work to bring change. I hope that their essays will help readers to better understand the atrocities that we collectively cause nonhuman animals, and will allow readers to see our complicity in animal suffering. This book features many ways that we can help alleviate this ongoing, egregious animal exploitation, and I hope that readers will be inspired to get involved.

My hope is that readers will support the animal advocacy organizations represented in this anthology (most of which can be found online), and/or a local organization, such as a spay-neuter van operating in your area. As you read these stories, please choose from among the many organizations represented in this anthology and send a donation. (Proceeds from this book will be returned to animal advocacy as well.) Animal advocates—

social justice causes in general—*always* (desperately) need donations *and* volunteers ... and almost always have job openings. Battered-women's shelters and spay-neuter clinics alike depend on volunteers to help with letter campaigns, protests, and educational activities. They cannot function without our support and assistance.

I also hope that this anthology elucidates shared concerns among feminists and animal advocates, and stands as testimony to the importance of women to the animal liberation, animal rights, and animal welfare movements. I hope that readers will come to better understand the many links that connect different forms of oppression—that connect social justice activists working for seemingly different causes—and the important contribution that women have made, and continue to make, on behalf of such causes. Indeed, the same patriarchy that oppresses women oppresses nonhuman animals. Farmed animals and "housewives," "lab" animals and prostitutes, dancing bears and girls in the sex trade—all have too long been exploited by the same patriarchal hierarchy wherein the comparatively weak are exploited for the benefit of the powerful.

Those who are aware of history, of patriarchy, and of the feminist movement tend to understand how difficult it is—and how important—for people to rethink basic behaviors in order to bring about deep and lasting change. We must rethink how we speak, how we spend our time, and what we consume. This is as true for fighting sexism as it is for fighting speciesism—or any other form of domination, exploitation, and oppression. We must change *our* lives first, and most fundamentally. I hope that readers working to improve the lives of girls and women, on reading these essays, will realize that they can and must choose not to continue to exploit nonhuman animals while working to liberate girls and women. I hope that feminist readers who do not already understand the links between sexism and speciesism will come to see that feminists must also speak up on behalf of nonhuman animals.

Oppressions are linked. We cannot free human beings without freeing cows, sows, and hens along with women and men who are systematically oppressed by those in power. Rather than seek to fight our way up the patriarchal ladder, those working for social justice need to dismantle hierarchies, and cease to exploit *all* those who are less powerful—even if we must give up a few culinary favorites in the process. (Those who have taken up a plant-based diet for any measure of time never want for fabulous foods. From my experience, people who discover the vast array of wonderful plant-based foods that are readily available in most of our communities never look back.) Each of us decides, over the course of our daily lives, whether we will ignore the suffering of nonhuman animals who are caught in laboratories, veal crates, circuses, and slaughterhouses, or choose to invest in compassionate, healthy alternatives. I hope that readers will rethink their consumer choices, monies that have long been offered at the expense of nonhuman animals—overwhelmingly female and exploited *because* of their female biology. *We* choose where our money goes, and in the process, we choose whether to boycott cruelty and support change, or melt ambiguously back into the masses.

Activists such as those represented in this anthology can only point the way; they cannot change the world all by themselves. The rest of us must also take action, and we must first make the necessary changes in our daily lives. *You* ultimately decide, every day, whether or not your life will speak on behalf of the oppressed, or remain an inaudible but decisive tool for the status quo. The women in this anthology each made their decision, now you must make yours.

## NOTE

1. Information on factory farming is from VIVA! USA (http://www.vivausa.org/visualmedia/index.html) (or VIVA! in the UK), HSUS (http://video.hsus.org/), PCRM (http://www.pcrm.org/resources/), Farm Sanctuary (http://www.farmsanctuary.org/mediacenter/videos.html), PETA (http://www.petatv.com/), and Vegan Outreach (http://www.veganoutreach.org/whyvegan/animals.html).

## REFERENCES

Adams, Carol. "The Feminist Traffic in Animals." *Ecofeminism: Women, Animals, Nature.* Ed. Greta Gaard. Philadelphia: Temple, 1993. 195–218.

Adams, Carol, and Josephine Donovan. "Introduction." *Women and Animals: Feminist Theoretical Explorations.* Ed. Carol Adams and Josephine Donovan. Durham: Duke, 1995. 1–10.

"An HSUS Report: The Welfare of Animals in the Meat, Egg, and Dairy Industries." *Factory Farming Campaign.* Accessed: Aug. 7, 2008. http://www.hsus.org/farm/resources/research/welfare/welfare_overview.html#05.

"Cage-Free Hens Kept for Eggs." "Free Range Poultry and Eggs." *United Poultry Concerns: Promoting the Compassionate and Respectful Treatment of Domestic Fowl.* Accessed: Feb. 16, 2011. http://www.upc-online.org/freerange.html.

"The Cancer Project: Protective Foods: Ask the Dietitian—Milk and Dairy" *Physician Committee for Responsible Medicine.* Accessed: July 6, 2010. http://www.cancerproject.org/protective_foods/ask/milk_dairy.php.

Cobbe, Francis Power, and Benjamin Bryan. *Vivisection in America: I. How It Is Taught II.*

*How It Is Practised.* London: Swan Sonnenschein, 1890. http://www.indiana.edu/~letrs/vwwp/cobbe/viviamer.html#InU-CAP5357-p53.

Cohen, Robert. "Early Sexual Maturity and Milk Hormones." *Health101.org: The Realities of Health.* Accessed: July 6, 2010. http://www.health101.org/index.htm.

"Dairy's Dark Side: The Sour Truth Behind Milk." *Compassionate Living: The Magazine of Mercy for Animals* 10:6, Spring–Summer 2010. 10–14.

Davis, Karen. "Thinking Like a Chicken." *Women and Animals: Feminist Theoretical Explorations.* Ed. Carol Adams and Josephine Donovan. Durham: Duke, 1995. 192–212.

Dunayer, Joan. "Sexist Words, Speciesist Roots." *Women and Animals: Feminist Theoretical Explorations.* Ed. Carol Adams and Josephine Donovan. Durham: Duke, 1995. 11–31.

Ehrenreich, Barbara, and Deirdre English. *For Her Own Good: Two Centuries of the Expert's Advice to Women.* New York: Anchor, 2005.

"Factory Beef Production." *FactoryFarming.com.* FarmSanctuary. Accessed: August 9, 2008. http://www.farmsanctuary.org/issues/factoryfarming/beef/.

"Factory Egg Production: Laying Hens." *FactoryFarming.com.* Farm Sanctuary. Accessed: March 4, 2010. http://www.farmsanctuary.org/issues/factoryfarming/eggs/.

"Facts About Violence: U.S. Statistics." *Feminist.com.* Accessed: July 26, 2010. http://www.feminist.com/antiviolence/facts.html#statistics.

"Farm Sanctuary Challenges USDA's 'Natural' Labeling Standards." *Sanctuary: Farm Sanctuary's Compassionate Quarterly.* Winter 2010. 14.

"Francis Power Cobbe (1822–1904)." *Sunshine for Women. 30 of the Most Influential Women of the Millennium: A Women's History Month 2001 Celebration.* July 27, 2007. http://www.pinn.net/~sunshine/whm2001/cobbe.html.

"'Free-Range' Hens Kept for Eggs." "Free Range Poultry and Eggs." *United Poultry Concerns: Promoting the Compassionate and Respectful Treatment of Domestic Fowl.* Accessed: Feb. 16, 2011. http://www.upc-online.org/freerange.html.

"George Eliot Quotes." *FamousQuotes.com.* Accessed: Jan. 30, 2009. http://www.famousquotes.com/search.php?search=1&FirstName=George&LastName=Eliot&field=FullName.

Gruen, Lori. "Dismantling Oppression: An Analysis of the Connections Between Women and Animals." *Ecofeminism: Women, Animals, Nature.* Ed. Greta Gaard. Philadelphia: Temple, 1993. 60–90.

Kappeler, Susanne. "Speciesism, Racism, Nationalism … or the Power of Scientific Subjectivity." *Women and Animals: Feminist Theoretical Explorations.* Ed. Carol Adams and Josephine Donovan. Durham: Duke, 1995. 320–352.

Kheel, Marti. "License to Kill: An Ecofeminist Critique of a Hunter's Discourse." *Women and Animals: Feminist Theoretical Explorations.* Ed. Carol Adams and Josephine Donovan. Durham: Duke, 1995. 85–125.

———. *Nature Ethics: An Ecofeminist Perspective.* New York: Rowman & Littlefield, 2008.

Kirchheimer, Gabe. "US Cows: Sacred or Mad?" *High Times.* July 1, 2001. Organic Consumer's Association. Accessed: June 22, 2009. http://www.purefood.org/madcow/cows7101.cfm.

Morrissey, Christine. "Christine Morrissey, Director of East Bay Animal Advocates." *Poultry Press: Promoting the Compassionate and Respectful Treatment of Domestic Fowl.* 17:4. Winter–Spring 2007–2008. 12.

"'Organic' and 'Certified Humane' Eggs." "Free Range Poultry and Eggs." *United Poultry*

*Concerns: Promoting the Compassionate and Respectful Treatment of Domestic Fowl.* Accessed: Feb. 16, 2011. http://www.upc-online.org/freerange.html.

Scholtmeijer, Marian. "The Power of Otherness: Animals in Women's Fiction." *Women and Animals: Feminist Theoretical Explorations.* Ed. Carol Adams and Josephine Donovan. Durham: Duke, 1995. 231–262.

"Sexism." *Eastern Shore Sanctuary and Education Center.* Accessed: Oct. 26, 2010. http://sanctuary.bravebirds.org/wp-content/uploads/2009/05/speciesex.pdf/.

"Viva! USA Guides: Murder She Wrote." *Viva! USA.* Accessed: Aug. 14, 2008. http://www.vivausa.org/activistresources/guides/murdershewrote1.htm#.

"What Do Your Food Labels Really Mean? 'Free-range,' 'Natural,' 'Non-toxic,' and Other Myths." *Wallet Pop: Consumer Ally.* Accessed: Jan. 9, 2011. http://www.walletpop.com/2010/05/07/what-do-your-food-labels-really-mean-free-range-natural/.

Part I

# Pondering What I Put in My Mouth

CHAPTER 1

# Weekends at the Mall with a Pig

*Dana Medoro*

**Dana Medoro** *is Associate Professor of American Literature at the University of Manitoba, where she teaches and researches the subject of animals and ethics. Professor Medoro is also a member of the Farm Animal Welfare Committee with the Winnipeg Humane Society. Over the past decade, she has participated in many animal rights activities, from protesting the continued exploitation of wild animals in circuses to demonstrating on behalf of humane farming at the World Meat Congress when it came to Winnipeg. Since 2003 she has turned most of her attention to the necessity of banning sow stalls in Canada's factory farming of pigs.*

About two years ago *Harper's* magazine featured on its cover an illustration of pigs in profile set against an image of a large, black cog. I think that the accompanying article was called "The Price of Pork," but I don't exactly remember. Knowing the kind of information it would contain—the certainty of clear allusions to graphic cruelty—I didn't read the article. I figured that doing so would be like taking a large rock and smashing myself in the face. About two weeks later, the next *Harper's* arrived at my door, and it included a brief letter to the editor in which the writer recalled her childhood on a family farm. After noting the precise memory she had of watching a sow give birth to her piglets in the warm sunlight, she mentioned the sow's very purposeful grunting during her labor. She then concluded her letter with a quietly poignant statement about the article's effect on her: "a little piece of me died last week."

Something about this letter filed itself in the forefront of my memory, although I'm not exactly sure why. Maybe it was the way in which the writer managed, in about four lines, to set in juxtaposition the vast themes of life and death: the remote memory of the piglets being born against the sudden experience of dying inside; the inwardness of the laboring sow's own consciousness against the mechanized world that turns her into meat; the freedom to give birth in the sunlight against the enslavement within a dark, metal crate. I don't think that at the time of reading the letter, I actually registered all of those now-clear pairings; it's more accurate to say that the one sentence captured exactly how I felt. When I got an insider's view of the pork industry, a little piece of me also died and it will never come back to life again.

Most of the time I feel as though I'm carrying around a kind of cadaverous, rotten gloom about the lot of animals, particularly pigs for some reason. It takes a concerted effort to bury the images of their suffering in order to get on with my day. I think it's a kind of survivor's guilt, an acute awareness of the parallel universe that pigs inhabit—their lives in dark stalls, their sense of confusion at the entrapment as they push and push on the bars with their snouts. I once read an essay published by an eighteenth-century Jesuit who proposed that farm animals were the reincarnated souls of evil-doing humans in former lives. In an attempt to make sense of the animals' endless suffering, he reckoned that factory farms were a literal hell on earth.

Such arguments emerged during a time when philosophers and physicians felt unconvinced by René Descartes' famous declaration, a little less than a century earlier, that animals were purely mechanistic, devoid of the immortal souls and delicate sentience that animated the human body. Given that nonhuman animals—the brute creation as they were then classified—expressed emotions and possessed a capacity for communication, those who defended animals could not bring themselves to believe that they belonged to the realm of things. The barrier behind which humanity stood then cracked a little: either no living creatures possessed souls, or we all did. If frightening, nihilistic conclusions followed from the former premise, then perhaps sense could be made of the latter, and eighteenth- and nineteenth-century thinkers drew on Eastern religions and philosophies to do so. Emily Brontë, for instance, suffused *Wuthering Heights* with a vision of reincarnation and the souls of animals. On the other side of the ocean and around the same time, Ralph Waldo Emerson argued that like us—and he characterized us simply as "upward, heaven-facing speakers"—four-legged animals also sought out and deserved a spiritual footing on the earth.

I don't know. Part of me adores these ideas; even my attitude toward insects has changed, and I understand why the Jain of India are careful not to tread on these small beings. (Nathaniel Hawthorne once mused, however, that mosquitoes were particles of a satanic soul, and, living in a city plagued by the little fiends, I'm inclined to agree.) But a bigger part of me is just saddened by the fact that very little has changed in four centuries of thinking about animals. Some beautiful, thoughtful things have been said about animals over the past half-millennium to counteract the rise of factory farming and scientific experimentation—the same beautiful, thoughtful things that today's writers are still saying in the face of exactly the same factories and experiments.

I began researching the history of animal rights after I finished my dissertation on blood and menstrual blood in American fiction. I wanted to go back to the novels I had studied for my PhD in order to explore why the image of a menstruating woman was often combined with that of a slaughtered animal. I also wanted to figure out why Toni Morrison's *Beloved*—the novel I struggled most with—aligned slave plantations with slaughterhouses, the shipping of Africans across the ocean with the transport of hogs up the Mississippi. It wasn't enough to say that *Beloved* questioned why slaves were treated like animals, because that question opened onto another one: why did such brutality against animals exist in the first place? When I prepared my first graduate seminar on American Literature and Animals, I was struck by how many writers put the subject of animals at center stage. Herman Melville's *Moby-Dick*, for instance, isn't a novel about God's wrath manifested in whale form, as it's been traditionally taught; it's about a big, intelligent whale pissed off at seeing his species hunted to near extinction. My students responded to the course material in such interesting ways, either by avoiding the painfully difficult issues it raised or by confronting them head-on. Some signed a petition that I once brought to class (protesting the treatment of pigs in factory farms); others did not.

I have learned not to force the issue. No one forced animal rights on me, and I came to where I am today in a rather slow and awkward way. My first encounter with animal rights information took place in 1989 when I was a second-year undergraduate at the University of Toronto. One day, as I wandered past a bunch of tables set up along a hallway to announce the different campus clubs—the ski club, the canoe club—someone had arranged to display information about the use of veal crates. I just innocently walked up to it, not really knowing what it was, and looked at the large photos spread across the table: I vowed never to eat veal again. That year I also decided to boycott McDonald's. The year after that, I read *Diet for a New America* and I stopped eating red meat altogether; another year later, chicken, having managed to suppress the images of the slaughtered birds in *Diet for a New America* for twelve months. I once asked a visiting professor who teaches philosophy and ethics concerning nonhuman animals if he pushed his students to read a book like that and he answered, "I put the information out there and let people come to it in their own way."

When I attempted to force the subject of animal rights on a group of people, I just ended up getting myself called a terrorist and a propagandist. This was about three years ago, when I was asked to give a lecture on campus on the concept of animals as thinking subjects. I titled my paper "Animal Sentience/Human Subjectivity" and set about exploring recent philosophical perspectives on the separation of the human mind from the animal body. As I researched material for my paper, I became increasingly unhinged. I read too much all at once: too much about vivisection and meat production and terrible cruelty. When I showed up to give the paper, I was in a rotten state of mind and I veered all over the place, showing pictures I had photocopied from Sue Coe's *Dead Meat*, quoting sources comparing concentration camps to slaughterhouses, handing out leaflets. It's not that I regret having done all of this; it's more that I wish I had kept my wits about me better. If I had just kept a cooler head, if I had just scaled back the mountain of information I confronted, then I might have handled the question period more professionally and I might not have been asked, by a colleague who called the next day, why I had become a "bomb-thrower" and not an intellectual. I remember feeling terribly embarrassed—just dreadfully red-faced—for a long time afterward. The story doesn't have an entirely bad ending, though. I still like the ideas I came up with for the talk and I still get asked to give on-campus talks about animals and ethics. I've learned to become more strategic, more cunning maybe, and less messianic.

It's important to be dexterous when advocating for animals because it's difficult for people to absorb the shock of the information about all the hateful ways in which humans treat and use animals. Because we humans are equipped with such a strong capacity for psychological repression, it's hard to unseat deeply ingrained ideas or behaviors. It's like showing someone a sphere—what someone has been calling a sphere her entire life—and then shifting it, just slightly, into a different light so that it is revealed to be in fact a cube. The onlooking person would then have to stop herself from calling a cube a sphere; or, she might avoid that particular angle of light, so that she could persist in calling it a sphere for a little longer. I understand the resistance—as someone who really did shuffle, all stiffly and sideways, sort of like a crab, toward the cause of helping animals, and I would hate to be told that I arrived too late or that I didn't do enough.

When I finally decided to do some advocating for animals, I thought I'd help out at the Winnipeg Humane Society (WHS), cleaning cat cages and walking dogs. I filled out the forms, put "professor" under the category for occupation, met with the manager, and was promptly steered toward the Social Action Committee and the Farm Animal Welfare Committee. A few months later, I attended a meeting with the WHS Director, Vicki Burns, about the Quit-Stalling campaign she had started. We met in her office, with other volunteers, and she introduced us to Penelope, a life-sized sow that an art student had made out of papier-mâché. Penelope stood, looking very real, in a metal stall purchased from a Manitoba hog farmer. When Vicki handed us the information, explained the campaign, and told us that millions and millions of sows lived in those stalls their entire lives, I started to cry (and I wailed inarticulately all the way home, while my confused husband silently drove the car). I knew the industry was bad, but I didn't know it was *that* bad. I had no idea that pigs were kept in cages so small that they can't even turn around or lie down properly; that right now, as I write this, millions of them are confined in such a way, forced to defecate through the metal floors of their crates, forced to receive food from so-called swine technicians.

So, I agreed to volunteer several weekends a year to take Penelope out to the shopping malls and ask people to sign petitions. The very first weekend, Vicki sent me and another woman to a mall in the meat-packing district of town. (She and I still refer to this first outing as the time when we were parachuted in and dropped behind enemy lines.) Big men in leather jackets who owned hog factories and who worked for the meat company nearby were not happy to see us in their local shopping venue. We quickly learned to remain calm in the face of their sputtering outrage. When people shout, "Get a real job, you (expletive deleted)!" I refrain from barking back, "That's *Dr.* (expletive deleted) to you," and simply ask, "What is it that you think you have to hide?" We also learned, in the future, not to make any eye contact with any hostile-looking men in leather jackets (especially, for some reason, the kind with cloth arms) who stalked past the table. That's just asking for trouble.

Making eye contact with these guys is as good as extending an invitation to skirmish on an uneven battleground. Decked out in jackets that signify toughness, masculinity, and an allegiance to sports or hunting (or both), they view a glance in their direction as a reason to approach us. The only advantage we have lies in our ability to ignore them, which they tend to broodingly reciprocate; otherwise, it's man versus woman, big versus small, the heavy leather jacket (with tribal symbols stitched all over it) versus the light cotton t-shirt (with a weeping pig printed on it). I have been caught off-guard several times, though, because sometimes they smile as they move toward the volunteer table. For example, on a recent shift, I started talking to one of these gents, only to find out that he approached me to discuss both his proprietorship of several hog barns and his singular opinion of me. He started roaring, "Do you know what's wrong with you? Do you know what's wrong with you? Do you want me to tell you what is wrong with you?" Pretty sure that I did not want to hear what was wrong with me, I abruptly stood up, shouted something about knowing what was wrong with *him*, and walked away. I'm not sure how the other volunteers handled him afterward; when I returned, they were talking with some other people, busily handing them pens and offering them information.

Some malls are easier for animal advocacy than others, but sitting with Penelope is always a difficult thing to do. Some people put their hands into her stall and whack her; others tell us that our efforts are futile because the world wants cheap bacon. It's painful to talk to the elderly people who approach the table in distress, exclaiming that farms were just not like that when they were young. Sometimes we meet young men who work in the barns and who confirm that, yes, it is exactly so and that they hate their jobs. We never call anyone over to the table; we sit near the heavy metal stall and we put signs on top of it that say, "This is not a temporary holding pen. This is how a breeding sow spends her entire life." We consider it a kind of public service announcement, and we are often overwhelmed with positive responses. My favorite moment is the one that took place about a year ago in a shopping mall near my house: a woman rounded the corner, saw Penelope, read the signs, and then shouted from about three yards away, "You've got to be (expletive deleted) kidding!"

Little by little, we're getting the message out there. It's a tiny sound against the roaring machinery of the meat industry, but I like to think that somehow the pigs can hear it, that somehow they know that they're not entirely without hope as they wait out their lives in those wretched, hideous hog barns.

If I had any advice for the next generation of animal rights advocates, I'd tell them to read a lot, join PETA, and try to keep their sense of humor. People I absolutely adore eat bacon in front of me all the time. If I fumed at every opportunity, I'd end up alone with my cats, who also eat meat in front of me all the time. Sometimes, a person just has to accept ridiculousness. To wit: Last Christmas, one of my best friends invited me and my family over for a festive dinner, where she lovingly served ham (because of tradition, she apologetically explained, because that's what her mother had always served). The next day, when another friend called for the obligatory social-gathering postmortem, she said, "What was Hilary *thinking* serving that ham? My husband said it was all pink and glistening and chubby, just like a warm little baby." Having just given birth myself, I snorted in delight. She said, "Truly, what *was* she thinking? Doesn't she remember that I'm a Jew who never eats ham-babies and that you spend your weekends at the mall with a pig?"

# Chapter 2

# On the Road with Open Rescue

## Patty Mark

*The second of twelve children, **Patty Mark** grew up in rural USA, in a small farming town where milk was on tap in the family dining room and meat was on the table twice daily. Nonetheless, she went vegetarian in 1974 after seeing the head in "goat's head soup." Settling in Melbourne, Australia, in 1975, she gave birth to three children: Noah in 1976, Elsa in 1977, and Animal Liberation Victoria in 1978 (www.alv.org.au). A vegan abolitionist for fifteen years, she pioneered Open Rescue, in which people "illegally" rescue animals, but do so publicly (www.openrescue.org).*

### HIDE AND SEEK AND RUN LIKE HELL

"Pick us up, *now!*" Deb's whispered voice yelled into the mobile phone, and I could hear her gasping for breath, her feet crashing through leaves and branches on the forest floor. Coming from Deb, I knew this was serious, so I turned the key in the ignition and pushed down the pedal.

Romeo took my mobile, but I could still hear Deb's frantic cries, "*Hurry, Hurry!*" Thankfully, my eyes were accustomed to the moonlit night, since we had been "standing guard" in the rescue van on a dirt track for over an hour. I made a sharp turn onto an old country lane and scanned the black bushland for Deb's flashing light. There it was, as well as two other flashlights bouncing frantically up and down as they closed in on Deb and Diana. Within seconds the side door of the van slid open, and Deb and Di both fell in yelling, *"Get out of here QUICK!"*

I pressed my foot to the floor. In the rear view mirror, I could see the whites of an angry man's eyes within meters of the van. Another vehicle appeared on a parallel track, and we could hear the door slam as it picked up a passenger then accelerated. Yes, they were coming after us—a chase was on!

Our rescue team had traveled more than four hours from Melbourne that weekend. First, we intended to dismantle duck hides ("blinds," behind which the hunter hides to fire at ducks) in a popular wetland, as it was nearly time for the annual duck shooting season. Second, we intended to check out what a local member suspected was a "white veal" factory farm.

The morning was warm and clear. We hit crown land wetlands early. Since it was pre–duck season, the hunters were not hiding inside their makeshift blinds, out of sight of their dangerous and fierce victims—the ducks. During duck season, shooters dress in camouflage gear and clutch big guns as they crouch inside their hides, where the gentle waterbirds, feeding on the lake, don't notice their presence. When the ducks wander near, the hunters blast them to pieces. Crown land is public property, yet these thrill killers brazenly erect their hides along the shore lines, complete with personalized ID tags. The hides, some built in the shallows, stood empty and vulnerable.

So we just as brazenly took their hides to pieces, flattening at least twenty before a ute (Utility Vehicle) appeared in the far distance, speeding to the scene, carrying an angry shooter. We figured this hyperventilating human had been alerted by the guy suffocating fish on a nearby shore, fishing pole in hand. He had noticed our good work! Though our work was exceptional, we thought the better of taking credit, and scattered. Those who were waist deep in the water headed to the other side of the wetland, while I made a direct dash for the van. (The first thing shooters do is slash tires.) I skidded off before the ute arrived, shouting to my coliberators that I'd collect them on the other side. It was a long wait, since they had to hide in the reeds while more shooters rushed to the scene, examining our exquisite handiwork.

Luckily, the police came, too. Seeing me parked on the roadside, an officer asked to see my driver's license, and what I was doing parked by the wetlands. I handed him my license and smiled, "Waiting for friends." He repeatedly asked for their names, but I refused, noting in a friendly tone that their names didn't matter.

The officer flashed a cheeky grin. "We have ways of finding out," he replied as he turned away. But he knew as well as I did that duck hides on crown land were no more personal or private property than sandcastles on a beach.

I picked up my trusted friends, and we had a good rest before setting out at midnight to track down the veal operation. The cruel overseas practice of "white veal" entails confining newborn calves in rows of wooden stalls barely larger than their bodies, then keeping them in darkness twenty-two hours a day, feeding only milk or formula from buckets. The lack of sunlight, iron, and roughage makes the calves anemic, ensuring that their flesh stays "tender and white." Luckily, this practice hasn't taken firm hold in Australia. We were determined to investigate, and if it *was* in operation, to expose it with video footage.

Deb and Di are the two bravest women I know. We'd been doing Open Rescue together for years, and with them I always felt we could do anything, once we put our minds to it. Each one of us is so very different from the other, yet working together, we were a tight unit. Deb doesn't know the meaning of the word fear, Di can do anything with a video camera, and I won't budge once I've made contact with an animal in distress.

All that aside, you could hear our hearts pounding as we sped down the Princes Highway, maxed out in our rattling van at 110 kilometers an hour, with an angry driver tailgating! Luckily, at two or three in the morning there wasn't much traffic. Still, I was surprised when their vehicle pulled up beside us, and naively, for a second, hoped they would be on their way. But they drove right alongside, still going 110 k's an hour, and I could see this extremely angry man motioning me to pull off the road. He drove his car *so close* that I soon had no choice. I pulled over. Two huge blokes (men) got out and headed our way. We could see anger, pumped up muscles covered in tattoos, all coming our way. We were terrified. I blurted out, "Oh no, guys, what should I do?"

"*Go!*" everyone yelled. I put my foot to the floor and got back onto the highway.

Of course they came after us. From the back seat, Deb rang the police and kept them on the line while these two furious men tailgated us and ran us off the road two more times. It took twenty minutes for the state patrol to reach us and apprehend our pursuers. They were booked for dangerous driving. Of course, it just so happened that these were police from the same station as the officer who had questioned me that very morning at the wetlands, and he took each of our names as witnesses.

Never mind; we had accomplished our mission. Safe back in our motel room, but still shaking, Deb explained that they never found any calves, but instead stumbled onto a "drug factory" hidden in the forest.

## In the Shit with the Hens

"The hens were trapped in their own shit?" I asked again. The woman on the phone confirmed. Those were her exact words, yet I couldn't make sense of what this employee on a battery hen farm was saying.

It was this call from Celia, in 1993, that tipped me off. Animal Liberation Victoria (ALV) was then fifteen years old.

I started ALV near the end of 1978, placing a handwritten sign in my local milkbar (as delis are called in Australia): "Help the Hens." The message called for a meeting. Luckily, a journalist from the *Herald Sun*, Melbourne's highest circulation paper, picked it up as an oddity, and wrote a paragraph on the proposed meeting to help hens, which helped to bring seventeen people to my living room on December 7.

At our first meeting I remember saying that the battery cage industry was huge, and that it might take us two years to shut it down. I said this so no one would be discouraged if we didn't manage to ban battery cages in just a few months. Such was my naïve enthusiasm.

I was the second of twelve children growing up in a small town in southern Illinois, in a rural community. Even so, I had little knowledge of factory farming. My father was a builder, and my mother loved kids and animals. More specifically, she looked after stray dogs who happened past, while feeding us meat and dairy in huge quantities, like many mothers of that era, in that part of the world. We even had a milk machine in the dining room—cows' milk on tap.

The two "treasures" from my childhood were my dog, Randy, my best friend from age four to seventeen, and the nuns and priests who taught us every day at school. Until years later, however, it didn't dawn on me that all their wonderful and genuine talk of love, compassion, and doing good work for others seldom mentioned animals. In their minds, as in our general culture, animals were there for us to use and enjoy—items of property like bikes, toys, groceries, clothes, and shoes; *things* we could buy, sell, loan, or eat. We must look after them of course, just like all of our other possessions.

When I posted that sign at the milkbar, I had never known a hen. In the months before, I had been reading a book that my Australian husband brought home from the library. I was extremely distressed by this author's descriptions of battery cages, where four and five hens were permanently crammed together in row after row of tiny wire cages, unable to walk, without *ever* getting out—*ever*—until they were sent to slaughter. This was torture and constant torment for these small birds. The blind ego of my species, which either didn't know or, worse, didn't care how these animals suffered, frustrated and shamed me. I was determined to *stop this cruelty*.

For fifteen years we marched in the streets, petitioned, met with Agricultural Ministers, spoke at schools, did street theater, handed out leaflets, erected and stood in battery cages in the city square ... whatever we could think of.

Then Celia rang.

"Yeah," she continued, pausing to draw on a cigarette, "the hens get out of the cages and fall down into the manure pit, there's no food or water down there, so I'm always throwing eggs down there for them to eat. But most starve to death, stuck in their own shit. At lunch break the blokes use them for target practice, but some only get wounded and flap around, which makes them laugh, it's disgusting."

"What do you mean 'manure pit'?" I asked. I had been taken to a few battery hen factories by the Department of Agriculture, but the ones I had seen contained a single tier of cages, about four feet above the ground. Celia was describing double-story, windowless sheds, with an enclosed excrement pit on the ground floor that collected the droppings of 52,000 birds. Five tiers of cages were crowded above.

Celia added, "There's a gap that runs along the length of the bottom tier of cages. Sometimes birds squeeze out, or when dead hens are pulled out. Workers don't close the cage properly, and birds escape into that space. Also, during partial depopulation, birds always escape, and they drop through this gap into the shit pit below." She kept pausing to pull on her cigarette. "Lots of the cages hold five, six, and even seven hens, though they're only meant for four. The cages up front have only four hens, just in case someone comes to inspect."

Though I had been working to ban battery cages for fifteen years, I had never seen or heard what this stranger from the country was describing, and I didn't know whether to believe her or not. She seemed genuine, and genuinely concerned, so I asked a friend if he'd take a job at that factory farm to confirm or deny her story. He agreed.

The battery operation was four hours north of Melbourne, and he only lasted three days. He discovered that conditions were every bit as horrible as Celia had described. Diana, who owned a country property nearby, offered to video the manure pit conditions.

I'll never forget how Diana went to this factory farm *alone,* at night, to get footage of these hens in distress. I was awed by her courage. When she brought the tape back to Melbourne, the footage stopped my heart. Stooped on a ledge of concrete, leaning against a floor support beam in a dark manure pit, a pitiful white hen slumped, with her pale, anemic comb flowing down over her entire face. She had nothing left, no hope, and no life. At the base of the concrete, where she sat dying, were mounds of chicken excrement, including a slurry created by a leaking water pipe. A dozen dead bodies swirled around in this shitty soup, once desperate thirsty birds hoping for a drop of fluid to ease their painful dehydration. Instead, they sunk in their own feces, and died. Other hens were roosting on top of the mounds of excrement that piled up under each aisle of cages. The little frail hen would be an easy target for the next lunchtime shooting session.

I'd *never* felt so propelled and compelled to take action. "We have to go straight there and get those hens!" I cried to Diana. "This is beyond belief." I called a few other people who I thought would help, then I rang the top rating current affair program, told them what we were going to do, and asked if they wanted to come along.

"Of course," they said, after viewing Diana's footage. On November 8, 1993, *Hinch at Seven* televised nationally across Australia "The Dungeons of Alpine Poultry." For the first time, the public saw with their own eyes the dead and dying hens in the manure pit, as well as the twenty debilitated hens we openly rescued that night; "Open Rescue" reclaimed its first desperate hens.

Open Rescue teams around the world now continue to find and save hens dying in manure pits, as well as sick pigs lying in their own filth, calves left for dead, and countless other exploited and neglected animals. Open Rescue activists are united by compassion and nonviolence, and are fueled by integrity and an unwavering duty to give aid to those in dire need.

Shortly after our story aired, a young, single mother showed up at the ALV office with two lovely daughters. "I saw the story on *Hinch*," she announced, "and want to help." The compassion and fire in Debra's eyes were unmistakable, and we have been partners in "crime" ever since.

## Grieving with the Pigs

Bolts of jagged lightning ripped open the black sky for what seemed an entire minute, followed by rumbling thunder that shook the ground. My twenty-year-old daughter had never accompanied me on a piggery rescue, but that night she had asked to come along. We held tightly to each other as we maneuvered our way across the rock-strewn paddock and through the barbed-wire fences in a crashing storm.

We were both grieving; I didn't want to leave her alone. Her dad, my estranged husband, had been buried the week before, three months to the day after doctors discovered his brain tumor. He and I were close, but nine years of nonstop animal advocacy had taken its toll. He couldn't cope. I was challenged by our marriage as well: He was eating the animals I worked to save. So we separated. His death and dying, eleven years later, was a tragic way to reunite; the kids and I kept vigil at his bedside until the end.

I wasn't sure if a pig rescue was what my daughter needed at the time; everyone handles grief differently. An animal activist's life is routinely heavy with grief. We know *too much* about how animals suffer and die. Counterintuitively, my antidote to this grief, when it becomes too much to bear, is to go where the animals suffer, to be there at their side, and to help however I can.

That night, now ten years ago, I felt closer to my daughter than I had in years. We were both consumed by sadness, but we were bonded and in some inexplicable way, transforming our personal pain into something positive.

The piggery was rundown, worse than most. The last time I was there I was with Deb, Diana, and Fiona. When the four of us had visited, it was freezing cold. The pigs, kept on bare concrete covered with excrement and urine, were filthy, smeared with their own waste. Leaking water turned pig droppings into a slurry, in which they stood and shivered. Some had bleeding prolapses and huge hernias. We walked past "grower" pigs, those in group pens who were being fattened for slaughter. We were filming in the "finishing" shed that night, which means that the pigs were around five months old, and ready for slaughter. They were already large animals and crowded.

In one of the finishing sheds Deb, Diana, Fiona, and I came across a pen with a couple of dead pigs, and another very weak pig, obviously near death. We wondered if this was a "sick bay." The huge, dying animal was black with feces, and shivering with cold. She was unable to stand up, and could barely move. Part of her body lay across a dead pig next to her. The whites of her eyes shone as she looked up at us, gleaming against the background of her filthy body. I pressed my water bottle to her mouth. She immediately grasped the bottle and *urgently* sucked every last drop of water. I stood patiently at the leaking water nipple, tears streaming, refilling the bottle for her.

We were distraught. It was heartbreaking. There was no way four women could carry this dying, 300-pound pig across four paddocks and over barbed wire fences to our rescue van. In a sane world, we could have driven to the nearby farm manager's house, explained that the pig needed to be seen by a vet, and asked for help. Wait, I take that back. In a truly sane world *there would be no pig factories.*

I had a large towel in my backpack, which I clumsily placed over her wet body to keep her warm. We were heavily dressed. She was visibly shaking from the cold, laying in a sludge of excrement next to two dead pigs, and dying.

Pigs are very intelligent animals, and they are extremely sensitive to cold and heat. Deb (a nurse) and I used the towel as a makeshift stretcher, and the four of us laboriously dragged her, inch by inch, to the central aisle where it was at least dry. This wasn't enough, but it was all that we could manage. We then made the long trek back to our vehicle, drove until sunrise, and rang the Department of Agriculture to lodge a complaint. As usual, they did not respond. But when we returned on that stormy night, my daughter and I grieving in unison, we brought an ABC film crew with us. It was too late for the dying sow on the previous visit, but we exposed the general public to the horrors that factory farmed pigs endure.

## THEY KILL BABIES

Fifty-two billion animals (this does not include sea creatures) are killed *every year* to feed the world's 6.6 billion flesh-eating humans (United Nations Food and Agriculture Organization 2004 figures). The overwhelming majority of these animals, 90 percent (or approximately 47 billion), are chickens. Billions of baby birds are killed each year so that humans can feast on their bodies, especially their legs and wings.

These figures are incomprehensible to most of us, yet they escalate as the human population swells, and nations such as China jump onto the factory farming, flesh-eating bandwagon. Meat consumption in China has grown from 23 kilograms to 54 kilograms per person, per year, since 1989 (still under half of the United States's consumption, which is 124 kilograms per person per annum).

So, who and where are these 47 billion chickens the world washes down with a soft drink or glass of wine? Many people who eat chickens assume that the flesh they swallow comes from the remains of exhausted battery hens (egg-laying hens). But the bodies of egg-laying hens (including barn laid and free range hens) *are too bruised and damaged* to sell as meat. "Egg-laying" hens are processed into stock cubes, fertilizer, or landfill.

The chickens people eat are called "broilers." These chickens are genetically selected and bred to gain weight as quickly as possible, making a normal, healthy lifespan impossible. The bodies of these hens and roosters literally outgrow their hearts, lungs, and legs. They are slaughtered at only six to eight weeks old, yet they are already the size of adult birds. Feed laced with antibiotics promotes their growth and also keeps them alive in putrid and dimmed sheds, where they spend their short life crammed alongside 40,000 other chicks, all sitting on top of their accumulated excrement.

Chickens, by far the largest number of land animals abused and killed every year, are only seen as a product, a package in the grocery store, a dripping delicacy on the deli spit, an item on our shopping list. Very few people know or care who these birds are, or how they lived and died, and they definitely don't want to know they are eating unhealthy, sickly, and genetically manipulated baby birds.

Our rescue teams have been inside numerous broiler chicken sheds, including recently the "parent bird sheds." This is an area of animal exploitation that animal activists are just discovering. Did we imagine that a stork delivered the billions of baby chicks born each year on factory farms? We came across a "parent bird shed" by accident, by following the screams of thousands of birds—wretched wailing sounds we'd never heard before.

Walking into that inferno of suffering and pain solidified my commitment to abolition and a vegan lifestyle. Campaigns against factory farming, cage eggs, feedlots, sow stalls, white veal ... all are important yet peripheral battles in the war against animal agriculture. The birds we heard screaming in pain that night are also the parents of free-range and aviary produced chickens bred and raised for consumption.

Aviary produced chickens, a system of intensive farming that was established as an alternative to battery cages, are common in the European Union and Britain. Aviaries are a way to intensively house thousands of birds without keeping them in individual cages, which appeases the public but does little for the hens. In this system, thousands of birds are permanently confined in sheds with perches and laying boxes, often several tiers high. The problems of manure, ammonia in the air, and crowded conditions are no better than conditions in large sheds used for the broiler industry.

## Reflections on Open Rescue

There's not enough room in this essay to introduce the special stories of all the birds we have met, but this I will tell you: Chickens have captured the minds and hearts of our rescue teams. Their intelligent and amiable personalities are largely unknown among humans. Chickens are wonderful beings.

The current trend toward animal welfare (humanely produced animal products) is not acceptable. Animal welfare won't get us where we need to be, it won't move us forward. More importantly, it will continue to put animals where they *don't* need to be—in abattoirs.

The most pain I've ever personally witnessed was a *free range* pig being killed at a slaughterhouse. She screamed, kicked, panicked, and frothed at the mouth in terror and desperation to avoid the knife being stabbed into her throat.

For my part, I will continue to engage in Open Rescue. I will continue to work to expose the horrors of factory farming to the general public, and I will continue to fight for animal liberation. Billions of lives hang in the balance. There can be no compromise.

CHAPTER 3

# No One Left Behind

*Kymberlie Adams Matthews*

**Kymberlie Adams Matthews**, *a long-time animal activist and vegan, was raised on a small animal sanctuary where she was taught to respect all living creatures. Kymberlie has worked with several national animal advocacy organizations and most recently served as the Managing Editor of* Satya *magazine, a publication dedicated to animal advocacy, environmentalism, social justice, and vegetarianism. She lives in Brooklyn with three misbehaved dogs, four schmaltzy cats, and a cantankerous bird named Larry.*

## SEPTEMBER 2001

Turbulence. Our plane was about to land and the bumpiness brought me to attention. I tightened my seatbelt and glanced out the window at a just awakening Ohio. It was barely morning as I had flown the red eye. Yet, despite knowing I had a very *long* drive ahead of me, I hadn't been able to get a wink of sleep on the flight. My mind was preoccupied. My thoughts were on the chickens.

It had been national news when it happened. Deadly tornadoes swept the Ohio valley, striking down twelve Buckeye Egg Corporation chicken warehouses. The media provided ample images of the millions of birds trapped in the rubble. Shocking were the number dead. But more grisly were the millions still alive. Topsy-turvy cages, mangled limbs, loose feathers everywhere. Squacks and screeches and fading peeps told of the suffering these birds felt. Broken and bruised without food, water, or shelter, this was tragedy.

Like most typical egg farms, each of the Buckeye chicken buildings held up to 150,000 birds cram-packed into wire "battery cages" stacked three rows high. All together, Buckeye, one of the largest egg factories in the country, housed over *15 million* hens. After the disaster hit, they tried to call the trapped hens "a loss"; discards that idling bulldozers waited to carry off as "debris."

So there I was, about to land in Croton only to take the pilot seat of an eighteen-foot U-Haul. My load: 500 of the Buckeye birds. Rescuers had been out for days, fighting to get as many chickens out of the wreckage as possible. My job was to bring some of the survivors home, driving them from Ohio to northern California where a farmed animal sanctuary eagerly anticipated their arrival.

Nebraska, Utah, one of the Dakotas ... I drove through eight states stopping every half hour to check on the birds who were desperately trying to find some comfort in the truck. Hay covered the truck floor. Food tins and water buckets had been nailed to wooden planks for support. I wore a bandana around my mouth and nose. It was cold and I couldn't stop shivering, but the windows remained open to keep the air fresh and cool for the birds. I didn't sleep. I couldn't eat.

Only a bit of fencing wire separated my driver's seat from hundreds of chickens; they were my passengers not my cargo. Together we managed to make the 1,000-mile drive in under thirty-two hours, but not once during those hours did my thoughts waiver from the images of those who never made it out—those left behind.

Soon after we drove away Buckeye embarked on a massacre. Hens were gassed, crushed by bulldozers, and suffocated in huge trash bins.

## KAPURRR-ING

"Cluck-cluck here girls! Suppertime." As a child, feeding the chickens was simply part of my daily chores. So was collecting their eggs. And mucking the goat stalls. *And* watering the rabbits. *And* so on. Growing up on an animal sanctuary I shared my life with all types of rescued critters—dogs, cats, goats, rabbits, ducks, chickens, and others. We were a family, sharing a little piece of the world, loving and taking care of each other. While I most certainly didn't always like my chores, often wanting to be playing games instead of pitching hay, I knew the work had to be done. And despite my artful attempts at dodging my chores, I knew they were important and that the nonhumans deserved to be taken care of.

Many of them had been through the unimaginable. Two of our pygmy goats were found mite-ridden and rotting away at a roadside zoo. One of our dogs was a fighting ring rescue. A dozen factory-raised rabbits, liberated from a live slaughter market in the city, roamed our yard. And a section of our barn had been converted into a ramshackle hospice for rehabilitating wildlife—litters of baby squirrels, rabbits, a fawn, and even skunks all passing through.

"Cock-a-doodle-doo!" A girl must admit when she has an affinity for chickens as strong as mine. I have spent countless hours lying in the grass, doing homework to their cooing and clucking. Sounds of happy and content purring, gurgling, "kapurrr-ing." Gathering around me, they would nestle in. White billows, gentle beak nibbles, my perfectly humane feather pillows. Who could not love these gentle creatures?

*You'd be surprised.* Many of our chickens were discards of the factory egg farm located several miles from our home in upstate New York. Every week or so, Ace Farms would proudly display a large box of baby chicks in the front window of their country market. Just picked blueberries, fresh sweet corn, home-style apple pie, and a box of baby chicks. A nearby stool made it easy for every child (and interested adult) to manhandle, squeeze, pinch, and drop the babies. Oh, how cute they were! Soft and fuzzy. Warm and yellow. Too young to know any better.

Ace Farms did their best to sex their chicks. Dumping all the little girls, beaks freshly singed and sliced, into crates warmed by artificial heating lamps, and all boys into big black plastic bags perfect for mass suffocation. They weren't worth two pennies to an egg farm. Randomly chosen, ten or so lucky chicks would be saved for the infamous store display.

As soon as the boxed chicks began to trade fluff for feathers, the folks at Ace Farm would gently gather them all into a black bag of death and place them outside as garbage. Discarded. Whenever possible my mom and sisters would go to Ace Farms, sort through the garbage, and find a few chicks alive. They were the lucky ones.

Grade A Jumbo, Medium Brown, Extra-Large White, known throughout surrounding counties as having the largest assortment of farm fresh eggs, Ace Farms was a hot spot for locals and tourists alike. Cute country-style signs of smiling chickens in blue stripped bonnets dangled from wrought iron hooks. "Get Your Farm Fresh Eggs!" Yet, I could never understand why people didn't ask the most obvious of questions of all: Where are the chickens?

Aside from the chicks in the display box, none was ever seen. Where was the farm? And why on earth didn't anyone ask what those enormous sheds were for? You know, the ones located behind the field where we seasonally gathered to pick our own pumpkins? At the age of thirteen, I made up my mind to find out.

## Turning Point

It was dark outside. Almost 11 p.m. Way past bedtime for a small town like Highland Mills. But for young teenagers anywhere, it was the perfect time to sneak out of the house undetected. Dressed in black, flashlight in pocket, my sister and I began our walk to Ace Farms. We were going to find out once and for all what the inside of the massive sheds looked like.

It wasn't hard to get in. This was still farm country and no one would worry about those animal rights "terrorists" for quite some time to come. Besides, we weren't out to destroy or steal. We just wanted to understand. In silence, we crossed the pumpkin patch and arrived at the doors to the first shed. I twisted the handle. "Click," the door was unlocked. Fear had engulfed me, filling my belly with acid. My mouth was dry. And when the smell hit me, I almost vomited. I have smelled animal waste my whole life, but nothing, *nothing* prepared me for the smell. It was death. Decomposition. Buzzing filled our ears as flies began swarming around our heads, dogging in and out of our noses. We couldn't breathe and could barely see. We turned our flashlights on. Hundreds of thousands of hens were crowded together in small, decrepit wire cages. Dead hens scattered the floor. Manure mountains and piles of broken eggs littered the aisle. Young and scared, I never could have imagined the horror before me. I knew it was bad, but this ... this was worse. Turning, we ran.

It was only later, after I caught my breath and was sure I had gotten all the flies out of my hair did I realize what we had done. What we didn't do. We had left them all behind.

## October 2005

The stench was indescribable. For days after the rescue I could smell it in my hair and on my skin. It is hard to imagine being a chicken and living day after day in this aroma of suffering. There had been hundreds of them, crammed into plastic crates, stacked one on top of another. Many were severely dehydrated, while others suffered from injured limbs and eyes. Many were dead. Strewn around the parking lot, black garbage bags full of dead and decomposing birds awaited the sanitation truck.

It was a makeshift market, set up in a Brooklyn parking lot to sell chickens for the Jewish kaparot ritual, which is observed around Yom Kippur and involves waving a live chicken around one's head while saying a prayer. These birds, they were the ones left behind. Simply abandoned and left to die in stormy weather. Almost all of the birds on the bottom layer of crates had drowned in the flooded parking lot.

Rescuers got to work. Bird after bird after bird was pulled from the wreckage and transported to sanctuary. Filthy and skeletal, their feathers stiff, encrusted with dried feces and urine. Toes broken. Wings sprained. Eyes and flesh torn.

Hours later we were done. We were exhausted. Our noses and sinuses full of stink and gunk. Voices all but gone from breathing in the noxious fumes of feather particles and bits of dried feces. But there they were. Over 300 chickens. I watched as many began to stretch their toes out, cautiously touching their feet to the ground and walking freely for the first time in their lives. I watched others huddle together, drifting off to sleep. Were their dreams good? I noticed one bird whose eye only minutes before had been encrusted shut with muck blink and look around. Did she feel relief? I know that I did. They were fed, free, and safe.

## Coming to Terms

I cried for days after entering the shed of Ace Farms. I cried for what I saw. For what I did. And for what I didn't do. My emotions were tangled. I was fragile. And I was determined to set things right. As a child, I didn't quite understand that I couldn't save them all. Hell, I was still coming to terms with the fact that not everyone cared about nonhumans. While I had certainly seen my share of cruelty, I felt I had always been able to do something about it. Even if it was picking out the live chicks from the suffocation bags. But that night was different. I had failed. I hadn't made things better for even one bird.

## June 2007

I look at a wall mirror and examine my face for evidence of deepening creases. Are those double lines between my eyes widening? The bags under them darkening? My face is catching up with my life. Knowledge and compassion are downright exhausting. Rescuing takes its toll.

It has been twenty years since that fateful night at Ace Farms. And while it took some time and some hard-learned lessons, I have come to terms with the events that took place. Indeed, I now have understanding. It's brutal. It's unfair. But it's true: There will always be those I cannot save. There will always be those I leave behind. And they will forever haunt my dreams, leaving profound scars on my heart and creases in my brow.

But I have found a way to keep them alive. I share their stories. Those hens are remembered because we have read about their tragic lives and senseless deaths. Putting pen to paper has become my way of making sure that no one is left behind.

# Chapter 4

# That's Some Sheep

*Lorri Houston*

**Lorri Houston** *is a pioneer in the farmed animal sanctuary movement. She opened the country's first shelter for farmed animals as cofounder of Farm Sanctuary. Lorri has directly saved thousands of nonhumans from the cruelties of factory farming, and has brought national attention to the plight of nonhumans used for "food production." Her work has been featured in hundreds of national and state news reports, and she has been featured in several documentaries. In 2005, Lorri Houston formed the nonprofit organization, Animal Acres (www.AnimalAcres.org), opening the Los Angeles Farmed Animal Sanctuary and Compassionate Living Center.*

In 1986 I discovered a living sheep on a stockyard "dead pile" and her rescue led me to cofound Farm Sanctuary, the first shelter in the country for farmed animals. Hilda the sheep was my first teacher, and set me on a path to rescue thousands of other suffering farmed animals and establish the farmed animal sanctuary movement.

I was investigating the Lancaster Stockyard in Lancaster, Pennsylvania, which bought and sold thousands of nonhumans each week. I found Hilda on the stockyard "dead pile." She had been thrown on a pile of dead and decaying farmed animals, and at first I didn't know she was alive, but she lifted her head as I approached. My partner and I rushed her to a nearby veterinarian, who determined she was suffering from heat exhaustion. One hour later, she was standing.

Though I didn't expect to see farmed animals treated well, I never expected to see them treated like "trash." I was shocked to find Hilda abandoned at the stockyard, and I was appalled to learn that dumping "downed" animals (nonhumans too sick or injured to stand) was *not* illegal in the state of Pennsylvania. We took photographs of Hilda on the dead pile. Through her identification tag we determined which trucker had dumped her, and that she had been on the dead pile for about 16 hours before we found her. Yet local authorities would not prosecute the trucker or stockyard for cruelty because abandoning sick and injured nonhumans was considered a "normal animal agricultural practice." Most states, including Pennsylvania, specifically exempt farmed animals from state anti-cruelty laws. Any act, no matter how cruel or inhumane, is legal for farmed animals.

Hilda enjoyed twelve blissful years at Farm Sanctuary. During our years together, she showed me how much can be accomplished when people care enough to be a vital participant in programs and campaigns to stop farmed animal suffering. In 1986, very few organizations were advocating for farmed animal protection, most people thought the word "vegan" was a character from *Star Trek*, and there were no farmed animal shelters in the country. Today we have over twenty-five farmed animal sanctuaries. The newest is Animal Acres, which I opened in Los Angeles in 2005.

Animal Acres is a unique twenty-six-acre farm, just forty-five minutes from Los Angeles. With its proximity to a major metropolitan area and the entertainment capital of the world, Animal Acres is in a strong position to bring our message of compassion to millions. In our first year of operation, I saw how much an urban farmed animal sanctuary can do—and how much people wanted to have farmed animal sanctuaries in their cities. A dedicated team of over 200 people came out to help us build the sanctuary. We saved over 200 nonhumans from slaughter, welcomed thousands of sanctuary visitors, and reached millions of people with news coverage of our efforts in the *Los Angeles Times*, the *Daily News*, and other major media. Dozens of Hollywood's famous friends of farmed animals joined Animal Acres to lend their voices and support. The comedian Bill Maher stated it best when he wrote, "I'm pleased to be a supporter of Animal Acres, L.A.'s new farmed animal sanctuary. This special place is giving city slickers an opportunity to get to know farmed animals—and it's hard to eat a pig after you've given one a belly rub."

Within one year of opening, we had raised the funding needed ($1.2 million) to purchase property. Animal Acres is now forever owned by the cows, pigs, chickens, and other farmed animals who desperately need a home of their own—and the organization continues to grow. Although I have been involved in the farmed animal sanctuary movement since 1986, the success of Animal Acres was a reminder to me of the crucial role played by farmed animal sanctuaries—both for nonhuman advocates and the general public.

In our own animal protection movement, farmed animal sanctuaries are helping teach animal advocates that cows, pigs, and chickens need our help, too—and the new and growing interest in farmed animal protection issues continues to prompt campaigns to ban cruel factory farming and marketing practices. Humane enforcement agencies are more willing to intervene to stop farmed animal cruelty if there is a shelter facility in the area for these nonhumans. Shortly after Animal Acres opened, a California humane agency was able to conduct the first U.S. raid on a slaughterhouse for cruelty to animals, and subsequently confiscated dozens of severely neglected nonhumans, who were then brought to Animal Acres for rehabilitation and refuge.

For people who come into contact with farmed animals only at breakfast, lunch, or dinner, farmed animal sanctuaries provide a positive way for the public to learn that farmed animals are friends, not food. Sanctuary visitors interact with the "animal ambassadors" while being educated on the harsh truth of how farmed animals are treated to produce meat, milk, and eggs. It's just a little easier for people to hear about the cruelties of dairy production when they are getting a big cow lick. Even the youngest sanctuary visitor "gets it" after giving a pig a belly rub and sampling a veggie hotdog. Farmed animal sanctuaries make it fun—and profound.

As a founder of Farm Sanctuary, and now Animal Acres, I have personally seen thousands of people "touched" by a farmed animal, and then make the decision to save *all* farmed animals by going vegetarian or vegan. More than anyone, those of us involved in direct rescue efforts for farmed animals recognize the only way to "be the change" is to use the sanctuary to open peoples' hearts and minds to the plight of farmed animals.

Every year, over 10 billion nonhumans are raised, transported, and slaughtered under the most inhumane and cruel conditions possible. During my own investigations of the meat, dairy, and egg industries, I have witnessed more suffering than I could have imagined in my worst nightmare. At hatcheries, I have seen tiny day-old chicks thrown alive into trash dumpsters because they were male and could not be used for egg production. I have given water to thirsty "downed" cows who were left suffering for hours, in parking lots, with temperatures over 100 degrees. I have looked into the many hopeless eyes of calves chained to veal crates, unable to walk or even turn around. I've watched in horror as pigs with broken legs dragged themselves to the killing floor, as they were kicked and shocked by slaughterhouse workers.

People often ask me what the hardest part is of doing farmed animal rescue and sanctuary work. Witnessing animal cruelty is very difficult, but leaving suffering beings behind is devastating. Over the years, I have had to make hundreds of "Sophie's Choices"—choosing which ones to save, and which ones to leave behind. I remember the hardest rescue I ever worked on like it happened only yesterday—the Buckeye Egg Farm Rescue.

The Buckeye Egg Farm in Ohio is a typical egg production factory farm. To produce eggs, four to five hens are crammed into a bare wire cage about the size of a folded newspaper. The confinement is so severe, the hens cannot walk, stretch their wings, or even lie down comfortably. The Buckeye Egg Farm was one of the largest egg production facilities in the country, housing 14 million hens in large warehouses which held 80,000–100,000 birds per building. Tornadoes struck the Buckeye Egg Farm facility, and overnight, over one million birds became trapped in demolished buildings.

There was no way to prepare myself for the devastation and the suffering. The warehouses that housed the birds had been severely damaged, and most of the buildings were missing sides, roofs, or both. Most of the birds were still trapped in the mangled cages without access to food or water. For several days, we tried to rescue as many hens as we could, while urging the owners of the facility to remove hens from cages as quickly as possible and humanely euthanize the ones who could not be taken to sanctuaries. On my last trip to the Buckeye Egg Farm, the birds had been in the cages without food or water for twelve days. I expected to see birds weak and near death—what I saw instead were birds who were very much alive and moving frantically in their cages.

The Buckeye Egg Farm would not allow animal groups to help release birds from cages, claiming it was "too dangerous" to allow nonemployees to enter demolished areas. They agreed to let us have as many hens as we could take, but we had to agree to this stipulation. Still, there were times I had to make a mad dash to a cage of hens. I approached one cage that was smashed in half and reached down to pick up a bird who was caught in the wire of a mangled cage. I tucked the hen safely into my shirt, and then I tried to pry open the cage bars to rescue another hen who had her wing caught in the wire—but I was forced to leave the area before I could get her. The look on her face will never leave me. I also had to break the rules when I saw birds stuck in the manure slurry pits that accumulated under the cages. The live birds were slowly sinking into the wet manure. I got three birds out of the pit before I was stopped.

After a great deal of pressure, the Buckeye Egg Farm agreed to remove trapped birds and euthanize them. The "bird removal" crew consisted of six to eight workers to remove almost 100,000 birds from piles of debris and mangled cages. It was agonizingly slow, and cruel. The workers grabbed the birds by the legs and threw them into a tractor loading bucket. The tractor then drove to a large trailer, and dumped the live birds into it. The birds fell, flapping their wings and screaming, onto the other birds in the trailer, who lay dead, or dying. A tarp was then pulled over the trailer, and $CO_2$ gas was pumped into it for five minutes. When the tarp was pulled back, many of the birds lay gasping until the next loader full of birds was dumped on top of them.

After attempting to remove and euthanize birds for a few days, Buckeye Egg Farm halted its bird removal effort, and sent in bulldozers. Hundreds of thousands of birds were crushed and buried alive.

We documented all of this cruelty and death. The endless rows of trapped birds. The nonhumans stuck in quicksand-like manure pits. The birds being thrown into gas chambers and left suffocating, gasping for breath. We tried to convince authorities to prosecute the facility for animal cruelty, but we were unsuccessful. It was considered a "natural disaster," though it was clear the suffering was caused by the "unnatural" confinement of millions of nonhumans. In the end, there was nothing I could do but save as many as possible. On the last day we were allowed in, I drove off with 500 hens. I didn't glance back as we pulled away ... I couldn't.

It is hard to witness animal cruelty and leave suffering nonhumans behind—and when I am struggling to cope with my anger and grief, I try to remember another nonhuman teacher who crossed my path, a hen named Henny.

When I was directing Farm Sanctuary's shelters, I received a call from the American Society for the Prevention of Cruelty to Animals (ASPCA) that a chicken needed a home—a chicken who had somehow managed to escape from a factory farm and end up on a New York City bus. Fortunately, the kind driver knew this was a chicken in trouble, and drove her to the ASPCA. At the time, our New York shelter was completely full because of the Buckeye Egg Farm rescue. We didn't have any rehabilitation pens open at our shelter, but after hearing about her heroic escape, I just couldn't say no. So, until she was healthy enough to be with the other shelter chickens, "Henny" moved in with us.

At the time, my family consisted of four dogs, three cats, two humans (and now one chicken), and we were all residing in a small, one-bedroom cabin. I didn't want Henny to be locked alone in the bathroom, so I cautiously let her into the main room, keeping a particularly watchful eye on the dogs. I was concerned that Henny would be intimidated and not "fit in," but I didn't have to worry for long—at least about the chicken. The dogs were the first to learn that Henny would rule the roost. The minute my largest dog KJ stuck her nose into her, Henny gave KJ a peck on the nose—clearly there was going to be no dog "nosing" in this household. This chicken had attitude—she was from New York City all right. Later that night, after everyone seemed to settle in and things were starting to get peaceful, I was relaxing on the couch with Pierre (cat) in my lap. Henny walked over to the couch, surveyed the situation, and then jumped on to my lap—which of course meant she also jumped on to the cat. Pierre leaped into the air hissing and screaming and Henny didn't ruffle a feather. She just calmly settled into my lap, ignoring the glaring cat, and started cooing.

The first night, I put her into a bedded carrier so she (and the rest of us) could sleep soundly throughout the night. She didn't seem to like this idea, and I felt a little guilty as her eyes followed me into the bedroom. That night, she must have worked her way into my dreams, because I woke up knowing I couldn't put her in the carrier again. By now, everyone had accepted Henny into the household, so it seemed safe enough to just let her find her own sleeping spot in the house. The big dogs grabbed the couch, the cats and small dogs jumped on our bed, and we all crawled under the covers. Within seconds, I heard the tiny "click-click-click" of Henny's feet, and they were coming closer and closer. I peered over the side of the bed, and there was Henny, looking up. I'd seen this look before—Henny was going to jump on to the bed. I went to the bathroom and grabbed a towel for the bed, and Henny jumped up and slept with us until dawn. (In case you're wondering, Henny was "housebroken" and never had an "incident" on the bed or furniture.)

At night when Henny and I cuddled together, I was amazed by her trusting and loving nature. She was, after all, a hen who had lived her entire life under cruel factory farm conditions. She had suffered "debeaking" a painful mutilation that involves cutting off the tip of hens' beaks to reduce pecking injuries because the birds are so severely overcrowded. Then, for months, she endured intensive confinement in a bare wire cage with several other hens—a cage so small that she could not even stretch her wings. Finally, when she was no longer "productive" she was literally torn from her cage and thrown into a transportation truck headed for slaughter. Bruised, battered, and worn-out laying hens are ground up and used for pot pies and baby food.

In the few weeks she stayed with us, I discovered that Henny was curious and intelligent (she learned in one night to stay on the towel in her corner of the bed). Henny was fearless and self-assured (I learned this when I saw her "take on" a ninety-pound growling dog because *she* wanted the chew toy). Henny was friendly (she greeted me at the door each day after work and then followed me around like a puppy dog). And, Henny loved to be loved (and gave me enormous amounts of love in return).

Henny had never known a kind touch from a human. Humans had only inflicted fear, pain, and endless days of torment. Yet, she had chosen to bring us into *her* family—a family filled with generosity, forgiveness, and hope. It was a sad day when Henny was ready to be with her own people (well, maybe not so sad for my companion dogs and cats), but I was grateful for the time I had with this remarkable teacher, who reminded me of all that one chicken, or person, can be.

My biggest mission in life is to teach people that farmed animals *are* animals—animals who feel pain or comfort, or joy or sorrow, just like a dog or cat. Farmed animal sanctuaries provide the opportunity for people to learn and love. Colin, a newborn goat brought to Animal Acres, taught us to love, even when our hearts are breaking.

Colin was taken from his mother when he was just a day or two old. Like male calves, male goats are taken to livestock auctions as soon as they are born and sold for meat production. We don't know who bought Colin, but we do know little Colin was purchased by humans whose hearts had turned to stone.

Colin was abandoned in a canyon late at night—with both of his ears cut off. One ear had been completely severed and the other ear had been cut off halfway. His cries were heard by two responsible individuals who intervened to help, and took Colin to local authorities. Within twenty-four hours, Colin had found safe refuge at Animal Acres. After determining that he needed immediate medical attention, our veterinarian performed corrective surgery and repaired both ears. Because of his condition, Colin couldn't be with the other goats and sheep, so he lived in the sanctuary ranch house or offices at night, and the visitor courtyard during the day.

Despite all he had been through, Colin was one of most loving and friendly nonhumans we have ever met. He always wanted to be near people, and liked to sit in visitors' laps. At night, he would sleep on the couch or his fluffy "blankie" on the floor. Our little "house-goat" became a beloved member of our sanctuary family, and he deeply touched everyone who met him.

Sadly, surgery, veterinary care, and hours of love weren't enough to save Colin. Since he lacked essential nutrients from his mom's milk, his immune system was weak. Colin passed away peacefully in his sleep one night on his favorite blankie. We were devastated. Our grief turned into anger as we gathered to bury him. His grave was filled with roses from the sanctuary courtyard, and locks from our hair (he loved to chew on peoples' hair). Then, one by one, we started remembering how Colin had done so much in his short time on Earth to teach people to extend compassion to farmed animals too. It was as if our littlest angel was watching, and reminding us never to let hate or anger consume our compassion and love.

We remembered that Colin loved humans even after humans had tortured him.

We remembered how Colin would smile when people were petting him.

We remembered how Colin wanted to be a part of our Country Hoedown and stood for hours to be kissed and cuddled.

We remembered his last day on Earth, when he helped to teach over sixty visiting schoolchildren to be kind to *all* beings.

And we remembered how he motivated people to protect farmed animals. Everyone who met Colin wanted to help. When we asked the schoolchildren what they should do if they see someone hurt an individual like Colin, the kids replied, "Tell someone who can help," "Call the police," and "Take the animal to a safe place like here (Animal Acres)."

One Animal Acres member posted Colin's picture and story on a message forum, and the responses brought more tears to our eyes. One person wrote, "It is always uplifting to me that with everything an animal can go through, they can still respond so readily to love and care." Another wrote, "I'm so sorry his life was so short, but at the very end, the horrors he had gone through were replaced with love overflowing beyond measure. I hope those schoolchildren will take that lesson with them for the rest of their lives and use it to do good for animals."

Colin knew that hate and anger don't change the world—and he reminded us that we must always turn anger into compassion and compassion into action.

People are now seeing cows, pigs, and chickens as living, feeling beings, and it is changing the way society views and treats farmed animals. When people learn about the suffering farmed animals endure, they are shocked and appalled, and they go vegetarian, and/or vote to stop abusive farming practices. In addition to the creation of dozens of new farmed animal sanctuaries, the past ten years have ushered in laws and initiatives banning cruel animal agriculture practices, along with the introduction of vegetarian and vegan food options at almost every major supermarket and restaurant throughout the country. Through farmed animal sanctuaries, farmed animals themselves finally have a voice. They are their own advocates—and perhaps that is why the farmed animal sanctuary movement is so successful.

At times, working on behalf of 10 billion suffering nonhumans is heartbreaking, and daunting. But Hilda, Henny, Colin, and the other farmed animals have touched my life, and have given me hope—because each and every person *can* do something to stop the suffering *now*, simply by choosing what, or whom, to eat.

# Chapter 5

# Slaughtergate

## Investigating Nonenforcement of Farmed Animal Laws

*Gail A. Eisnitz*

*Gail A. Eisnitz, 2004 winner of the Albert Schweitzer Medal, is chief investigator for the Humane Farming Association. Her work has resulted in exposés by ABC's* Good Morning America, PrimeTime Live, *and* Dateline NBC, *and has been featured in the* New York Times, Los Angeles Times, *and* US News & World Report. *She has been interviewed by more than 1,000 radio stations. Eisnitz was the driving force behind a front-page exposé documenting slaughterhouse atrocities for the* Washington Post, *one of the highest reader-response pieces ever run, after which a* Washington Post *reporter described her as "the most courageous investigator I've ever seen."*

I think about some of the more fortunate nonhumans I've encountered over the years. Like Chloe, the rescued turkey with the abscessed foot the size of a baseball, whose eyes dreamily close and who drifts in and out of sleep when you gently pat her head. Or Spanky, the abandoned domesticated wild boar, who barrels from his shelter 150 feet away to greet you when he hears his name, then carefully drops to his side so you can use his 400-pound body as a giant cushion to lean up against. And Romeo the rooster who pecks at ankles until you pick him up and carry him during rounds to visit the other nonhumans on the refuge. And I think of my friend Patty's parrot, who communicates his demands and initiates conversations in English, and who has taught his mate, and now his offspring, how to converse in English. And then I think about the 10 billion nameless, faceless, and voiceless beings who are raised and slaughtered for human consumption each year just in the United States.

\* \* \*

I was seduced into the animal protection field by a PBS television documentary, produced by Quaker Oats, about polar bears and wildlife conservation. I was fourteen years old. The name of the documentary was "Say Good-bye." The last scene was filmed from a helicopter. It was of two polar bear cubs stranded on an ice floe. Their mother had been shot, and they were staring up at the camera in abject terror. Their helplessness cut me to the *core*. That was thirty-seven years ago. You might say that particular TV show sealed my fate. From that day on, I knew I would save nonhumans as a career.

Next, when I was in high school, I wrote a paper on endangered species. I learned about the Passenger Pigeon and the Carolina Parakeet and how they had been wiped out by zealous hunters. It was hard to fathom Passenger Pigeons once so plentiful that they blackened the sky. Yet they had been blasted into oblivion. I was deeply touched and felt that something had to be done to save endangered species. I was going to be the one to do it.

As a result of these happenings, and my interactions with my beloved cat H.R., who was with me for twenty years, I decided to study wildlife management and natural resource conservation in college. Little did I know that I would be indoctrinated by a bunch of hunters masquerading as professors, and I would graduate from college with the erroneous belief that wildlife had to be "managed for maximum yield."

Just out of college, I worked for the U.S. Forest Service in Oregon, and for the New Jersey Division of Fish, Game, and Wildlife. I found myself leading hunters into the "wilds" of New Jersey to kill nonhumans, contrary to my beliefs. I was promptly fired for refusing to stock domestically raised pheasants for hunters to shoot.

\* \* \*

I headed to Washington, DC, pounding the pavement over the course of several years in search of work within the animal protection movement. When I couldn't land a job in animal protection with any of the national groups in DC, I taught myself how to draw, and became an animal illustrator. This enabled me to work for groups like Audubon, HSUS, and Defenders of Wildlife until such time as I convinced somebody to hire me full time.

Then "the exterminator" arrived and further changed the course of my life. Unbeknownst to me, our landlord hired an exterminator to spray the house where I lived with several young women. Instead of catching the ants and putting them outside, as I did, the landlord wanted all the ants dead. The exterminator sprayed along the baseboards of each room and directly over an illustration of a baby bald eagle I had drawn for a story I'd written on New Jersey's endangered eagles. The story I *subsequently* wrote, which compared the destruction of my illustration from pesticide to the demise of New Jersey's bald eagles from DDT, was published in the *New York Times*. That was my first *New York Times* article. I was in my mid-twenties.

I traveled often to Washington, DC to attend "Monitor" meetings, weekly gatherings of representatives from the major animal protection organizations to discuss news and events. I would hand out my résumé, ever hopeful that someone would hire me. At each meeting, I would see the elegant, yet matriarchal Christine Stevens, president of the Animal Welfare Institute and in many ways one of the founders of the animal protection movement. (Christine was the first to fight successfully in the U.S. Congress to protect nonhumans.)

One day, while living in New Jersey, I visited a large veal producer in the northern part of the state and interviewed the farmer. With the help of a sympathetic editor at the *New York Times,* and with assistance from my mentor Michael W. Fox, then vice president for farm animals at the Humane Society of the United States, I spent almost a year working on my first exposé documenting the mistreatment of calves exploited for milk-fed veal. Shortly after the piece was published, I was hired by Christine Stevens at the Animal Welfare Institute.

As staff writer and lobbyist, my first project—a graphic feature for the *New York Times* about trapping—influenced passage of New Jersey's controversial anti-trapping bill following an eighteen-year battle. The morning of the vote, the story I'd written was placed on the desk of every senator in the New Jersey Senate Chamber. By the end of the day, the senators passed the bill banning the steel jaw leghold trap. This marked my first victory in my career in animal protection.

Eventually I found myself working at the Humane Society of the United States as a writer, and then, after years of scout work, as a national field investigator. At the time, I was the only female national field investigator. In that position, I could both investigate and then write about my findings for various publications. I investigated a wide array of animal abuses, including the mass production of dogs at commercial puppy mills, the use of live lures by the greyhound industry, the sale of debilitated horses to killer buyers, and finally, the intolerable abuses to nonhumans on factory farms.

In 1992, Bradley Miller, national director of the Humane Farming Association (HFA), hired me as the organization's chief investigator. At HFA, my investigations took me to see one of the most debased sides of human society—the way we treat and slaughter farmed animals. First, I investigated the smuggling and widespread distribution and use of an illegal, toxic substance known as clenbuterol, used in the production of calves for the U.S. milk-fed veal industry. Realizing that concerns about consumer safety could draw attention to the plight of calves in the veal industry, I traveled from slaughterhouse to slaughterhouse collecting eyeballs and bladders from calves exploited for veal, slaughtered for human consumption. I shipped these samples to the world's leading testing lab in Holland, for elaborate testing for clenbuterol. While the United States Department of Agriculture (USDA) had claimed it could find no traces of clenbuterol in tested veal samples, the Dutch lab found the toxic drug in more than one-third of my samples. I turned over my evidence to federal authorities and assisted in the convictions of four drug kingpins in the veal industry. After months of pitching the story, I finally convinced ABC's *PrimeTime Live* to expose my findings. I would later climb into dumpsters to retrieve pig carcasses for testing, and cut out eyeballs from the carcasses of pigs at rendering plants and slaughterhouses in order to have them tested for drug residues. Again, even samples from slaughterhouses that were selling pigs for human consumption tested positive for toxic drugs.

\* \* \*

Then I received a tip from a USDA employee in Florida that cattle at his plant were being skinned and dismembered alive. I spent the next five years crisscrossing the country documenting the routine dragging, strangling, skinning, scalding, and dismembering of fully conscious beings at essentially every slaughterhouse I visited. It became apparent that the federal Humane Slaughter Act (HSA), a law that had been on the books for forty years, was altogether unenforced. With my documentation and follow-up, I gained the support of the 6,000-member meat inspectors union—comprised of the very individuals who were required by law to enforce the HSA.

Even with reams of documentation and the support of the meat inspectors union, I was repeatedly disappointed by the media. All three television networks worked with me to expose my findings, and then ultimately nixed those stories on the grounds that the subject matter was "too disgusting." That's when I wrote *Slaughterhouse*, a book exposing violations of the Humane Slaughter and Federal Meat Inspections acts in U.S. slaughter plants. The result: For the first time in the law's history, funding was appropriated by Congress, and personnel were delegated, for enforcement of the HSA.

\* \* \*

During the course of my investigations, I've seen much grisly abuse. With individuals required to kill as many as 1,100 nonhumans an hour—one slaughterhouse I visited kills roughly *192,000 hogs a week*—workers were resorting to brutality to keep the slaughter line running smoothly. I've seen live pigs arrive in winter at the slaughterhouse frozen solid like rocks, and who had to be pried off the sides of trucks with knives and chains; live cattle whose legs were caught in chutes or trucks and workers chain sawed or blow torched their limbs off; conscious hogs who could no longer walk, who had meat hooks inserted into their mouths or anuses to drag them to the stunning area.

Among the most horrendous of violations I encountered was the complete skinning and dismembering of cattle while they were still conscious. I was able to expose and stop the skinning and dismemberment of hundreds of thousands of fully conscious cattle at a slaughterhouse operated by the world's largest meat packer. The "down puller" had stripped all the skin from the farmed animals' bodies—except on their heads—and their legs had been removed. They were still struggling. At another plant, I exposed and halted the immersion of hundreds of thousands of conscious hogs into the scalding tank for dehairing while they were still kicking and squealing.

I think the worst cruelty I observed, however, was inside factory hog farms. As Humane Farming Association's chief investigator, I had the unique opportunity to work with three other women on a campaign to stop construction of the world's third-largest hog factory. It was to be built on the Rosebud Sioux Indian Reservation in South Dakota, and it was to "finish" nearly one million pigs a year. I joined forces with Prairie Hills Audubon President Nancy Hilding in Rapid City, South Dakota Peace and Justice Center President Jeanne Koster, and Concerned Rosebud Area Citizens President Oleta Mednansky, a tribal member, to combat the building of the immense facility. Four women, with the help of environmental lawyer Jim Dougherty in Washington, DC, with financing from HFA, were able to stop construction of the factory farm after only two of thirteen sites were constructed. The litigation went all the way up to the U.S. Supreme Court, but we prevailed because the Supreme Court refused to hear the factory farm's argument.

Later, HFA investigated conditions inside the two sites that had been constructed. There were pigs with huge infected abscesses and hernias the size of volleyballs limping across their pens. Those who were sick and trapped in pens with other pigs were cannibalized—a problem that surfaces when pigs are housed in hostile environments. Hundreds of pigs had their hindquarters eaten out while others had bloody faces from eating their penmates. There were pigs scooting on their hindquarters because they couldn't walk. Emaciated pigs. Scores of dead piglets whose legs had become entrapped between floor slats, and thus had starved to death. Dying beings. Piles and piles of dead pigs.

Pigs who were sick were sometimes taken out of pens and left in aisles to die of starvation, dehydration, or disease. If wounded pigs were not removed quickly from the general population, the only remains would be bones and hide, which employees referred to as "rugs."

"A rug basically looks just like a bear rug on the floor," explained a worker. "A rug is a pig who has been rotting, sitting there, where the ribs have actually come apart and it is basically flat except for the head. It's basically the skin and bone. The meat is usually broken down, ate up by maggots and it's basically just a rotten carcass.

"Basically, pigs have been eating on them, and laying on them, and that's how they get crushed down and flat, because other pigs will lay on them, and that's another reason why they call them rugs—is because the other pigs will actually use them for a rug, you know? And they will sleep on them, lay on them, eat them up off the cement."

Other instances of extreme animal cruelty involve the housing of sows in gestation crates. At one operation, sows, weighing roughly 450 pounds, were sentenced to life inside crates that were only nineteen inches wide. As with most sows housed in gestation crates, they could never walk or turn around. Covered in massive open sores from rubbing against the crates' metal bars, and living above the noxious fumes of the waste pit, the sows were essentially going crazy. These nonhumans suffered so much from their inability to perform the most basic and natural of behaviors that they engaged in activities that are clinically exhibited by humans with severe psychiatric disorders. Looking down a row of crated sows, one could see a variety of repetitive behaviors known as stereotypies being performed: methodical head bobbing, air chewing, bar biting, nosing the bars of the crates. These pathetic nonhuman animals were trying to soothe themselves, releasing endorphins in their brains in an effort to ease their pain and self medicate.

Downed sows who can no longer stand are left in their crates to die slowly of infection, starvation, and dehydration. "Some of them have problems with their feet," said a worker. "Some of them lay in those crates so long their legs just rot off. It's a real atrocity how many sows die in their crates."

And finally, there are the piglets who fall into the waste pit below and struggle to stay afloat. This is a standard problem in farrowing operations. "Once they fall in there, some of them were so far in the 'soup' that you could just see bubbles coming up through the manure. And I saw bubbles coming up and I knew that something was in there. I could barely see this one's snout crack through the manure, and I snared him. He did not survive." Next to them were piglets who had already drowned in the liquefied waste. The Humane Farming Association successfully closed this particular breeding operation.

\* \* \*

I am often asked how I can repeatedly expose myself to horrendous animal cruelty. I find support in unexpected places. For example, my beloved cat, Bobby Rae, is one of the highlights of my life. Bobby is a fifteen-year-old tabby who was abandoned as a kitten at my apartment complex. It took Bobby a long time to trust me. He was afraid of most things. With love and time comes trust, and he is indeed my best friend. I see spirit in him every day. While I've taught Bobby that it's okay to trust, he's taught me unconditional love, and how to live in the moment.

Aside from Christine Stevens—who was integral to the passage of the Humane Slaughter Act in 1958 (and many other pieces of legislation)—Dr. Jane Goodall has been supportive of a number of my projects and an amazing friend to animals destined for the slaughterhouse. Without her kind help behind the scenes, working with members of Congress, we would have little or no funding to enforce the federal Humane Slaughter Act.

The sorrow that attaches to those who witness animal abuse is lessened by my commitment to change these practices. In addition, every day in my job is a new experience. I might work undercover to document violations at slaughterhouses or factory farms, interview witnesses, determine creative ways to obtain videotaped evidence of offenses, talk with the media, or simply write up complaints for local or federal law enforcement officials. Then again, I can be crawling inside dumpsters and removing pigs' eyeballs for drug samples. Trust me, it's never dull.

\* \* \*

I recently read this parable:

One day a farmer's sow fell into a well. The pig cried piteously for hours as the farmer tried to figure out what to do.

Finally the farmer decided that the sow was old, and that it wasn't worth it to retrieve the old sow, and that the well was also dried up and needed to be covered. He invited all his neighbors over to help him. They grabbed shovels and began to throw dirt into the well.

At first, the sow realized what was happening and cried horribly. Then, to everyone's amazement, she quieted down. A few shovel loads later, the farmer looked down to see what had happened, and was astonished by what he saw.

With every shovel of fill that hit her back, the sow would simply shake off the dirt, and take a step up.

Everyone was amazed when the sow finally stepped up over the edge of the well, and ambled off!

\* \* \*

Meat industry officials, eager to increase profits, can throw one obstacle after another at animal protectionists, and we will keep shaking those obstacles off and using them as stepping stones for the nonhumans. We are going to use them to show the world just how ruthless the meat industry is. With every being whose suffering is ended because of our efforts, we take a step up. With every person who reads this anthology because he or she cares about nonhumans, we take another step up. We have taken some pretty enormous steps in the last few years, and we're just going to keep stepping up!

This brings me back to those fortunate nonhumans, like Chloe, the rescued turkey; Spanky, the abandoned domesticated wild boar; and Romeo, the rooster who pecks at your ankles until you pick him up. The fact that these beings are loved and respected individuals suggests that the following prayer, written by humanitarian, missionary, and Nobel Peace Prize winner Albert Schweitzer, may not be beyond our grasp:

> Hear our humble prayer oh God, for our friends the animals. Especially for animals who are suffering. For all those who are overworked and underfed and cruelly treated. For all who are hunted and frightened and lost. For those who beat their wings against bars. For all who must be put to death.
>
> We entreat for them all Thy mercy and pity and for those who deal with them, we ask a heart of compassion, kind words and gentle hands.
>
> May we, ourselves, be friends to Animals, and so share the blessings of the Merciful.

# CHAPTER 6

# The Art of Love

*Sue Coe*

**Sue Coe**, *born in England, attended the Royal College of Art in London, then settled in New York. As an animal advocate and artist, Sue lectures, gives workshops, and has displayed her work in exhibitions in Japan, Austria, France, England, Ireland, Scotland, and all over North America. She has written many articles and eight books, including* Dead Meat, *winner of the 1991 Genesis Award. Philosopher Tom Regan has chosen her artwork for recent animal rights book covers, and the Culture and Animals Foundation awarded Sue the 1994 Outstanding National Activist Award. Her paintings are now housed by art museums, institutes, libraries, foundations, and universities internationally.*

Just today, I looked down from my meadow and into the farm (pharm) below—pharm being a modification of "farm" that recognizes contemporary "pharmaceutical farming."

This farm has black and brown cows. Last week, the owner slaughtered some of the nonhumans to sell at the October Fest celebration. Their flesh is advertised as home grown. The stench of barbecue, and the sickly greasy smell of smoke, suffocates the beauty of autumn, the orange and red leaves, the migrating geese, the large pumpkins, and late tomatoes.

But back to the farm. Each day I go down and look, because there is one cow who always looks back at me, makes eye contact. She stands out from the rest because she is a very unusual and beautiful light dusky brown color, a Brown Swiss, with no white splashes. The orange tag in her ear also stands out.

When summer was in full heat, the farmer, who also owns a veal farm a few miles away, brought two tiny calves (Holsteins), barely as big as cats, and dropped them in the meadow with the herd. The corn field had just been harvested, and the herd was eating up the chaff, the leavings. The two little calves were distinctive, being black and white, and they were so young that they could barely stand. I went down to watch every day, to see what would happen.

One day I saw that the two orphans were suckling from the dusky brown cow and following her everywhere. She always looked back up the hill to see me looking at her. In the past, the cows would come to graze on my land, as far as they could run away from the tin sheds of the farm. They would run nearly up to the woods; sometimes they even escaped into the woods and would hide for days, until the men with ATVs hunted them down.

All summer I watched her with those calves. I was awed by her willingness to be a foster mother, and I was filled with a deep sadness that their lives are merely a manipulation by men, "animal husbands," who profit from a cow's opulent supply of milk and calves, and a cow's endless supply of compassion. Even in the death camp of the modern farm a cow will extend herself to help little calves. She followed her instinct to nurture two babies who would have died without her, and yet I knew they would die anyway.

Yesterday, when I went to see her, the exploiters had put electric wire between her and the calves. The cattle had gotten as close as they could to each other without being shocked. Apparently, the time had come for them to be forcefully separated. They were not eating; they just yearned for each other. Three strands of hot wire separated them physically, but they were not separate; her breath was still their breath.

Again the brown cow looked at me. Every nonhuman knows the gaze of human eyes, and is wary. Even across a quarter of a mile, she knows I watch her. I want to tell her that I will never eat her, drink her milk, kill her and her babies—that I am not part of what is laughingly called humanity, yet I am.

In the winter I drive past the "other" farm, the Veal Farm. Temperatures can dip to thirty below in these parts, and yet the calves who will be exploited for veal are kept in white plastic kennels, chains around their tiny necks, separated from each other. Never a soft kiss from the muzzle, or a lick of kindness, never the warmth of any other living being. These calves are never to be touched, except by "man" when they are torn from their mothers, when holes are punched in their ears for tags. They shiver, and they lie in the snow. They move as far as the chain allows, only a few feet. Their breath is icy.

The mothers, crammed together on the other side of the electric wire, distraught, watch their calves, bending their necks as far as possible over the wire, in the hope of a scent or glimpse of their babies. I have heard them bawl for days, all day and night, for their calves. They are treated like machines, with no feelings. I rarely see any human being at these farms. No one observes the nonhumans, or checks that their drinking water is not frozen. Sometimes the calves who will be slaughtered for veal become tangled in the chains, and I slither under the wire to untangle them. The chain is so cold that it freezes to my skin.

People generally do not eat veal, yet they eat cheese and drink milk. They do not make the connection: for every drop of milk there is blood, and there is unbelievable suffering—a cow raped and made continuously pregnant, a baby stolen so the milk (mother's milk, the kindness of mother's milk) can be harvested, and a young calf taken to slaughter.

Hunting season will begin soon, and the sounds of gunfire will echo in the mountains. The herd of cows will stay in the upper pastures until the deep snow forces them down nearer to the filth of the milking barn and their rickety sheds. Until that time, the cows sleep together in the grass in a tight group, and when the deer and the fawns run out of the woods, frightened by the gunfire, the cows hide them. The deer mingle with the herd, concealed from hunters. When it is dark and the moon bright, the coyotes come out to play and tease the cows, who for the most part ignore their teases. Nonhuman animals have their secret lives, away from us.

I do not believe in biological determinism. We are *socialized* to behave as we do, our behavior is learned. Our brains are too big, our souls too small.

What is a soul? Is it a large slithery thing, like a liver, that hides between the heart and rib cage?

It is amazing that in this day and age, we are still murdering other species for food: imprisoning them, then slaughtering them in the cruelest way. In the process, we are destroying ourselves and our planet. It's not just insane, it's ideology: Profit over life. The crime is economics.

Does our empathy only extend to our immediate family? Why are human females ever on the alert for disaster—always one step ahead, fearing the worst, to protect offspring? Perhaps those less likely to profit from this economic system, those closest to the heel of the boot, are better equipped to see reality, and more likely to desire change.

To be in reality, to examine it, to analyze it, to learn from it, is one of the greatest gifts of being alive. There are people who languish in unreality; they want lies. They want to be served the bloodless flesh of their victims in neat plastic packages; they want to support sanitized wars; they want to remain in the dark. As long as they do not personally see the blood and death, they are contented. Maybe there is something in our makeup that desires a benign dictator, totalitarian rule, a Daddy who will wash away all those pesky contradictions, look after us, make the world safe, simple, and neat—just as long as we follow orders.

There are others who crave the truth, in all its messy glory. They want to see behind the curtain, to witness and intervene. They are not satisfied with collusion and compliance.

When I was a girl, we had a girl-gang that was devoted to raids and rescuing nonhumans. We raided the school biology class, rescuing mice and guinea pigs. Somehow we kept these successive generations of nonhumans hidden, safe, and well fed, in our parents' sheds and gardens. When my younger sister went to school, she did the same. *We never read any books about animal liberation, we didn't know anything about animal rights, yet we knew what to do, what was right.*

We lived a block from a slaughterhouse, next door to factory farmed pigs. The pigs were kept in steel sheds. At night, when they were rounded up for slaughter, they would scream. This sound really was not something one could ignore, or pretend did not exist, yet most adults *did* ignore this screaming in the night.

Our society does not feel empowered to make change (ironically, since we pride ourselves on individualism). We have been trained to consume, not create. We have been trained to keep quiet, not make waves. The apex of Western civilization is the art of denial.

When my sister and I were older, our time came to be farmed out to the local boys so that *we* could breed our 2.4 children, and become lifelong purchasers of plastic furniture and mortgages. The highest dream available to young women in those days was to be an airline hostess, or join the military and "see the world."

Between the slaughterhouse and the factory farm in our neighborhood, there was a meadow filled with abandoned car parts, used condoms, broken beer bottles, foxes, hedgehogs, owls, and moles—free creatures. This meadow was freedom for us, too, a place where we could hide and play. Something about a being yearning for freedom captured me, while the programming for short skirts and high-heeled shoes, with blue eye shadow and mascara, did not take. When the gang of girls started to think about boys, I started to think about being free, and art was my way to freedom.

I prefer to work in narrative sequence, using a modest pencil, which is simple and cheap. As an artist, my mission has been to record and document how nonhumans are treated at our hands, to obtain access to places that are concealed, and expose them to the viewer's eye. I witness firsthand what goes on, wherever possible. The first state of growth and awareness is to witness without power. This puts us in the same position as most of the earth's creatures.

Just gaining entry to a slaughterhouse, or following a truck of nonhumans bound for slaughter, is a considerable journey. These experiences are lessons in humility. Other animals have dignity and courage when they die. When they know they cannot save their friends, or offspring, they bow their heads, their legs shake, but they do not fall to the ground. They stand and look at us, their killers.

Always, I want to draw nonhumans as unique individuals, not units with numbers punched in their ears, but as they are: idiosyncratic, unique, special. Each face I have drawn and painted is different, even in drawings with hundreds of sheep, or pigs, each one is an individual.

Through art I started to meet women who were revolutionaries, like Patty Mark of Australia. I realized that she had solved something, fixed a bit of violence, mended a tear in our lives—she had *saved lives*. She knew that there was another pathway, and with clarity of mind, she found it.

Today I went back down the meadow to visit the brown cow. She does not look at me, does not seem to see me. How many calves have been stolen from her? When her time comes, as dictated by the meat industry (a small fraction of her natural life span), she will be taken in a truck to slaughter, stand in line with her own kind, hear the clanking of the chains, the shouting of the men. She will be forced—with an electric prod—to move forward in single file, stand on concrete puddled with blood and water. At her end, she will be in a steel restraining pen, and shaking, will look into the eyes of the man, who will put a bolt into her brain. Then, still alive, she will be hoisted into the air by one back leg, and her throat will be cut. As her blood gushes out, as she moves to the next disassembling of her life, she may be able see other skinned and decapitated cows, some might be her own calves, her own mother, her favorite friends.

This killing, a process unnecessary for our survival and damaging to our health, and the health of the planet, happens billions and billions of times each year. It happens repeatedly so that a few mega-corporations can make huge profits, profits from their blood, from our ignorance.

We now share a global network of vegans—still, it sounds like the planet Vega sometimes, and feels as though we are from another solar system. A vegan diet is a real way to save nonhumans, a baseline for any thinking person. Changing what we eat is one way to do something positive for the environment and to help other people. We can control what we put into our mouths, what we put on our bodies, and with this starting point, who knows what is possible?

> *Who Killed the Harrier?*
> By Mandy Coe (Commissioned by BBC, author's rights)
>
> Who shot the Harrier?
> I, said the gun, with my hair trigger.
> I shot the Harrier.
> Who stole his flight?
> I, said the crosshairs, with my telescopic sight.
> I stole his flight.
> Who silenced his cry?
> I, said the bullet, straight as a die.
> I silenced his cry.
> But who held the gun?
> I, said the hand, the hand of The Man.
> I held the gun.

CHAPTER 7

# Here I Stand, by Faith

*Linda Elkin McDaniel*

**Linda Elkin McDaniel,** *born in Natchez, Mississippi, baptized in the Methodist Church, and an ordained minister in the United Methodist Church, teaches Christians about God's claim upon them to honor all God's creation. Women's studies and liberation theology inform her ministry of teaching and animal advocacy; she is particularly concerned about the atrocities of farmed animal factories. Linda lives with her husband, Fred, two dogs, and ten cats in Cope, South Carolina, where they enjoy family, gardening, reading, music, and nature. Linda is a board member in the Christian Vegetarian Association (CVA, www.ChristianVeg.com).*

When my sister and I were little girls, our parents got us a puppy. I suppose they felt that a pet was a good way to teach the young ones to be responsible. Looking back, it must have been for this reason alone, because my mother was afraid of nonhumans, period. Furthermore, my father had no heart for other beings. I can still remember vividly and with great pain how he lured a starving, homeless dog out from under our house with stale leftovers *in order to shoot her* as soon as she got her first mouthful. This memory, which I have lived with for forty-six years, is so awful that I have blocked out most of the details. I vaguely remember that Daddy, being a minister and not a hunter, had some trouble killing her. In other words, he botched the shot, and she not only lost her life, *she died in terror and pain.* But for Daddy dogs were, nevertheless, a good way to teach your children responsibility.

We named our puppy Frisky, then took a four-week trip across the country, to visit relatives in California. We left the puppy on our screened back porch. My Christian parents paid a neighbor to feed Frisky *once a day* (puppies need to be fed three times a day). I remember vividly that Daddy told the caretaker to "heap" *one spoonful of food* for Frisky: starvation rations for a puppy, who needs more food volume than an adult dog. We always bought the cheapest brand of dog food, and looking back, it seems remarkable that Frisky grew at all while we were gone. Still, I remember that he looked a little bigger when we got home. My guess is that he was stunted by our unwillingness to feed him. No arrangements were made to clean up Frisky's urine and feces, and a puppy who needed companionship was left alone, in his own waste, for a month.

It was not until thirteen years later, when I was twenty and no longer living at home, that I discovered the wonder of a cat's paw—little hairs between each pad, claws that retract and extend—and how that purr sounds *and feels.* Daddy always said a cat would "bite the hand that feeds it," (not "feeds him" or "feeds her," but "feeds *it*"). Furthermore, he said that cats were always walking over his just-washed car, leaving muddy paw prints. Daddy always took great delight in his "rolling stock."

At age forty-one I was still a meat-eater and hadn't thought about any incongruity between eating meat and loving nonhumans. I had heard about people roaming the neighborhoods, calling cats, then scooping them up and selling them to labs for experiments. Because I loved my two cats, I kept them inside. I thought about my cats, but I never thought about *farmed* animals. I began to hear about factory farming from my sister. I also learned that my Uncle Jesse and his daughter Becky both had an extraordinary love for other creatures, considering nonhumans as part of their family. And thus it was that in that forty-first year of my life I came to believe that God endows certain people with the gift of extra sensitivity to nonhuman beings. I decided that, despite my parents' oblivion—even hostility—to nonhumans, I and my sister Evelyn had received a gift of sensitivity intended to be used to help God's creatures. It was the beginning of my journey toward living vegan.

I felt God's call to the ordained ministry in 1984 when I was thirty-five. In 1988, fresh out of seminary, I received my first ministerial appointment in the United Methodist Church. I served ten years in parish ministry. As pastor I shared with my people times of joy and celebration, sadness and grief, and profoundly redeeming experiences. Yet I also struggled with parish ministry. I struggled because I was an introvert engaged in highly social work, and I struggled with disillusionment about the Church as an institution. Much of my time was spent maintaining the status quo: weekly worship, hospital and home visitation, committee meetings, and administrative reports. While these are important ministries, something vital was missing. In 1998 I took a personal leave of absence from the parish. Ultimately, I questioned my personal source of meaning and purpose. *What was I passionate about?* As I look back now, with hindsight, I see what I could not see then—God was blessing me with discontent, moving me in a new, uncharted direction. God needed me in another place.

When I requested leave I did not know what lay ahead. In three years of leave, I steadily expanded my knowledge of how nonhumans are treated in this world. Most people don't realize what happens to nonhumans before they buy their body parts and products from Bi-Lo and Kroger. Hens live in cages so small they cannot turn around, the floors of which are wire, so that their feces drop down on the birds below. (I have read of baby pigs stacked in cages that allow feces and urine to fall down on piglets below.) Farmers force hens to molt by removing food for up to twenty-one days, so that a new egg-laying cycle can begin, so that more eggs can be sold, so that more *profit* can be made. Many of the birds die during this stressful time, which is not at all like their natural molting cycle. The industry accepts these losses as inevitable in their quest to maximize profit.

Farmers cut tails off of pigs and notch their ears, and cows are branded and castrated, all without anesthesia. Because chickens peck at one another when living in unnatural proximity, farmers debeak them (cut off ends of their beaks with a hot knife) without anesthesia. Chickens are genetically bred to gain weight rapidly, and to have gigantic breasts, so that we can fry larger, juicier chicken breasts. Chickens and turkeys bred for their breast meat often topple over from the unnatural size and weight of their breasts. They get sores on their feet and broken leg bones from carrying so much unnatural weight.

Farmed animals are given hormones to stimulate muscle development. Beef steers are given hormones to increase weight gain. Cows exploited for dairy products are given hormones to increase milk production and to regulate their reproductive cycles. Though cows given hormones are milked regularly, it is not often enough to relieve the excessive engorgement of their udders, and thus the cattle often get an infection, mastitis, in their teats. Cows exploited by the dairy industry probably should be milked more often to prevent mastitis, but the trauma of the milking machines is also a factor. Their udders are now so large that they often step on their own teats, which leads to further infection. As a result, antibiotics are frequently administered.

The use of antibiotics in cattle contributes to bacterial resistance to drugs, resulting in fewer ways to treat human and nonhuman illness.

Male calves are taken from their mothers and confined in crates so small they cannot turn around or lie down comfortably. They are kept immobile so that muscles do not develop. They are fed an iron-deficient liquid diet so that their flesh is pale from anemia. No bedding is provided, because they would eat the straw, out of desperation. They live amid urine and diarrhea caused by the unnatural diet and bacterial infections. They receive no water and remain constantly thirsty so that they will drink excessive amounts of their artificial liquid diet, designed to rush weight gain. After slaughter, they are sold in restaurants as the delicacy we call "veal." So severe are their living conditions that 10 percent to 20 percent die before they reach four to six months, when they are slaughtered. Like the egg industry, the veal industry accepts this suffering as necessary for maximal profits. Veal is a byproduct of the dairy industry, created by unwanted male offspring born to cows who are milked by the dairy owners. I had to have it spelled out for me before I grasped that these cows are perpetually impregnated, because this is the only way they will produce milk. *Only cows with young produce milk.*

Farmed animals trucked to slaughterhouses are denied food and water during shipment, which can last several terrifying days. "Downers" (those too sick to pass meat inspection laws) are dragged aside, usually by one leg, and left to die. Farmed animals are exempt from the Animal Welfare Act. Humane slaughter laws for livestock, where they do exist, are poorly enforced, if they are enforced at all.

Complex, global distribution practices developed by agribusiness to maximize profits are a large part of why "the least of these," as Jesus has referred to the world's poor and powerless, remain poor and powerless. Farmers in small and/or poor countries raise and sell their meat to large, international agribusiness corporations at a better price than they could receive "at home." The practice keeps poorer countries economically dependent and robs them of the ability to develop self-sufficiency, raise their standard of living, or combat hunger.

Raising meat uses up precious water resources, pollutes rivers and streams with animal wastes, and converts grain protein into meat protein, which provides *96 percent less protein than would grain itself.* Forests must be sacrificed for land required to graze cattle, contributing significantly to global warming.

Some people, somewhere, may need to eat nonhumans in order to survive, but no person in the United States of America needs to eat nonhumans. Nonanimal protein is plentiful (see www.vrg.org). The amino acid content of plant protein is not lower in quality than animal proteins, and eating a balanced diet of plant foods will provide all the essential amino acids in adequate amounts (The Vegetarian Society, www.vegsoc/health.org). (I encourage readers to visit www.All-Creatures.org, and the Physicians Committee for Responsible Medicine, www.pcrm.org. Recipes and nutrition information may be found at Vegetarian Resource Group's www.vrg.org.)

Because many Christians support meat and dairy industries and their lobbyists, and enjoy the taste of flesh, they defend the marketing of nonhumans and nonhuman products, excusing cruel behavior by disassociating these acts from the compassionate standard Jesus Christ taught. The question to ask, when considering the use of animal products, is not, Do nonhumans have souls? but rather, Can they feel pain?

Eating meat, dairy, and egg products undermines the Bible's teaching that the body is the temple of the Holy Spirit. Scientists have linked these products with heart disease, diabetes, and several kinds of cancer. Allergies are linked with lactose (in milk), which many people can't digest. The fat in cows' milk contains much more fat than does human milk. Humans are the only species that drinks milk after infancy.

Over the past ten years I have come to understand that, even if I had not been given a special sensitivity for nonhuman animals—even if I were not Christian—I would nevertheless be severely disturbed by the existence of our meat, dairy, and poultry industries, which breed nonhumans as *commodities* for *profit*. In addition, damage to human health and the environment, caused by farming, are entirely unacceptable. However, I *am* Christian and must object to these atrocities out of my understanding of Jesus Christ. Jesus is *peaceful, just, and compassionate.*

During my leave of absence from organized ministry, I studied what the Bible says about God's relationship with creation, and became better educated concerning Christian Tradition over the past two millennia on the issue of nonhumans. Though relatively few, some Christians, including Saint Francis of Assisi, Hildegaard of Bingen, and John Wesley have taught the innate value of nonhumans. I even explored pagan influences on the Church's perspective, noting that pagan ideas concerning nonhumans were contrary to what Jesus taught, and to Hebrew scriptures recording God's covenant with nonhumans.

It is important to me that strong *theological* responses be put forth to recent arguments that have been leveled against Christianity by the secular animal rights and liberation movement, because I know God has called me to ministry *within* the Church, and that the Church has affirmed *through my ordination* that I am called. I cannot, however, defend the institutional

Church. For the most part, the Church has accepted the suffering of nonhumans in the service of our needs and pleasures; it has given tacit approval to animal abuse, citing the dominion given us in Genesis 1:26.

For many, living as a vegetarian seems odd. For me, living as a vegetarian is a blessing, and is my Christian witness. I have volunteered with the nonprofit Christian Vegetarian Association (CVA) since 2003 to bring the Christian/nonhuman message to the media.

I have not found the Church receptive to a theology that includes the redemption of nonhumans, a theology that includes nonhumans in the possession of immortal souls. Indeed, these ideas have been met with hostility and fear within the Church. My response is many-faceted. First, I still love the Church, even with its imperfections, but *this love is more an act of will than a love affair.* Second, I am sad that so many creatures continue to be victims of Christian shortsightedness: our *human*-centered conception of the Cross and Resurrection of Jesus Christ. Third, I consider it my challenge to bear the Cross of Christ for the sake of "the least of these" for whom Jesus gave his life, and to whom Jesus sent his followers ("... just as you did it to one of *the least of these* who are members of my family, you did it to me" [Matthew 25:40]).

I want to *build up* the Church, fostering a deep appreciation of the cosmic Christ of Colossians, Ephesians, and Revelation, a Christ who reveals the breadth and depth of God's universe. I want to lay these biblical strands alongside biblical strands that present Christ's work as solely for humanity. I am not interested in debating texts to "prove" one perspective right and the other wrong. I believe the Bible must be received as a whole, and all voices held together, if we are to have the complete picture of God that the Bible is meant to reveal.

Jesus demanded that disciples be peaceful, just, and compassionate. No matter what one believes about humanity's relationship to nonhuman animals, *if* one believes in the values of the "Prince of Peace" (prophesied in Isaiah 9:6) who taught us to pray, "Thy will be done on Earth as it is in heaven," one must see that factory farming, cock fighting, dog fighting, bull fighting, rodeos, and animal circuses cannot possibly be justified. None of these activities is peaceful, just, or compassionate. Each robs the creatures, including the human creature, of the respect and peace God intended for them. Each robs other creatures of their God-given desires and needs: to play, enjoy one another's company, explore, dust bathe, and/or forage for food.

The Hebrew prophets prophesied that nonhumans will be present at Christ's final advent and throughout his eternal rule of the universe (eternity), when all is gathered back to God and made complete. Nonhuman "living souls" are found in the book of Revelation, taking their place alongside human "living souls," praising Christ the Lamb around the throne of God (a portrait of heaven) (Revelation 5:13). Genesis describes nonhumans as having *neh-fesh* ("life" or "soul") just as do humans (Genesis 2:7, 19; Genesis 9:4, 7). The same Hebrew word, *neh-fesh*, is used to describe both humans and nonhumans.

Further, the Hebrew prophets warned the Hebrews not to offer animal sacrifice in ritual as atonement for human sin. Speaking through Jeremiah, God specifically says, "… in the day that I brought your ancestors out of the land of Egypt, I did not speak to them or command them concerning … sacrifices. But this command I gave them, 'Obey my voice, and I will be your God, and you shall be my people'" (Jeremiah 7:22–23a).

In his own time, centuries after Jeremiah lived, Jesus became angry and turned over the tables of those in the temple who were selling nonhumans for sacrificial slaughter. By the time of Jesus, the temple sacrificial system had become institutionalized to the extent that priests depended on bloodletting for their livelihood. The people were dependent on the priests to mediate through sacrifice between themselves and God. During Passover, the temple ran with blood, and the crowds waiting to offer sacrifices were so thick that only so many could be allowed in at any one time. I can imagine the screams and the stench of slaughter! *It was an abomination to God. Of course Jesus was angry!*

I can see how experiences from childhood on have blessed and prepared me for ministry to and for both nonhumans and humans. My parents, who were faithful servants of God from Methodism's strong Wesleyan roots, though insensitive to God's joy in the animal nations of the world, taught me to read the Bible alongside the newspaper. Christian faith must inform our politics. Hunger, and all other social problems, are interconnected. People who are hungry are affected by *my* lifestyle choices. Eating flesh contributes to hunger, so I must not eat flesh (www.ivs.org). Further, I must not utilize any product for which nonhumans have suffered: food, leather, cosmetics, or scientific research. I have old leather shoes, but will buy no more. I do my best not to buy personal care products and cleaning supplies made by companies that test on nonhumans, or that use nonhuman animal ingredients. I try to live vegan: I try not to use any animal products. Our markets are saturated with animal products, and I constantly find that products purchased, which I thought were vegan, contain animal products, or are connected to painful and needless animal testing (www.aavs.org: compassionate shopping guide).

God continues to call all of the world into a future in which lambs and wolves, snakes and little children can play together, a time when "they will not hurt nor destroy in all [God's] holy mountain" (Isaiah 11:6–9). When people fail to follow this vision, the Lord's vision, our wounds will not heal. God's original will for the world was that nonhumans be *companions* to humans, not "meat" to be eaten. For food, God gave to humans "every plant yielding seed, ... and to everything that has the breath of life [God gave] every green plant for food" (Genesis 1:29–30). After the Flood, the first thing Noah did was offer sacrifice, killing some of the dear nonhumans with whom he had lived closely in the Ark. *But the blood was not to be eaten* (Genesis 9:1–5). The Hebrews believed *"life"/"soul"* resides in the blood. Can all blood be removed from a dead animal? I think not. Scripture notes that for the blood of another, humans will have to give an account. In other words, God strongly advised against eating nonhumans. Genesis indicates that both humans and nonhumans eat other creatures because of human willfulness (our sinful nature). That God has redeemed us through Jesus Christ from our sin is not a license to ignore God's plan for a vegan world. It is, rather, our *primary* incentive to live *now* as we will delight to live when we finally understand completely God's perfect love. God, help us to see the need for this work and to take it up!

There are stories throughout the Bible descriptive of the place to which I've come to stand. For example, in the book of Acts (Acts 5:27ff), the high priest and the Council charge the apostle Peter not to teach in Christ's name. Peter responds, "we must obey God rather than any human authority" (Acts 5:29). This story supports the idea that if the Institution (the Church) tries to silence God's plan, God's ministers must speak out. When it comes to connecting animal slaughter with Christ's name, religious authorities are still resisting God's plan. But I am with Peter, and I am with Martin Luther, "Here I stand; I can do no other."

Christ is still building the Church; the Church is not finished. There is more to be built; there is more for us to learn. Therefore, we must consider new ideas. "There will be other sheep, too," Jesus said, "that do not belong to this fold.... They will listen to my voice. Then there will be one sheep herd, one shepherd" (John 10:16) (Brown). How can I build awareness that nonhumans, like ourselves, are part of the one flock of the shepherd Jesus Christ, and that they, too, listen to Christ's voice?

Is it a new idea that sheep and goats and chickens have unique, individual personalities—just like our companion dogs and cats? Can we not see that cows and pigs have families, that they must feel something akin to what slave families in the American South felt when rounded up and sold? These are the truths about nonhumans, and about the Church, and about ourselves, about which I hope to raise awareness. *Children* instinctively know these things. Children have to be *taught* to accept the slaughter, to eat nonhumans, to hunt nonhumans, and to view them as commodities. Jesus said that unless you become like a child, you cannot enter the Kingdom God has prepared (Mark 10:14–15). When choosing ministers, God sometimes asks us to do things that we would not otherwise choose. *I* didn't choose this particular ministry. *Christ* has chosen me. Christ has chosen me to speak for him. The Church is wrong to participate in chicken fries and barbecues. Christ is saying "no" to animal slaughter and "no" to animal abuse, just as Christ says "no" to human slaughter and "no" to human abuse.

I have been guided to a place I would never have imagined, from which I can see Christ transforming the status and material conditions of the powerless, *including nonhumans*, into something qualitatively better. This transformation is what Liberation theologians like Jurgen Moltmann describe as "the work of *the Church* in the power of the Spirit" (emphasis added). Moltmann was writing about the Church at work among Latin American peasants. I am thinking of the Church at work among animal nations. Moltmann's insight into the Church at work among peasants can be *broadened* to include nonhumans. Christ intends the Church, led by the Spirit, to work to bring humans and nonhumans into one community. God is reshaping me in this new and different ministry to lead a skeptical Church to a broader understanding of God's plan for creation. This is the story of my journey to this point. I am confident the work begun in me God will bring to completion according to God's plan and purposes, and so I open myself to God's leading into the future.

Reading about Strongheart in Allen Boone's true story, *Kinship with All Life*, was a significant milestone on my journey toward appreciating nonhumans. Strongheart, a former war dog turned Hollywood actor (by his owner), stayed with Boone one summer while his owner was away. Upon Strongheart's initiative, the dog and Boone took turns selecting the path and destination for their daily walks. Strongheart often led the way into the hills overlooking Hollywood, where he would sit transfixed for long periods, staring out and *up* into the sky (not down at the view of the town at the bottom of the hills). Boone finally came to understand from Strongheart that he was communing with God. Boone did not come easily to the understanding that a dog could worship his Maker or that this dog was teaching wisdom. When I realized that Strongheart worshipped the same God whom I worship, it spilled over into my thoughts about nonhumans raised as commodities for profit, and about companion animals. *The dog who took up under our house when I was little, the dog Daddy ineptly shot after luring her out with food, was a worshipper of the same God Daddy was serving as an ordained minister.* I didn't know, after I finished reading *Kinship with All Life,* that I was one step closer to that broad place where God has called me to stand.

I dedicate this essay to the dog who took up under our house in search of Home. And to Frisky. Some day, I hope to meet them anew.

## References

Boone, J. Allen, *Kinship with All Life.* San Francisco: HarperSanFrancisco, 1976.
Brown, Raymond E., S.S., Trans. *The Gospel According to John.* Garden City: Doubleday, 1970.
*NRSV Harper Study Bible.* Grand Rapids, MI: Zondervan Publishing House, 1991.
Wesley, John. "The General Deliverance," preached Nov. 30, 1771. From *Sermons on Several Occasions,* Public Domain, 1771. www.ccel.org/ccel/wesley/sermons/txt.

CHAPTER 8

# The Fiercest Predators of the Sea

*Heather Moore*

**Heather Moore** *is a freelance writer and a research specialist for the PETA Foundation, 501 Front St., Norfolk, VA 23510; www.PETA.org. She is a Baltimore native, currently living in Sarasota, Florida, who has been a vegan for almost twenty years. Her work has appeared in many publications, including the* Philadelphia Inquirer, Houston Chronicle, Las Vegas Review Journal, IMPACT Press, Colorado Dog, Chicago Dog, New Mobility, Earth First Journal, *and* The Encyclopedia of Human-Animal Relationships.

Sharks are commonly thought to be the most ferocious predators of the sea—bloodthirsty monsters who attack and eat everything in the water, including humans. Of the more than 400 species of sharks, only 11 have been known to attack us, but when you think about all the sea animals that humans eat each year, it would seem that people are the fiercest predators of the sea. We're causing sea life to suffer immensely, and we're decimating fish populations.

Every year in the United States alone, approximately 21.7 billion sea animals are killed as a result of commercial, recreational, and aquacultural fishing. About 17.4 billion of these animals, including fish, shrimp, lobsters, and crabs, are eventually eaten by humans. Even octopuses—live ones, no less—wind up on people's plates. Some people line up at all-you-can-eat "seafood" buffets—making an "extreme sport" of eating fish, lobsters, octopuses, and other sea animals. These animals are not swimming vegetables—they're sentient, intelligent beings, who have more in common with us than many people realize.

When I was a child, one of my best friends was a goldfish named Squirmy. I loved that fish; he was full of character, and though I doubt that he was happy living in a tank, he certainly entertained me with his antics. When he died, I somehow sensed that there was a connection between my beloved goldfish and the fish sticks in the freezer. Something clicked in my young mind, and for months after Squirmy's death I refused to eat fish. Being a kid, my resolve didn't last, and I occasionally ordered fish sandwiches or shrimp or scallops in my teen years, when my family went out to eat.

But now, having worked in the animal rights movement for fourteen years, I know much more about fish and other sea animals, and I have too much appreciation—and empathy—for sea life to eat these fascinating individuals. Tuna, salmon, shrimp, scallops, crabs, lobsters, and other sea animals don't belong on our plates any more than do goldfish. Each of these beings is a fascinating creature who has feelings and many of them construct civilizations, as we do.

## Fish Are Friends, Not Food

Fish, for example, can recognize their "shoal mates," "talk" to one another, and gather information by eavesdropping. The journal *Fish and Fisheries* cited more than 500 research papers demonstrating that fish have impressive long-term memories and sophisticated social structures. The introductory chapter said that fish are "steeped in social intelligence, pursuing Machiavellian strategies of manipulation, punishment and reconciliation" ("Scientists Highlight"). That sounds a lot like us!

Fish gently rub against one another as a sign of affection and males will sometimes woo potential partners by singing to them. Fish build nests to raise their babies, and gather small rocks to make hiding places. They "garden," weeding out the algae types that they don't like. Some fish even use tools, including the South African fish who lay their eggs on leaves, then carry them to safety.

Red groupers are the architects of the sea. They excavate and maintain crevices by laboriously removing sand from the ocean floor, exposing rock that is necessary for the spread of coral and sponges, which they use for shelter. Excavation sites, which can be sixteen feet across, attract both prey and beneficial species, like shrimp, who pick parasites off of groupers. "So it is no surprise that [groupers] are remarkably sedentary. Why move if you are clever enough to make everything you need come to you?" (Coleman).

Groupers are not only clever; they are unique individuals who suffer when they are treated unkindly. Marine Biologist Dr. Sylvia A. Earle recently appointed chief scientist of the National Oceanic and Atmospheric Administration, one of the world's most skilled divers, and one of the first to take a one-person submersible vessel to a depth of 3,000 feet, commented, "I wouldn't deliberately eat a grouper any more than I'd eat a cocker spaniel. They're so good-natured, so curious. You know, fish are sensitive, they have personalities, they hurt when they're wounded" (Orenstein).

## Fish Can Feel Pain

Extensive research confirms that fish feel pain, just as do other animals (including people). Dr. Donald Broom, scientific advisor to the British government, reports that

> Anatomically, physiologically and biologically speaking, scientists have found that the pain systems in fish are virtually the same as in birds and mammals. They too experience increases in heart and breathing rates and release adrenaline and pain-reducing substances like enkephalins and endorphins. Marine science professor Tom Hopkins of the University of Alabama likens the experience of being hooked to "dentistry without Novacain, drilling into exposed nerves." The physical pain is also accompanied by psychological distress, as researchers at Edinburgh University found that fish engage in "a 'rocking' motion strikingly similar to the kind of motion seen in stressed higher vertebrates like mammals." ("Sports")

Morally speaking, ethicists conclude, not surprisingly, "Just as do other animals, fish require proper consideration for their welfare" (Lembo 4). A team of researchers at the University of Guelph in Canada reviewed scientific literature on fish pain and intelligence, and concluded that "the welfare of the fish requires consideration" (Chandroo 241).

Yet, for some people, taking the sentience of fish into consideration means choosing to eat a fish that was killed in a more conventionally cruel way, rather than eating a live flounder. To prepare live flounder, chefs fillet the fish down to the bone, leaving the head and tail intact. Then they chop and season the fish's flesh, return the flesh to the skeleton, then pin the flounder down with wooden skewers to prevent the still-living fish from thrashing off the plate.

Most fish are killed in more "acceptable" ways for human consumption. For example, every year, billions of fish, along with unintentional victims like dolphins, turtles, and sea birds, are hauled onboard huge, commercial fishing vessels. Fish who are dragged from the ocean depths by bottom trawlers suffer from excruciating decompression—which can rupture swimbladders, pop out eyes, and push stomachs out through their mouths. Removed from their ocean homes, the fish are often thrown on ice to slowly suffocate. Some are still alive when their throats and bellies are slit open onboard the fishing liners.

Another conventional way of killing fish is trapping them in gill nets, which hang like curtains in the oceans. Fish caught in gill nets bleed to death because mesh catches them by the gills and fins, slicing into their flesh. Some fish are strangled when they try to escape. It is difficult to tell which conventional fishing method is the worst.

Farmed fish fare no better. They are forced to live in filthy, overcrowded enclosures. Land-based farms raise thousands of fish in ponds, pools, or concrete tanks. Ocean-based farms are situated close to shorelines, where fish are packed into net or mesh cages. Conditions on some farms are so deplorable that 40 percent of the fish die before farmers can kill and package them for food. Those who manage to survive must go without food before they're sent to slaughter in order to reduce waste contamination in the water during transport. U.S. fish slaughter plants do not stun the fish before "gutting" them, so they are conscious when they start down the "slime line," where they are cut open while still convulsing with life and pain.

## CRUSTACEANS: SEA LIFE VERSUS SEAFOOD

Like fish, crustaceans feel pain, and suffer when they are cut, broiled, or boiled alive. Being sliced apart and bled to death is no more palatable than being boiled alive, which is how lobsters, crabs, shrimp, prawns, and other crustaceans are typically killed. Common sense tells us, along with scientific studies, that this is an agonizing death. When dropped into scalding water, lobsters whip their bodies wildly and scrape the sides of the pot. When watching a lobster in boiling water, "it is hard to deny in any meaningful way that this is a living creature experiencing pain and wishing to avoid/escape the painful experience" (Wallace 7). In fact, "lobsters are maybe even *more* vulnerable to pain" than are other animals since they lack opioids, which are the "mammalian nervous systems' built-in analgesia" (Wallace 6). According to invertebrate zoologist Dr. Jaren G. Horsley, "The lobster does not have an autonomic nervous system that puts it into a state of shock when it is harmed. It probably feels itself being cut [open, and] is in a great deal of pain" (Brown 4). She concludes, a lobster "feels all the pain until its nervous system is destroyed" during cooking (Brown 4). In Reggio, Italy, boiling lobsters alive is illegal, and offenders face fines of up to $600 (Berger).

In 2009, researchers at the School of Biological Sciences at Queen's University in Belfast, Ireland, conducted a series of tests to determine whether or not crustaceans feel pain. The researchers documented hermit crab reactions to mild electric shocks. They found that hermit crabs not only react adversely to electrical shocks, but remember pain and attempt to avoid such experiences in the future. Crabs who had already been shocked once were more likely to move out of their shell when they experienced a second shock. Shocked crabs also showed stress-related behaviors, including repetitive grooming of the abdomen, and rapping their abdomen against an empty shell—neither of which is a typical crab behavior unless stressed ("Crabs"). (While it is by no means excusable to shock crabs for studies, at least in this case the crabs survived and were later released back into their native habitat.)

In another test, researchers daubed acetic acid on prawns' antennae. The animals, who are similar to shrimp, survived, but responded by vigorously rubbing and grooming the affected areas for up to five minutes, attempting to remove the irritant. According to Dr. Bob Elwood, one of the researchers, their findings suggest that crabs, prawns, and, by extension, lobsters and other crustaceans, are sensitive to pain (Hance). A man with few scruples about causing extreme pain to other creatures conducted a study in which he noted that when a crab's legs were twisted off the animals' stress response was so profound that some did not survive, or were unable to regenerate the lost appendages (Viegas).

How many times will we allow researchers to cause nonhuman animals pain and trauma just to prove that they can experience pain and trauma? Common responses, for those willing to see, make it obvious that all living beings feel pain (not all living things, but all living *beings*). Shouldn't we *start* with the assumption that all creatures are sentient, rather than harm other creatures to demonstrate the obvious? Perhaps Elwood's team can be forgiven, since their intent was to give sea-life eaters food for thought.

Elwood, along with researchers Stuart Barr and Lynsey Patterson, wrote a paper outlining seven reasons why we know that crustaceans suffer. For one thing, the scientists assert, crustaceans possess "a suitable central nervous system and receptors" (Viegas). They learn to avoid a negative stimulus after a potentially painful experience, and they engage in protective reactions, such as limping and rubbing, after being hurt (Viegas). Crustaceans possess "high cognitive ability and sentience"; they release adrenal-like hormones when pain or stress is suspected, and they make future decisions based on past events (Viegas). Researchers have also observed that crabs, when given medicine, appear to feel relieved, showing fewer responses to negative stimuli (Viegas). Research highlights the need to rethink how we treat crustaceans in our kitchens and shops. Dr. Elwood concludes, "With vertebrates we are asked to err on the side of caution and I believe this is the approach to take with these crustaceans" (Hance). If crustaceans suffer, should we eat them?

While evidence overwhelmingly indicates that lobsters, crabs, and other crustaceans feel pain and suffer when captured and prepared for human consumption, few people err on the side of caution. Basic biology and research both demonstrate that shellfish, like finfish, belong in the oceans, not in people's mouths, but there "seem to be a multitude of reasons that stop people wanting to enquire about pain in invertebrates" (Hanlon). It is likely that our tendency to enjoy eating these sentient individuals prevents us from honestly assessing who these marvelous creatures actually are.

## Lobsters Value Their Lives

Thanks to those who have found ways to investigate pain in crustaceans (without destroying their lives), more and more people have been forced to accept that, in morally critical ways, crustaceans are more like us than they are different. They're smart, sentient, long-lived beings with distinct personalities, who form families and friendships.

Paula Moore of People for the Ethical Treatment of Animals (PETA) notes that lobsters are highly developed. They carry their young for nine months and, when left in peace, can live for more than 100 years. They recognize other individual lobsters, remember past acquaintances, and have elaborate courtship rituals. They take long seasonal journeys, often traveling for hundreds of miles. Elder lobsters help guide young lobsters across the ocean floor by holding their claws in a line that can stretch for many yards (Moore).

Crustaceans are clever animals. Underwater cameras have informed humans that lobsters wander in and out of traps at will, grabbing a bite of food, and propelling themselves to freedom (Watson 416). In late 2007, dozens of lobsters in an Asian supermarket in Germany crawled out of their poorly secured crates, scuttled across the floor, squeezed under the metal shutters at the front of the store, and made it out onto the street. Although the lobsters were eventually apprehended, their escape saved their lives: PETA Germany whisked all of them off to an animal sanctuary ("Lobsters").

Based on the above information, marine animals value their lives, just as we value ours. Crustaceans show preservation instincts and behave in ways that were once attributed only to humans. Crabs, for example, are capable of learning from their mistakes. They retain information to help them avoid making the same mistake again. They adapt to cues indicating change in their environment, and they avoid foods that have made them ill—which is something that many people can't seem to do! On reflection, why would we have thought that sea life, just because these individuals live in the sea, would not have evolved with brains that would help them to survive—just as we have? They need to remember dangerous foods and risky situations so that they can avoid these items and situations in the future. As Darwin noted, between animals there is only a difference in degree, not in kind.

In general, animals are smarter than people give them credit for. For instance, with regard to pigs, Professor Stanley Curtis (Penn State University) said, "There is much more going on in terms of thinking and observing by these pigs than we would ever have guessed" ("Ten"). Similarly, commenting on chickens Professor Christine Nicol (University of Bristol) noted, "Chickens have shown us they can do things people didn't think they could do. There are hidden depths to chickens, definitely" (*Chicken*). It seems the same can be said of sea life, including fish, crustaceans, and even cephalopods, such as octopuses.

## Amazing Octopuses

Most of us do not think of octopuses as brainy animals, despite their large heads, but octopuses have been observed using tools. Scientists filmed octopuses in Indonesia collecting discarded coconut shells, emptying them out, and scrambling into the shells to hide from predators ("Scientists Discover"). Videos show these ingenious creatures carrying these coconut shells about for emergency shelter, and even pulling two half shells together to form a complete octopus armor ("Coconut"). Octopuses have also been caught on tape using clumps of algae for cover, and taking on the shape of algae in an ingenious imitation, walking on two legs with the other limbs bent like plants, scurrying away from danger ("Octopus"). Octopuses are, in fact, extremely intelligent, curious, and playful.

These miraculous animals are also expressive. Otto, an octopus confined to a tank at the Sea Star Aquarium in Germany, was apparently irritated by a light that was left on all night, and repeatedly shot squirts of water at the light, destroying the mechanism and bringing the desired darkness ("This"). Otto is clearly bored in his home, and tries to find ways to entertain his active mind in stale confines:

> Otto gets bored and causes mischief for attention and stimulation. In addition to the dangerous act of vandalism [putting out the lights], Otto has been seen juggling the hermit crabs that he lives with, damaging the glass of his tank by throwing stones at it, and obsessively rearranging the items in his tank. ("This")

Some of these "items" are alive, and would no doubt prefer not to be "rearranged." Another captive octopus, who was fed a slightly spoiled shrimp, stuffed the offending morsel down a drain while maintaining eye contact with his keeper to make sure he made his displeasure known (Johnson). Octopuses are best known for their eight legs, but it is time we recognized their well-developed brains and charming personalities as well.

## Extreme Eating

The aforementioned anecdotes and expert opinions suggest that these and other sea animals have self-awareness, social structures, and a keen interest in prolonging their lives. Despite our growing understanding of marine animals, and our admittance that these fellow creatures are sentient, our eating practices have not changed accordingly. "Live seafood" is increasingly popular in restaurants. In addition to live flounder, extreme eaters are ordering live shrimp, freshly vivisected lobster (the lobster's eyes watch the fierce human predator consume his or her body), "drunken prawns" (live prawns are plucked from a tank, doused in alcohol, and set ablaze), and live octopus (who writhes as the chef clips off his tentacles for diners to consume while the octopus's limbs wriggle in pain and desperation). In order to call attention to the cruelty of eating fish, lobsters, octopuses, and other sea creatures—whether they're still alive and twitching or dead and dismembered—PETA, an animal protection organization that advocates a vegan diet, has coordinated numerous protests at restaurants and aquariums, designed an informative FishingHurts.com Web site, given away delicious mock seafood at fairs, helped to liberate several lobsters, and even organized a tongue-in-cheek "Sea Kittens" campaign, in which people were encouraged to refer to fish as "sea kittens" in an attempt to remind others that fish can feel pain just as our furry friends can.

Ultimately, PETA wants people to extend compassion to *all* animals, whether they have fur, feathers, or fins, whether they walk, fly, or swim. By refusing to eat sea animals, people can help reduce animal suffering, and alter their current status as savage predators of the sea. While *Jaws* and other fictional movies have portrayed sharks as crazed killers who devour everything and everyone in sight, the most destructive feeding frenzy takes place every day at restaurants in our own communities. The way we're mindlessly consuming fish, humans ought to star in the next *Jaws*—or change our ways.

## Note

Many thanks to the editor for extensive editing, including tracking down references for quotes, adding in-text citations, and creating a bibliography.

## References

Berger, Keith. "Sea Life Not Sea Food." *Examiner.Com, Miami: The Insider Source for Local.* April 30, 2009. Accessed: Oct. 19, 2010. http://www.examiner.com/animal-rights-in-miami/sea-life-not-sea-food.

Brown, Stuart. "Do Fish Feel Pain? The Science Behind Whether Fish Feel Pain." *FirstScience.com: Your First Stop for Science Online.* Accessed: Oct. 10, 2010. http://www.firstscience.com/home/perspectives/editorials/do-fish-feel-pain-the-science-behind-whether-fish-feel-pain-page-4-1_1818.html.

Chandroo, K. P. et al. "Can Fish Suffer?: Perspectives on Sentience, Pain, Fear and Stress." *Applied Animal Behaviour Science* 86 (2004): 225–250. Accessed: Oct. 15, 2010. http://www.aps.uoguelph.ca/aquacentre/files/research-publications/Fish%20Welfare%20Review.pdf.

*Chicken Intelligence.* "Compassion Over Killing: Exposing Routine Animal Cruelty in the Chicken Industry." Accessed: Oct. 15, 2010. http://www.chickenindustry.com/cfi/intelligence/.

"Coconut-Carrying Octopus Stuns Scientists." *AFP: Youtube.* Accessed: Oct. 20, 2010. http://www.youtube.com/watch?v=RUN6c5yWJhQ&NR=1.

Coleman, Felicia, and Christopher C. Koenig. "New Study Reveals Red Grouper to Be 'Frank Lloyd Wrights of the Sea.'" *Physorg.com: Science, Physics, Tech, Nano, News: Biology: Ecology.* Reprinted from *Open Science Fish Journal.* Accessed: Oct. 16, 2010. http://www.physorg.com/news183186896.html.

"Crabs Not Only Suffer Pain, but Retain Memory of It" *ScienceDaily: Your Source for the Latest Science News.* "Science News." March 28, 2009. Accessed: Oct. 19, 2010. http://www.sciencedaily.com/releases/2009/03/090327072759.htm.

"Curious Octopus Floods Calif. Aquarium." *USAToday: News: Offbeat.* Feb. 27, 2009. Accessed: Oct. 19, 2010. http://www.usatoday.com/news/offbeat/2009-02-27-octopus-flood_N.htm.

*Gordon's Corner—Blog.* "An Environmental View on Food Industry: Animal Einsteins." Oct. 7, 2010. Accessed: Oct. 19, 2010. http://gordons-corner.com/gordon/index.blog.

Hance, Jeremy. "Crabs Feel Pain, and Remember It Too." *Mongabay.com: Environmental News.* March 30, 2009. Accessed: Oct. 19, 2010. http://news.mongabay.com/2009/0330-hance_crabpain.html.

Hanlon, Michael. "Claws for Concern? Scientists Suggest Prawns and Lobsters Feel Pain Just Like Humans." *MailOnline: News.* Nov. 9, 2007. Accessed: Oct. 19, 2010. http://www.dailymail.co.uk/news/article-492557/Claws-concern-Scientists-suggest-prawns-lobsters-feel-pain-just-like-humans.html.

Johnson, Darragh. "Crafty Octopuses Keep Kids, Caretakers Entertained." *Washington Post.* Aug. 22, 2006. Accessed: Oct. 20, 2010. http://www.azcentral.com/arizonarepublic/arizonaliving/articles/0822octopus0822.html?&wired.

Lembo, Pino and Walter Zupa. "Fish Welfare: A Key Issue for Organic System Standards." Accessed: Oct. 10, 2010. http://www.ifoam.org/about_ifoam/around_world/eu_group-new/positions/publications/aquaculture/IFOAMEU-Fish_welfare_a_key_issue_for_organic_system_standards_P.LemboW.Zupa.pdf.

"Lobsters Escape Supermarket." *NPR.* Oct. 27, 2007. Accessed: Oct. 19, 2010. http://www.npr.org/templates/story/story.php?storyId=15691327.

Moore, Paula. "Leave Lobsters Out of Pot; Go Veggie Instead." *The Voice of Tucson: TucsonCitizen.com.* "More Letters to the Editor." Oct. 4, 2008. Accessed: Oct. 19, 2010. http://tucsoncitizen.com/morgue/tag/editorials/page/23/.

"Octopus Walking—Algea." *YouTube.* Accessed: Oct. 19, 2010. http://www.youtube.com/watch?v=ynLHkhVV7Gg.

Orenstein, Peggy. "Champion of the Deep." *New York Times.* June 23, 1991. Accessed: Oct. 2010. http://www.nytimes.com/1991/06/23/magazine/champion-of-the-deep.html?pagewanted=1.

"Scientists Discover Coconut Shell-collecting Octopus." *NYDailyNews.com: Lifestyle: Pets.* Associated Press. Dec. 15, 2009. Accessed: Oct. 20, 2010. http://www.nydailynews.com/lifestyle/pets/2009/12/15/2009-12-15_scientists_discover.html.

"Scientists Highlight Fish 'Intelligence.'" *BBCNews.* Aug. 31, 2003. Accessed: Oct. 20, 2010. http://news.bbc.co.uk/2/hi/uk_news/england/west_yorkshire/3189941.stm.

"Sports Fishing: Bad for Fish and Other Living Things." *Pittsburgh Independent Media Center.* July 27, 2005. Accessed: http://pittsburgh.indymedia.org/news/2005/07/19545_comment.php.

"Ten Good Reasons Not to Eat Piggies." May 17, 2009. *World Wildlife News: A Step Ahead in Saving Another Endangered Species.* Accessed: Oct. 20, 2010. http://news.worldwild.org/.

"This Just in: Mollusks Are Still Creepy." JGordon. *ScienceBuzz.* Oct. 31, 2008. Accessed: Oct. 20, 2010. http://www.sciencebuzz.org/blog/just-mollusks-are-still-creepy.

Wallace, David Foster. "Consider the Lobster." *Gourmet.* Aug. 2004: 56–64. Accessed: Oct. 10, 2010. http://www.gourmet.com/magazine/2000s/2004/08/consider_the_lobster.

Watson, Winsor H. et al. "Use of Ultrasonic Telemetry to Determine the Area of Bait

Influence and Trapping Area of American Lobster, *Homarus americanus*, Trap." *New Zealand Journal of Marine and Freshwater Research* 43, Feb. 2009: 411–418. Accessed: Oct. 10, 2010. http://win.unh.edu/publications/pdf/watsonareafished.pdf.

Viegas, Jennifer. "Lobsters and Crabs Feel Pain, Study Shows: Findings Add to Growing Evidence That Virtually All Animals Can Suffer." *MSNBC.com: Science*. March 27, 2009. Accessed: Oct. 10, 2010. http://www.msnbc.msn.com/id/29915025/.

Part II

# Working for Wildlife

# Chapter 9

# Pinnipeds in Peril

## Marine Mammal Rescue

*Sue Pemberton*

**Sue Pemberton** *works in the field of health care, and has long been a champion for nonhuman animals of all sorts. She has volunteered with animal rehabilitation organizations for sixteen years, and currently cares for marine mammals with The Marine Mammal Center of Sausalito, California (http://www.marinemammalcenter.org). Sue is mother to a young daughter (both are vegetarians) and houses "quite a few" companion animals, including a rescued tarantula and "a flock of lovely pet chickens." She finds peace and happiness with other creatures, and advocates educating youngsters about how animals live, what their rights are, and how we can ensure their survival.*

I never really understood how some of my fellow seal savers could work so hard at taking care of our flippered patients only to turn around and eat a slice of pizza with sausage. Why would someone save one animal and eat another? There's some sort of disconnect among many who save animals.

I wish I could say I was one of those cool kids who, at the tender age of five, vowed to be a vegetarian. I wasn't. I was born to an average American family who ate what Americans were eating in the sixties: meat and vegetables. Meat was thought to be part of a well-rounded meal. Everybody

I knew ate meat. Our mothers worked hard to provide a nutritious meal every night, including beef, pork, or chicken. There wasn't any question about whether flesh was actually good for us. More importantly, we never talked about where meat came from. Sure, I knew it was an animal. When we would go to the grocery store I could see the butcher behind the counter cutting away at large slabs of meat, presenting them neatly in shrink-wrapped containers. Buying meat was tidy in spite of its journey to the butcher counter, and we never suspected the cruelty that took place behind the scenes.

It wasn't until I was ten or so that I got a glimpse of where meat *actually* came from. I went for a summer stay at my friend Sherri's grandparents' farm. While we were there, I watched them butcher an adult cow and two lambs. They shot the cow in the throat to bleed him to death since they wanted to eat his brain. They cut the throats of the lambs. I still remember (with great horror) what it sounded like to hear the little lambs bleat through their slit throats. It was awful. I think if my mother had known what I was going to see, meat eater or not, she wouldn't have allowed me to go. Even so, it took another sixteen years for me to make a change in my diet. Still, that cow, and those lambs, ultimately propelled me into animal rights activism.

In 1986, as a young woman, I was looking to lose a couple of pounds, and read a book called *Fit for Life*, in which the authors referred to meat as "flesh." *Yuk*!! I was eating the flesh of another being. Disgusting! From that day on, I have been a vegetarian and defender of *all* animals. Being a healthy vegetarian was a difficult task back then. I lived on plain tofu and salads. My diet was nothing like the veggie kids of today.

But I am getting ahead of myself. I have always loved animals—for as long as I can recall. I know, most kids love animals, but I was the little girl who gravitated towards every animal in the neighborhood. My family had a few cats and a couple of dogs; I remember them as part of my family and dear to my heart. My friends and I would dress the cats and dogs up and have parties. The poor critters were so tolerant. I was heartbroken when each individual died; each time I lost a friend.

I grew up in a coastal town just south of San Francisco. Though I ran all over the beaches, I never saw marine mammals. Being a kid, what I experienced seemed perfectly normal, and strangely enough, our school curriculum didn't include local wildlife. So I didn't know there *were* marine mammals nearby.

In 1993 I discovered a specialized care facility for marine mammals right in my own backyard: The Marine Mammal Center of Sausalito, California, the largest hospital of its kind anywhere in the world. I became an animal care and rescue volunteer, cleaning pens and pools, preparing meals, and most importantly, administering lifesaving medications and treatments to pinniped patients: seals and sea lions. I also volunteer at a local shelter that treats land and air dwelling animals, like raccoons, opossum, hawks, and small birds. I added this shelter to "round out" my animal efforts. This added work only deepened my love for and commitment to my animal family.

As caregivers at the Marine Mammal Center, we are trained not to interact with or speak to our wild patients; we read their behaviors. We can see their happiness when they swim, and how upset they are after a procedure. I perceive how they feel; as fellow earthlings, we are not so different. To date, my ability to read my patients hasn't let me down. Fourteen years of experience contribute to accuracy. Sometimes it's as simple as noting certain behaviors in the absence of outward symptoms, but most of the time I can see fear, pain, or the will to live in their rich eyes.

Talk about thankless labor ... I have learned to let go of any need for thanks. Sure, there was appreciation among staff members, but most of my efforts were spent helping sea lions, elephant and harbor seals, dolphins, porpoises, and sea otters. They were not usually thrilled to see me, which is a healthy response. Still, there have been many precious moments of connection: a simple glance back when released to swim free in the ocean, a bit of cooperation in caretaking (when none was expected), acceptance of food—with me pleading under my breath to *please eat*. Were these expressions of thanks? I like to think that these wild sea mammals realize that my intent is good (even though I must sometimes cause them discomfort), that my intentions are pure. I really hope they understand.

Over the years, a few animals stand out in my memory, animals that seemed to carry a message. Coneely was a harbor seal born six weeks prematurely. He was abandoned by his mother during a fierce El Niño storm. He cried out for his mother with a woeful "ma" (yes—they really say "ma") as he waddled around the beach attempting to suckle nourishment from whatever was available—a rock, my shoe, the muddy hillside. At a puny twelve pounds, he was at least eight pounds below his normal birth weight. He still possessed his natal coat, a white fur that is normally shed while in the uterus. For a full day we monitored him closely from a distance, hoping he would reunite with his mother. When she did not return, I transported him to our hospital for specialized care. We tube fed him a customized formula, and taught him how to eat. Against all odds, following a six-month intensive rehabilitation, he was released as a sixty-pound youngster—together, we never gave up.

Anniversary, an adult female sea lion, arrived comatose. Looking back at her symptoms, she probably suffered from domoic acid toxicity, caused by a neurotoxic algae. While this algae occurs naturally, it is thought by some to be exacerbated by organophosphates that we dump into the ocean. Prior to 1998, marine life was little affected by algae blooms. Now it's a chronic issue for sea lions and otters, who eat sea animals containing neurotoxic algae.

I pulled Anniversary from her kennel and administered "last ditch" medications in a desperate effort to save her life. Before I left I placed my hand on her head and whispered, "The rest is up to you!" I called the next morning, expecting to hear that she had died in the night, but she was alive, sitting up in her pen, and inspecting her unusual surroundings. The next time I saw her, she was standing at the pen door peeking out through a space in the fence with one eye. Her glare was intense, as if she recognized me. Perhaps she knew that I had worked hard to save her life. Anniversary made a full recovery and was eventually released. This beautiful sea lion taught me to always have faith.

There have been less fortunate animals, ones who failed to thrive in spite of top quality care. Anje, an endangered Guadalupe fur seal, was successfully rehabilitated and released with a satellite tag to track her movements. When her tag stopped moving, I was sent out to see why. I found her curled up on a hillside with a well-meaning member of the public petting her. I explained that wild animals don't seek human attention; human attempts to help only make a bad situation worse. Anje was emaciated, hypoglycemic, and cold. I rushed her to our hospital. In spite of hourly formula feedings, and the most intensive care I have ever seen an animal receive, she quietly died. For twelve hours I fought with her for her life, and when she was gone, I held her lifeless body and cried.

Northern elephant seals were hunted to near extinction in the nineteenth century, but have since rebounded, and now number in the tens of thousands. Gorgonzola was a young, underweight northern elephant seal pup. In a perfect scenario he would have received his mother's rich milk for thirty days, gaining around 200 pounds. He would have used his newfound weight for sustenance while he learned to eat and swim, but that is not how his story unfolded.

Gorgonzola, roughly one month old, turned up on a local beach with only his birth weight. He thrived in rehabilitation, and was soon released back to the ocean, where he ingested a fish with a parasite. Most parasites will live in a host at manageable levels, but sometimes they become too numerous and create problems. This is what happened to Gorgonzola. His parasites were so numerous that they caused him to bleed uncontrollably.

We readmitted him, but his condition quickly deteriorated. I made him as comfortable as I could with painkilling drugs, and he lost his battle for life just three hours later.

Both of these pinnipeds fought valiantly for life, and lost. Their passing was accompanied by the sorrow I have felt for every animal I have cared for who has not survived. Working to save sea life, I have learned to accept defeat with grace.

One of my favorite rescues (and probably the most difficult) was a teenaged male California sea lion named D-Day. He was initially reported at San Francisco's Pier 39, a popular hangout for sea lions. He had a salmon flasher hanging from his mouth, a piece of fishing gear consisting of a twelve-inch piece of plastic covered with flashy reflective tape. The plastic is attached to a length of fishing line, and a two-inch baited hook, designed to attract and capture salmon ... but sometimes sea lions will snatch this flashy "meal," swallowing the barbed hook.

D-Day had swallowed just such a barbed hook, and we monitored him at Pier 39, certain that this 400-pound sea lion was too big for us to rescue in a crowded city. After a few days D-Day left the Pier. Not long after, while working with our Water Rescue Team (who capture and free sea lions entangled in fishing gear), we sighted a sea lion who looked like D-Day in Monterey, where it is easier to handle large mammals. We decided to attempt rescue.

I didn't have much hope for capture, not because we weren't prepared, but because sea lions like D-Day don't reach adulthood if they are naïve enough to get caught. We had our work cut out for us, but the planets were aligned properly and the rescue gods were looking down on us: we successfully executed a textbook approach and capture. But getting a perfectly healthy sea lion into a kennel is a whole different story. It took us thirty minutes of wrestling and pushing to wrangle him into the kennel. At the rescue center, the hook, which was deeply imbedded in his stomach, was surgically removed, and he was released back into his watery home. The problem of fishing gear is frustrating because it is one of the most preventable, along with gunshot and overfishing. As a member of the offending species, I feel like it's my duty to make restitution by saving as many animals as I can.

On November 7, 2007, a container ship named *Cosco Buson* hit the San Francisco Bay Bridge, tearing open its hull and spilling 58,000 gallons of bunker fuel, a sticky, viscous, smelly oil into the water. Devastation to land and wildlife quickly followed.

The next day I, and other Marine Mammal Center rescuers, went to Rodeo Beach in Marin County to offer assistance. My heart broke into a million pieces when sea birds, wintering in the bay, began washing up onto beaches stunned and in shock. They looked as if they were literally dipped in tar. Some were still alive, and every effort was made to quickly transport them for treatment. I drove a van full of stricken birds to a temporary bird hospital. There were many birds in boxes, lined up waiting for help, and people kept coming in with carloads of gooey birds. It seemed surreal. It was a horrible nightmare.

Much of the rescue effort was focused on the San Francisco Bay and Marin County. Very little people-power remained to tend birds in neighboring San Mateo County, where I live. I decided to take matters into my own hands and walked local beaches in search of oiled birds. It didn't take long to find the victims of this tragedy. I found three on my very first patrol, but was unable to capture them without rescue equipment. I returned the next day, well prepared, and rescued eleven birds. I must have walked ten miles of beach that day. I was physically and emotionally exhausted, but I did what I could to give those birds a second chance. The next day I hit the beaches again and found a few more before I was told to stop or face arrest.

Bunker fuel is a cancer-causing substance that only specially trained personnel are allowed touch, even when it is coated on wildlife. That was quite possibly the dumbest reason I had ever heard, in a life or death situation, to stop rescue efforts, but since "official" people were starting to rescue in my area, I stepped aside. I was, however, prepared to face arrest to save oil-mired birds, and I ruffled some feathers (no pun intended) commenting to the press about rescue efforts neglecting animals near my home.

All told, almost 1,100 birds were rescued. Only 450 survived. Another 1,800 (or so) were found dead on bay area beaches. It is predicted that as many as 20,000 birds will ultimately be affected by this one spill. I don't know if any birds whom I rescued survived, but if I saved even one, it was worth it.

In my work I have learned a great deal about protecting sea life. Most of us do not know how important a few simple acts can be:

- If you care about sea life, clean up beaches and waterways; garbage is dangerous to sea life. Plastic bags look like jellyfish, and they are deadly to whales and sea turtles who swallow them. Pick up fish hooks and fishing line; always cut six-pack holders and packing straps into pieces to prevent entanglement.
- Know how to respond. If you see an animal who seems to need help, contact a local animal rescue organization; don't approach or attempt rescue yourself. (Marine mammals are federally protected, which makes

it illegal for members of the public to touch or handle them in any way. They are also dangerous because they are wild and will bite to defend their lives.) Protect wounded or sick animals from dogs and people; keep everyone away until trained rescuers arrive. If you can reduce the stress these animals experience (by leaving them alone), you will increase their likelihood of survival.
- Support organizations that rescue and rehabilitate wildlife. If you live near a facility, volunteer your time. The work you do will save lives!

Nonhuman animals are not the only loves of my life. My daughter, Eden, is my "replacement" on Earth. She has been a vegetarian all her life. She knows why I have chosen a veggie life: I openly discuss (some suggest too openly) the cruel and inhumane treatment of animals who are raised and slaughtered for food. When she is old enough, she will choose her way. My daughter and I recently watched a video revealing how turkeys are butchered at a major turkey factory. Afterwards, she asked how and where we could protest such atrocities. She wanted to rally all of her vegetarian friends at school to say something on behalf of turkeys. I see compassion in her actions. Hopefully, the experiences she has with me (and her father, who also rescues marine mammals) will build a lasting connection in her between humans and animals.

I live my life according to Buddhist principles. I believe people accrue a karmic debt for every living being they affect negatively. In Buddhism, all living beings are sacred, and ought to be treated as if they were family. I am obligated to help my "family," not only out of Buddhist compassion, but also because humans cause so much harm. I feel my work is the very least I can do to reverse a little bit of our careless damage.

Is what I am doing changing the world? Not in the way that I wish I could. Do I make a difference in the individual lives of the animals I care for? Absolutely! I am one of many people who work tirelessly to give wounded and sick marine mammals a second chance at life. And when they take one last look back at their caregivers, as they waddle back to the ocean, I sense gratitude: gratitude from our supporters, compassionate people everywhere, and from the universe.

CHAPTER 10

# The Pen Is Mightier Than the Sword

*Phaik Kee Lim*

**Phaik Kee Lim** *has been an animal advocate for twenty-five years. She lives and works in Penang, Malaysia, for Friends of the Earth Malaysia (FOEM, or Sahabat Alam Malaysia, SAM, http://www.foe-malaysia.org/), founded in 1978. Phaik Kee has worked tirelessly on behalf of nonhumans, particularly those captured from their homes in the jungles of Africa and Asia, and shipped to other countries for human amusements.*

I work for Friends of the Earth Malaysia (FOEM), known locally as Sahabat Alam Malaysia (SAM). SAM is a grassroots organization formed to look into environmental problems affecting humans and the environment. I have taken a particular interest in issues pertaining to nonhumans affected by human encroachment, greed, ignorance, and indifference. SAM's founder, Mr. S. M. Mohd Idris, is very much aware that Malaysia's flora and fauna need protection.

As a child I used to see my neighbor's dog on a short chain, left out in the sun and rain year-round. Having read about the Penang Society for the Prevention of Cruelty to Animals (then the RSPCA), I decided to write up a complaint against my neighbor for tying up his dog all day every day.

I was afraid that I could not express myself clearly in English, and that people would laugh at my writing. Finally I resorted to a phone call, only to put down the receiver at the last minute for fear that the society's phone operator would take down my name and address, exposing me to the owner. I gave up; the dog was eventually released, when the neighbor moved out. The unfortunate dog became a stray eventually.

I felt guilty because I had not done anything to help the dog, and this guilt lived in me through my late teens. After completing my studies, I volunteered at the Penang SPCA as a telephone operator. I joined the inspectors, rounding up the strays, assisting the vet in the night clinic to treat sick and injured nonhumans and spay/neuter dogs and cats.

It breaks my heart to watch unwanted kittens and puppies die when they are "put down." There are few kind caregivers in Malaysia, people who feed strays, and have them spayed or neutered. Such people are rare. Stray dogs and cats abound in Malaysia because of irresponsible pet ownership.

Later, I decided to work for a nongovernmental organization involved in animal welfare. I asked around Penang until one of my teachers introduced me to SAM. Twenty-five years later, I am still with SAM. I am committed to this job because of my passion for nonhumans, both wild and tame. I have always felt for them, even at a very tender age. I cannot stand the sight of starving strays, and detest cruelty and exploitation of nonhumans.

My work consists mostly of writing to the media and corresponding with local authorities. I create and send petitions, action alerts, and write-ups on issues affecting the environment and wildlife, such as nonhumans in entertainment, animal experimentation and vivisection, the wildlife trade, poaching, zoos, farmed animals, livestock, the pet shop trade, invasions by exotic species, the aquarium fish trade, the suffering of aquarium fish, and any other form of abuse or cruelty to nonhumans.

It is heartbreaking to read or hear about animal suffering, whether local or abroad. The *Malay Mail* told a heart-wrenching story that moved me to tears and prompted me to write a letter to the editor calling for a ban on hunting. This article told of a mother monkey, a spectacled or dusky leaf monkey, who was wounded by hunters. She was discovered dead, but still cradling her infant on her lap.

Estate residents speculated that the wounded mother had scurried to safety, clutching her baby, after being shot by hunters. Another monkey was found dead just 200 meters away, also shot. They believed that this mother escaped, and hid behind a rubber tree, where she used one of the cups that had been set out to collect rubber to offer her baby a drink. There she remained, waiting for death. It is possible that she cradled her baby with such protective vigor, no doubt tainted by pain and fear, so that her little one suffocated.

Defenseless creatures are always at the mercy of humans. Some countries eat dogs, while others hunt wildlife, or train nonhumans for the circus; people everywhere brutalize defenseless creatures. In this difficult work, I am often motivated by one of the sayings of the Buddha, which I read in a magazine, *Animal Citizen*: "As much as you value your own life, you must also value the lives of others."

Therefore I believe that nonhumans should not be killed for human vanity, for food, for luxury or decorative items, for aphrodisiacs, or for entertainment. I detest angling for pleasure because fish suffer for such mindless sport. Birds should never be caged for our pleasure. They value their life and freedom as much as we value our own life and freedom. I strongly discourage people from buying nonhumans from pet shops. Buying from pet shops contributes to the trade in wild-caught nonhumans.

I will not go to the circus, theme parks, zoos, or wildlife parks. Even these many years later, I cannot forget an incident that I witnessed at the Royal Indian Circus when I was a child. Everyone was looking forward to watching the much acclaimed pair of "counting dogs"—small breed dogs who could read and count. The audience was asked to give two numbers for the dogs to add. The numbers were written on a whiteboard, and the dogs were required to pick the correct answer, from one to ten, written on the cards. One of the dogs picked a wrong number, and was severely slapped across the face by the trainer. His violence reduced me to tears. I was traumatized by his anger and his viciousness. Since then I have never had a good word for circuses or any other establishments that exploit nonhumans for human pleasure.

Those who go to circuses have usually never given a thought to how the nonhumans live, how they are chained, caged, or tethered for most of their lives. They are trucked all over, and forced to perform unnatural acts on demand, for the sake of human entertainment. If they do not do what they are expected to do, they will be punished by angry circus men. Our self-indulgence and ignorance are pitiful and painful.

In 2005, when I was on an investigative trip to the Kuala Lumpur Bird Park, I discovered that orangutans there were forced to perform tricks. A young orangutan was slow to respond, and I saw the trainer pinching her under her forearm. As a member of SAM, I brought this to the attention of the office of Trade Record Analysis for Flora and Fauna in Commerce (TRAFFIC) in Petaling Jaya. Consequently, the Wildlife Department was forced to investigate how these primates were obtained. They conducted

DNA tests, and as a result, the smuggled orangutans were seized and they were sent back to their country of origin—Indonesia. The show at the Kuala Lumpur Bird Park has since stopped. When we see something cruel, we should always pause to think how we might stop the cruelty.

A famous resort in Malacca still forces orangutans to perform for the masses. Animal acts are neither entertaining nor educational; they devalue both the unfortunate nonhumans and the mindless viewers, who fail to recognize or see the deprivation that these nonhumans suffer. These practices continue because of human indifference and ignorance. We can change this, but we have to stop supporting (with our entrance fees and our silence) these forms of entertainment, which exploit and harm nonhumans.

SAM also works with primate groups such as the International Primate Protection League (IPPL). In 2002, IPPL notified SAM that four gorillas had been imported to Malaysia's Taiping Zoo. Both SAM and IPPL were doubtful that these primates were acquired legally. Primates cannot be caught from the wild and transported into Malaysia. IPPL had reason to believe that these four gorillas were exported from Nigeria with documents claiming that they had been born in captivity, at a freshly opened Nigerian zoo. IPPL also had reason to believe that the gorillas were illegally caught from Cameroon, and then smuggled across the Cameroon-Nigeria border. We were yet more suspicious when smugglers were apprehended and two baby chimpanzees were confiscated on the border between Cameroon and Nigeria.

SAM, in conjunction with IPPL and other international wildlife organizations, sent letters of protest and action alerts to the Malaysian Environment Ministry, demanding the return of the Taiping Four to their country of origin. Sustained international cooperation between activists was a great success for the Taiping Four; the gorillas were sent home in 2007.

In August of 2005, SAM received emails announcing that the Thai and Kenyan governments were planning to capture 300 wild animals from Kenya for the Chiang Mai Night Safari Zoo in Thailand. SAM is always against the capture of free, wild-roaming animals for imprisonment, whether for science or entertainment. SAM pondered how these wondrous nonhumans would be moved from the wide-open savanna to comparatively tiny, barren pens. What psychological, emotional, and physical damage would they suffer as a result of their capture and confinement?

SAM, in cooperation with other international wildlife groups, notified Thai Prime Minister Thaksin Shinawatra of our strong objection to the import of Kenyan wildlife for the Night Zoo. We sent letters to the Kenyan president and the Kenyan minister for environment, urging them to keep and protect their wildlife as part of the magnificent national heritage of all Kenyans. SAM action alerts were sent to many wildlife groups, calling for letters of protest to local Kenyan and Thai embassies. If enough people raise their voices in protest, officials will listen. The nonhumans cannot speak for themselves.

In February of 2006, SAM received news from Edwin Wiek, who was in Thailand, that Thailand's Safari World had, in their custody, more than 100 orangutans indigenous to Indonesia. In September of 2003, and July of 2004, a joint Thai-Indonesian government inspection of Safari World uncovered 115 orangutans constrained in squalid, cramped conditions. Many were not registered with the authorities. Safari World claimed to have a breeding program, which had produced these orangutans, but a disproportionate number of young orangutans suggested otherwise. As experts awaited DNA tests, many suspected that Safari World's orangutans had been smuggled in from Borneo and Indonesia, rather than captive bred in Thailand.

SAM joined forces with the global community of animal welfare and conservation groups to condemn the capture and transport of wild animals illegally—and demanded the repatriation of these orangutans to Indonesia for rehabilitation and release back into the wild. It was my privilege to coordinate a letter-writing effort to the president of Indonesia, their minister of environment, and Indonesian nongovernmental organizations, urging them to demand the return of their orangutans. SAM also asked Indonesian authorities to pressure Convention on International Trade in Endangered Species (CITES) officials to impose sanctions on Thailand, as well as Cambodia, Malaysia, and Saudi Arabia, for allowing orangutans to be smuggled across their borders. Letters and alerts were sent to the Thai prime minister, and the director general of national parks, requesting that they return the illegally captured orangutans to Indonesia. These letters were followed by an action alert, calling members and other interested parties to send similar letters both to Indonesian and Thai authorities.

Resources are limited for SAM; we do not have the means to establish a sanctuary. But we can speak out. When we feel strongly, as we do about animal rights, we can speak up or write letters to encourage change.

I will continue to work to educate others about what is happening with Malaysia's wildlife, and about any other exploited or abused nonhuman. I have found that the pen is mightier than the sword. We must all refuse to support industries that exploit nonhumans, and be willing to write letters and protest when nonhumans are treated cruelly. It would be a sad day indeed to see Malaysia's endangered species go the way of the dodo bird.

If people understood how much nonhumans suffer—if they had seen what I have seen—they would not support animal industries. If we do not understand what we cause with our money, if we do not understand the power of our support through entrance fees, through buying animal products, and through what we choose to eat and wear, then animal exploitation will continue, and wildlife will be exploited for food, clothing, and entertainment. The suffering and the dying will continue.

Where there is a demand, there will be supply. The killing will only end if we stop buying. Please think about where you spend your money, and what your money buys.

CHAPTER 11

# The Meaning of Life

*Deborah D. Misotti*

**Deborah D. Misotti** *has worked with nonhuman primates for many years, with particular emphasis on gibbons. Married for more than forty years to her husband, Thomas (a Leadership in Energy and Environmental Design [LEED] Accredited Professional), she is the cofounder and director of The Talkin' Monkeys Project, Inc. (www.talkinmonkeysproject.org,) a 501(c)(3) educational primate sanctuary in southwest Florida. This environmentally conscious rescue project is the logical culmination of a lifetime of volunteering to help nonhumans, youth at risk, and the larger community based on their shared desire to make a difference. They are longstanding members of the International Primate Protection League.*

The wooden screen door squeaks with a familiar sound as we enter the volunteer porch. It closes with a sharp snap and I smile a secret smile to myself. We—my family and twenty-two volunteers—have labored hard in preparation for an expected arrival. Working together, we erected steel panels and metal roofing, created a fire hose hammock, dug trenches, erected secondary fencing for safety, and laid pipe for water hookups and drinking lines. One of the volunteers is a welder, and he struggled mightily with our chute system and slider panel doors to create a secure holding pen. The night caging (in the night houses) was a feat in itself. We are always amazed at how much needs to be done to set up just one habitat for one expected resident! We were all worn out, and had accomplished a great deal, but I could see that it would take another two days to complete all that was required for our new arrival.

We are pleasantly exhausted, having worked in triple-digit temperatures. But this is the norm in southwest Florida, in the center of the state, in the middle of summer. The conversation and pleasant laughter continue as volunteers enter for a cold drink, and the screen door snaps sharply closed behind them, sparking memories from my past.

Growing up in a large family in the suburbs of Baltimore, Maryland, was perfect for me. Our large family meant that money was always in short supply. Outings were simple picnics in wonderful nearby places like the Smithsonian Institute museums, or zoos, which do not seem so wonderful now as they did when I was a child. When I was a toddler, I thought that zoos were exciting because I loved to watch the monkeys. I did not understand the seamy side of zoos, but simply loved to watch the nonhuman primates. Whenever I wandered off, my family knew where to find me: I would be at the monkey cages, singing with the gibbons. I loved the music they made and I marveled at their fluid movements. They were quite the gymnasts, and I often tried to emulate their acrobatics at home, leaping from the shed roof, over picnic tables, and onto ropes that I hung from trees in our yard.

My maternal grandmother, my Mom-Mom, had a wonderful farm in Carroll County, Maryland, and on her farm, as a preschooler, I began to develop a deep bond with nonhuman animals. I would burst into the old country kitchen, with its wood-burning stove and long wooden trestle table, through the old, wooden screen door, which snapped loudly behind me, announcing my arrival. My grandmother, always tolerant of my youthful energy, reminded me once again not to snap the screen door, then listened patiently while I breathlessly described my latest adventure. She encouraged my dreams for the future, and never hesitated to tell me that I could do anything I wanted when I grew up—be anything I wanted to be.

Mom-Mom was the only person who told me that I could work with monkeys if that was what I really wanted to do. She was a quiet woman, who listened to me chatter about animals while we shelled peas or husked corn on the steps of the kitchen porch. She showed great interest in my adventures, encouraging my babble, but never failed to caution me not to love farmed animals too much—they all had a job to do. She even reminded me that, perhaps, when I next came to visit, they would not be there to greet me.

My fourth year was full of life changes. That was the year my Mom-Mom died, and the farm was sold. I remember looking back, as we drove away down the long rocky drive, for the last time. I suddenly realized that my Mom-Mom, my friend, was gone. I cried for a very long time.

It was also in my fourth year that my mother began working as a secretary as the elementary school librarian. When I wasn't babbling at Mom-Mom, I was a quiet child, and very obedient, and was therefore allowed to take books down from the shelves and sit at the tables to look at them, as long as I put them back where I had found them. One day, Mrs. Ruth Matthews, the head librarian, said that if I found a special book, and I really wanted to know what the story was about, she would teach me to read. I had discovered the Curious George books just that week, and wanted desperately to know what this monkey was all about. I began to learn to read, and I entered a new level of primate exploration. I spent days perusing the library shelves in search of books that might have something to do with monkeys.

While I had many friends growing up, animals were my most special friends, and they were also my teachers. I loved dogs, cats, horses, and any other animal I could get to know. It was about this time that my favorite aunt pulled me aside and explained to me that some people have a different way of looking at the world, and I was one of these "different people." I would always understand nonhuman animals better than human animals. She also explained to me that this was something we needed to learn to hide in order to "fit in." Growing up in the fifties, I was told that "fitting in," was the goal of all good little girls. Nonetheless, when I was eight years old, I informed my mother that I was going to be an anthropologist or an archeologist. She was appalled, and told me never to use such words again—they were not for women. She told me I would be a teacher, a secretary, or a nurse until I got married and became a mother. This was apparently the primary purpose and meaning of a woman's life. If my mother said so, it must be true. I was devastated.

Later I learned that my mother was wrong, but I learned this difficult lesson the hard way. In my early twenties, when I had just one young daughter, my infant sons died. Jason was born with multiple birth defects, and never left the hospital. From my perspective, he was simply gone soon after birth. Two years later, Tommy was born, and died with identical birth defects. Tom and I had always imagined having a large family in a home ringing with the laughter of many children. Now, there could be no more babies. I was desolate and hollow as I lovingly watched my four-year-old daughter, my first and now *only* child, play with a consolation gift from

Tom, my husband—an Irish Setter puppy named Corky, whom we could ill afford. Grief is an overwhelming companion, lacking substance, yet always there. I walked with heavy heart over the surrounding hills, seeking solace, a shadow of my former self.

One day, I shadow walked across the crest of a hill, through cattle pastures in search of that bountiful comfort that can be found with animals, and in nature. I headed for the little meadow where, in the past, I had renewed my spirits, but this particular day the calves and cows were being forcibly separated by the farmer. The fearful cries of the calves, the mournful bellows of heartbroken mother cows, resounded in my ears. I fell to my knees, overwhelmed by our mutual agony of loss. The tears I had withheld for so long gushed onto the green grass, and my body was wrenched by sobs as I wailed with my new companions in circumstance: cow mothers.

Sometime during this grief-stricken tirade, Corky crawled onto my lap and started licking my face. I looked down into his soulful brown eyes, and I realized that my arms had never been empty, they were filled with my new son, Corky. I was sorry that I could do little to help the cattle—except rethink my diet—and I was content with my new lease on life: animal mom. Corky and I walked home. With the help of Corky, the door had opened to a new and more appropriate meaning for my life, and I have never looked back. Furthermore, since that day I have never hidden my special ability to commune with animals.

Over the next fifteen years I worked with volunteer projects for dogs, cats, horses, tigers, cougars, lions, wolves, and various farmed animals. While I enjoyed interacting with so many animals, nothing completely fulfilled me. I always remembered my first love, monkeys. After helping out at a project for capuchins in Costa Rica in the early 1990s, I attended a Jane Goodall lecture in Fort Lauderdale. When she was done, I spoke with her about the possibility of establishing a primate sanctuary. She mentioned a "project" in Miami, where I might volunteer to gain some much-needed experience with primates. I contacted the director of the Miami primate project, which held chimpanzees and orangutans who had previously been exploited by the entertainment industry. I was very excited to learn that there were gibbons and capuchins on the grounds—those wonderful acrobatic clowns with the beautiful songs, friends of my early childhood.

My husband and I were excited to meet the director, but we were even more excited to meet the nonhuman primates. Oddly, we were allowed directly into the pens, where we met two very young apes—an orangutan and a chimp. I looked into the chimp's face and found the most soulful, cunning, and intelligent eyes I had ever seen. It was a startling experience—deeply moving. The young orangutan walked straight at my husband, displaying an impressive set of teeth in a startling yet ominous smile. My husband went sheet white, and the director quickly called out, "He only wants a piggyback ride!" Luckily, we were not the average tourists! Tom allowed the young orangutan to pull himself up for a piggyback ride, and the little fellow's smile is forever captured in a picture that sits on Tom's desk at work.

Next, with Tom still carrying the young orangutan, we were ushered into another fenced area. Much to my surprise, a small rust-colored ape walked up and took my hand. She gave a gentle tug, and I looked down into the golden eyes of one of the finest teachers I would ever know: Ruby. Ruby gifted me with an invitation, subtle and yet incredibly deep. I felt as though I had fallen into a trance: Steeped in silence, I experienced a combination of gibbon call, the musky scent of orangutan, and the warmth of friendship as I had never known friendship before. I also felt a deep peace. It was as though I had come home in my heart and in my mind. Life had finally come full circle.

I was accepted as a volunteer on the spot, and Ruby became my first teacher. In time, Ruby also became a very dear friend, though she proved to be a tyrant. She pulled me through every emotion in the spectrum. She gifted me with hugs and kisses, and punished me with smacks and bites when I did not obey her rules. Unfortunately, Ruby succumbed to cancer a year later, but as my first truly dedicated nonhuman teacher, Ruby remains with me always, accompanying me whenever I offer lectures or presentations. Her gifts have proven incredibly important, and I will never forget her. She was the first of many primate teachers I was to know and love.

On my first day volunteering at the Miami project, I met two White-handed Lar gibbons, Abby (black) and Sandy (gold). I was told that very few volunteers were allowed near the gibbons because they can bruise and scratch those who come too near. I often visited their cage over the next few months, to interact with these prisoners. Abby, in particular, was visibly unhappy. Her mate, Sandy, loved clowning for the crowds, but Abby was private and did not like to be ogled. The primary primate caregiver taught me how to interact with these small apes: nonhuman primates are wild animals, unaware of human frailties, and humans can be severely injured. Nonetheless, I was determined to work with these fuzzy little individuals; when the primate caregiver realized that my inclination toward gibbons could not be suppressed, even at risk of bodily harm, she again taught me how to deal with gibbons, and then allowed me to deliver their food—noting that I might have my hair pulled, or be scratched or bruised. Still, I continued to deliver their food—receiving scratches and bruises in exchange. Week after week I tried to gain their friendship, to become acceptable in their eyes. Week after week I walked away rebuffed and disappointed.

About four months later, despite my best efforts, I had made no headway. One day, when I approached the bars behind which the gibbons were trapped, the black female, Abby, grabbed my bangs and rapped my head sharply against the bars of her cage, painfully bruising my forehead. I had grown used to their unwelcoming responses, and knew better than to come so near the bars. As I walked away, rubbing my head, I looked up to see an old man standing with his arms across his chest. I stopped rubbing my head and assumed a sheepish grin. He kindly asked, "Did she hurt you?" I replied that the hurt was not on my forehead, but rather in my heart. I told him how I was drawn to gibbons, how I loved them, and how they refused to accept me. He asked why I loved these obstreperous primates, and I told him that I loved their song. The old man smiled and nodded, and in that moment I was struck with inspiration.

I turned, jumped onto the wall that surrounded the gibbons, and softly crooned a lullaby. The song that I chose was one I had never expected to sing again; it was a lullaby that I had sung to my son the day he died. As I sang, tears began to flow, but through my blurry vision I could see Abby racing across the cage. I braced for her blow, but she did not strike me, or tear my clothing. Instead, Abby reached out her hand touched a tear on my cheek, then tasted the salt. She tasted another tear, then started crooning softly along with me, continuing to wipe my cheek, seeming to understand, and perhaps willingly sharing my sorrow. I felt so close to Abby. I vowed then and there to one day create a sanctuary and bring Abby home, away from the public eye, to a place where she could be a gibbon, not a perpetual entertainer.

After that, Abby and I sang together every day. She would begin singing even before I arrived, as I drove my Jeep down the long two-mile road to the facility. So I would sing, too, ignoring the gawking people as I drove by. Abby and I bonded yet more with each song. When visitors asked me why I sang with Abby, I would tell them, "Because I can." Not everyone is privileged to sing with a gibbon, and for me this was a gift beyond measure.

My strong bond with Abby eventually brought Tom and I to create our own primate rescue project—a home for Abby. The venture was a vast undertaking and gave us a whole new respect for the many projects we had volunteered with. Though we worked diligently to set up a sanctuary for Abby, it was not to be. Before we were able to complete our labor of love, Abby was sold to a breeder. Her loss to the horrors of primate breeding—of endlessly producing offspring to be exploited by capitalistic human beings—is one of my deepest regrets. A few years ago I learned that the greedy breeder had left Abby outside during Hurricane Wilma. She died of a heart attack when a large tree fell on her cage with her trapped helplessly inside. I was inconsolable for months. I failed Abby, and I had lost her forever. We had to again let go of our dream—our dream of one day bringing Abby home to a sanctuary so lovingly created with her in mind, and again rediscover what the center and focus of our lives might be.

And, once again, we found our way. We continued to work on our primate sanctuary, The Talkin' Monkeys Project, Inc., and it has become our pride and joy, our purpose and meaning. The Talkin' Monkeys Project, now a 501(c)(3), is a homey place, where volunteers are not judged by the amount of money they donate, or by their social strata. Everyone at the sanctuary is valued for their own unique qualities. Talkin' Monkeys focuses on eco-education, on sharing the hope of a greener lifestyle, and offers visitors the many rich possibilities that are available to all living beings through a closer understanding of nature. We try to inspire visitors to reflect on their daily choices, their lifestyles, and to recognize the effect that each one of us has on every other sentient being through our daily choices. We also encourage vision in young people, as my Mom-Mom did for me, and perhaps even stimulate lost dreams in weary adults. At Talkin' Monkeys, we are aware that all people have dreams as children, and we hope that we might provide an example of how, even after a half a century of life, people can live a dream they envisioned when they were children.

The Talkin' Monkeys Project has become a noninvasive educational center for several local colleges and high schools, and we welcome students from all aspects of academia. Students come from all over the United States, and even from other countries around the world. Some come for community service hours, some for academic credits or projects, and some continue coming long after they have completed their service requirements because they have come to love the sanctuary and its residents. At the Talkin' Monkeys Project we hope to rescue more than gibbons, spider monkeys, and capuchins. We hope to rescue anyone who needs us at the time, even if only for a little while. Visitors and volunteers sometimes come to us wounded, sometimes physically and sometimes in spirit, too often lonely and wary of strangers. Sometimes they leave for new homes healed and happy, with a bright life ahead, a life filled with new people and new experiences. Sometimes they leave us unwillingly, and we grieve for the loss of souls we have loved. These are the hardest partings, but we know, in our hearts, that each soul has been loved while they were here.

My life has been a spiral dance of highs and lows, but animal friends have remained a constant. As I grow older, I see that my life will end as it began, with gibbons, the friends of my youth. Each day I walk into our sanctuary and I am greeted with the heart music of gibbons calling, and I see that the dream of my childhood has become a reality, and we must prepare ourselves for another arrival—a gibbon.

Fortunately, this gibbon is not injured, and will not require extensive veterinary care and prolonged recuperation, as have other abused and mistreated new arrivals. This new gibbon, Webster, is coming to us from a home where he has been kept as a pet. The owners have decided to give him up because his vocalizations are bringing complaints from nearby neighbors. But Webster will have his own set of difficulties. He has only known one set of human beings, and one lifestyle—that of a "pet." We must anticipate his psychological difficulties as well as his physical struggles as he adjusts to his new home. He will have to learn to be a gibbon.

We have been working on Webster's enclosure with an extra measure of enthusiasm and special attention to detail. This habitat, originally designed in my mind's eye as a home for my beloved friend, Abby, is to become a home for this very special gibbon: Webster—Abby's only surviving son.

I wander outside and the wooden screen door snaps shut behind me as a young volunteer, filled with energy and enthusiasm, races up behind me, chattering about her hopes of working with apes when she finishes school. I tell her that she can do anything she wants to, and be anything she wants to be, and she scurries off to feed the gibbons. I return to complete the day's finishing touches on Webster's new home. Mom-Mom must be smiling.

## Chapter 12

# Little Dog of Safety Bay

*Lynette Shanley*

**Lynette Shanley** *abandoned a well-paying job and mainstream lifestyle for more meaningful work advocating for nonhuman animals. She founded two Australian organizations, one for wildcats and one for primates. By working slowly and meticulously through official channels, Lynette has been instrumental in developing new laws regarding both education and trade in exotic "pets." She has also closed down two zoos, and when necessary, has dodged laws, entering primate quarters to expose wrongdoing. Lynette explains the importance of patience to successful advocacy, and of preserving habitat. Hers is the story of how saving nonhuman animals can save one's own life.*

The dog was cornered against the brick wall of a shop. It was a small, white and tan dog, perhaps a Jack Russell. There were five or six young boys beating the dog, who looked at me as if to question why I did not help. But I felt glued to the pavement. I could not move. In that moment I felt victimized. I felt unfairness. My emotions swung between anger and disgust. I was very frightened by the group of boys who were beating the dog. In that instant I understood injustice, intimidation, and domination. I hated myself because I was a coward. I sat on the park bench and cried. I never told my family about this horrible experience because I felt guilty. I disliked myself intensely. I was eleven.

I made up my mind there and then that I would make it up to that little dog.

This year is my twenty-fifth year working for animals. Whilst I can name the month and year I came into this work, it is harder to name why. But the event with the dog stands out in my mind; I can remember every detail as though it were yesterday.

When I was a small child I traveled on the train with my mother between Fremantle and Perth in West Australia. I would see posters of dogs in the railway stations. These posters had a very unsettling effect on me. The dogs looked sad and tortured and the caption read, "This is vivisection." I learned later that the posters were placed on the railway stations by the British Union for the Abolition of Vivisection (BUAV). When I asked my mother about vivisection, with a concerned expression she said, "nothing for you to worry about." I can still recall those posters in detail, and I found out later that it *is* something for me to worry about.

Twenty years later I was working a well-paid job, and living in a unit with a view of Sydney Harbor. I had nice clothes, went to nice restaurants, and had an active social life. But I felt empty. I had what many others wanted, but I was not happy.

I took up voluntary work at the children's hospital, spending time with lonely children who had no visitors. I still felt empty. Pythagoras wrote that a man without a purpose is like a ship without a rudder. That is what I felt like: a ship sailing aimlessly without purpose.

Then, one day while I was shopping, I wandered into a pet shop. As I looked around I felt something gently touch my shoulder. I turned to face a black and white kitten. He looked right into my eyes. I said to him, "No, I do not like cats." Ten minutes later we were both headed for home with litter trays, feeding bowls, collars, food, bedding, and many other items the shop assistant assured me I would need. I named him Marcus, and what followed was my first real experience with an animal. He changed my world.

I learned from Marcus. He told me of his needs, and in the absence of other animals, he relied on me for companionship. He taught me that even though he was a cat, and I was a human, there was very little difference between us. He needed food, water, and fresh air. He could feel pain and sadness. He thrived on kindness.

Because of Marcus, I started thinking about the plight of animals—not just pet animals, but research, farm, circus, and *all* captive animals. Because of Marcus, I stopped eating meat. I joined an anti-vivisection group. And the number of stray cats in my home increased. It took another few years before I started to consider the plight of noncaptive animals, and problems such as smuggling, habitat destruction, and hunting.

A year after Marcus came into my life, I no longer kept the same company; I no longer mixed in the same circles; I no longer enjoyed the same social scene. I felt more settled and at peace. I knew what my life purpose was. Marcus showed me who I really am. And for the first time, I liked myself.

Over the next eight years I joined various animal groups, exploring ideas in the animal movement and pondering the actions of groups that I joined. We put a lot of effort into campaigns: anti-vivisection, animals in entertainment, circuses, and zoos. But I felt that our efforts never really amounted to much. There were lots of protests and leaflets; all of us worked hard, such long hours, but I felt that we did not see much success. On the large committees formed from these groups, many good ideas were set aside because the majority did not agree. I felt that more time was taken with committees than with animal welfare. I felt frustrated and demoralized. I felt there had to be a different way of bringing change. I resigned from all animal rights groups halfway through 1990.

I felt lost and disappointed, but continued to work with animals. I took in cats, spayed and neutered them, then placed them in secure homes. I looked after birds for a local group that cared for injured wildlife. I wrote letters and articles on animal rights and advocacy. But I wanted to eradicate the *cause* of animal problems. Once again I had that feeling that something was missing.

Everyone in the animal rights movement must find their own niche. I started to feel as if I really needed to work mainly on my own. Then, in October 1990, my life changed drastically once again, thanks to two people.

In one of the groups that I had joined, I came across a newsletter published by Dr. Shirley McGreal of the International Primate Protection League (IPPL). The IPPL newsletter was sent to our Australian group every four months, and I always waited impatiently for that newsletter to arrive. It was full of facts, not just opinions.

Dr. Shirley McGreal's life changed at the Bangkok airport, when she saw monkeys waiting to be shipped to U.S. labs. Since then, she has made a huge difference for primates. From the other side of the world, I had a deep admiration for her. I yearned to meet her and to talk to her.

One morning, in October 1990, I opened the newspaper to find that Dr. William McBride, the doctor who discovered the effects of thalidomide, was going to euthanize 240 marmosets. In desperation, I phoned Dr. McGreal. I never thought I would actually talk to her, but she answered the phone. Dr. McGreal gave me a few good ideas, and a few weeks later, suggested that

I focus on helping primates in Australia. Australia's first primate welfare organization, Primates for Primates, was born.

Primates for Primates encompasses all primate species, and all problems affecting primates. I also started up a branch of the International Society for Endangered Cats (now called Wild Cats Plus) in Australia, with the help of Pat Bumstead of Canada.

That was nearly eighteen years ago. Since then, I have worked mainly on my own, with guidance from Shirley McGreal, Pat Bumstead, and Professor Colin Groves. I learned quickly, out of necessity, and one lesson learned was that very little is achieved overnight. Patience, perseverance, and determination pay off.

Australian schools once used ducklings to teach children about imprinting. The duck eggs were taken from the mother duck, and when they hatched the chicks imprint on the children. The child was then expected to look after the duckling. Of course many of these ducklings are dumped into lakes, where they have no idea how to look after themselves. Most of them die young. Several groups tried to ban duck imprinting but failed because they had given up on the campaign too early.

One day a woman I worked with told me about a duck whom she had kept after her son had used it for an imprinting experiment. I did not turn to press coverage, as others had done. Instead, I engaged in a two-year campaign with the Department of Education. It all boiled down to the meaning of a handful of words in education guidelines. A solicitor (lawyer) helped me out, and two years later the practice of duck imprinting was abandoned by every school in Australia's New South Wales.

Through a two-year campaign, I was also able to stop the Australian trade in pet monkeys. This was a campaign in which I had to learn how to compromise, an emotional campaign that often reduced me to tears. For two years I campaigned, met with government officials, and took part in a government committee examining monkeys as pets. The strain and effort paid off: Monkeys are now classified so that they may no longer be taken as pets.

Some people urged me to ban monkeys as pets altogether. But this would have required monkeys currently kept as pets to be removed from homes. We have no primate sanctuary in Australia, so these primates would likely be euthanized. This was not an option for me. Some of the people tending to these monkeys cared deeply for these primates, and it would have been emotionally traumatic to have the monkeys removed by force. Those owners are now allowed to keep their original pet monkeys, and the law includes guidelines that make it difficult for primate keepers to breed monkeys. Over the last twelve years, since the legislation was changed, the number of people keeping primates as pets has dropped to less than twenty, and of course the trade in monkeys has stopped altogether.

I have also been instrumental in closing down two zoos, and have successfully urged the federal government to adopt a national code that will improve conditions for captive animals throughout Australia. The lesson I learned in this campaign was to fight fire with fire. Attempts failed until we employed professional zoologists and primatologists to inspect zoos and write reports. It was harder for zoo supporters to dismiss our campaign when the reports against zoo conditions were written by experts in the field.

Twice I have entered into a primate breeding colony without permission. An informant tipped me off regarding conditions and treatment of baboons in a nearby breeding colony. Staff were exposed for taking pot shots at monkeys with air rifles. Managers did not answer my letters of concern. The first entry brought vast improvements in housing and general conditions for the monkeys. The colony, and the running of the colony, came under scrutiny because I was able to gain inside information. The second time I entered with a reporter from *The Bulletin*, an Australian current affairs magazine. This resulted in much-needed coverage about xenotransplantation. Xenotransplantation is the transplanting of organs from one species to another such as pig organs to baboons or organs from nonhuman animals to human animals.

Some years ago I was appointed to the Microsearch ethics committee. Microsearch is the medical research company that pioneered microsurgery (surgery on minute body structures or cells performed with the aid of a microscope and other specialized instruments, such as a micromanipulator). This ethics committee assessed whether or not experiments should be performed based on whether or not the experiments were morally acceptable, and also based on the importance of anticipated results. I would not pass experiments that exploited animals. I find all animal experiments morally unacceptable, so I just could not pass experiments. It made no difference whether the animals were monkeys or mice, I could not give permission to go ahead with any experiments that exploited animals. I was under pressure to stay on the committee from other animal rights activists, but I would not give in to what others wanted. I followed my own conscience; I stayed with my own feelings and my own beliefs, and was sacked from the committee. I believe that I am the only person in Australia to be sacked from an ethics committee for refusing to pass experiments that I argued were immoral.

One Australian activist who has my admiration and whom I respect is Christine Pierson. Australia has many cat haters, but Christine is working to bring change. She has spayed and neutered more than 80,000 cats. She also works with councils, changing attitudes. It is the combination of political pressure and practical work that has lead to results for Christine. She is also not well known as there is no ego and she does the work purely to make life better for animals.

Pat Bumstead, Shirley McGreal, and Christine Pierson are all determined women, who focused on what they want to achieve, and who have greatly influenced my life and work. Professor Colin Groves, a primatologist, has also had a large influence over the work I do. He took much time out of his usual activities to teach me about primates and to help me in many ways.

My work with Pat Bumstead taught me about the problems that small cats face in South America and Southeast Asia. Because I sometimes do not see things as Pat does, my contact with her is thought-provoking and has expanded my horizons. Pat taught me about conservation and the importance of protecting natural environments.

Margays are small South American wild cats, slightly bigger than house cats. The fur trade in the seventies and eighties caused hundreds of thousands of them to be killed for their pelts. When this trade was outlawed, their population slowly began to recover; unlike most wild cats, they only have one kitten at a time, rarely two. These highly arboreal cats rely on the trees of the rainforest. As large portions of the forest are cleared, the cats are stranded, as they will not cross open areas. This leaves small, isolated populations of margays stranded, unable to find mating partners who are not their relatives. Through this I learned that protecting the environments where animals live is necessary to ensure their survival. Protecting environments is not just conservation; it is also animal rights—they have a basic right to their natural habitat. We do not have a right to take this from them. We all share the planet.

Though I work mostly with primates and wildcats, I have not forgotten dogs and little domestic cats. Recently I helped a dog named Bronson find a new home. He spent much of his life at the end of a chain. He is now happy, with people who love him. Those people are very special people to take on such an emotionally injured dog. Seeing such generous love makes this work worthwhile.

Though I have worked on primate issues since 1990, it wasn't until 2005 that I actually saw a primate in the wild, in his or her own habitat. They are very different from the primates I have seen in labs, circuses, and zoos. They are a joy to watch. At a hotel in Jaipur, India, I felt I was being watched while I unpacked. The feeling grew more intense, and I grew uncomfortable. When I looked out the window, I saw a group of langurs in the tree outside my room, looking back. They were as fascinated by me as I was by them.

In 2000, at an IPPL conference in South Carolina, I first held a primate, the blind gibbon, Beanie. Gibbons are such gentle primates—and they sing! It was the first time I had ever touched a primate, and I was holding such a special gibbon. Sadly Beanie has since died. When Shirley McGreal told me of his passing, I could feel her pain.

I find I am of no help to the animals if I become depressed over the way they are treated by humans. So keeping my spirits up is a must. I spend time in the bush, and often just sit and watch birds. I feel complete happiness when I see Australia's native animals in their natural environment. Recently I watched a small echidna try, over and over, to climb an embankment, then finally reach the top, and go on his or her way. Driving home from a conference, I stopped to watch a wombat cross the road. Seeing animals go about their day, as they were meant to, without human interference, inspires me to keep working for animals. I love the Australian bush and every creature therein. I find complete peace when I go into the bush on my own and just listen to the sounds of the birds, smell the smells, and take in the beautiful sights.

I studied ancient history and archaeology at university, and I keep an active interest in both, including Australian history. I also love reading, scrapbooking, going to photography exhibitions, painting, and writing about animals. Sometimes in the early evening I like to sit in the garden with a glass of wine and my cats, and just watch the night take over. We must all take time out to recharge our batteries and to just sit with our own beloved animals.

When I started in animal welfare in 1982 my aim was to help correct the wrongs inflicted on animals. I wanted to change attitudes and legislation. I wanted to educate people so animals would be treated more fairly. When I adopted Marcus, I wanted to protect him, and the dogs I had seen in the BUAV posters, and of course the little dog who was beaten in Safety Bay. I never thought that one day *they* might help *me*.

In 1998 I was diagnosed with breast cancer. I survived, but in June 2002 the cancer returned in my bones. I was told I was not likely to see another twelve months of life. I made preparations for death, but kept working when I could. The pain was sometimes so bad that I would not have gotten out of bed were it not for my cats and the work I do for animals. The pain went on day after day, month after month. Morphine no longer helped. I was urged to hand my cats over to the Royal Society for the Prevention of Cruelty to Animals (RSPCA) and go into a nursing home to wait for death.

The pain several times tempted me to take my life. But I kept thinking of all I wanted to achieve. I was not willing to give up.

One day I fell to the floor in pain and just could not get back up. The pain was too much. I lay there for what seemed hours. The cats sat with me patiently. Seeing the look on their faces, I eventually dragged myself over to the phone and called an ambulance. After I was in the hospital for a week, I came home to find Jenny (one of my cats) would have nothing to do with me. She walked away, under the house. No amount of coaxing would bring her out. This was unusual for her; she was upset that I had abandoned her for a week. As evening started to settle in, I became concerned about her welfare. Once again I lowered myself to the ground and pleaded with her to come for dinner. She refused. I started to cry. I told her I had been in hospital, and was sorry, and wanted her to come for dinner. I told her I was worried about her. When I started to cry, she came out and rubbed against me. She followed me into the house, and that night she slept next to me, as close as she could. Perhaps sensing my agony, it seemed that all was forgiven.

In 2004 I was given a clean bill of health, only to have cancer return in 2005 in yet more places. I was in India when the pain returned. I thought, "What I'm going through is nothing compared to what some of the people and animals in India go through." This helped, but it was my work for animals, and my own beloved animals, who kept me going. *I never thought animals could give so much back.* Animals give life meaning and hope. They can help us to face pain, and to understand that life is a gift to be cherished.

Sometimes when I make a difference for animals, I say quietly, "this is for you, little dog of Safety Bay." I know that tomorrow the cancer may take off again and this time I might die. I will go to my death able to say "I did *what* I could *when* I could." I will have no regrets. My life is wonderful even now. It is made wonderful because of the work I do, because of my own cats, and because I know my purpose.

CHAPTER 13

# A Whole New World

## Rescue and Re-Education in Southeast Asia

*Amy Corrigan*

*Amy Corrigan is Director of Research and Education for the Animal Concerns Research and Education Society (ACRES, www.acres.org.sg), a Singaporean animal welfare charity. Amy is also Project Manager for the ACRES Wildlife Rescue Centre (AWRC). ACRES has run a number of campaigns both in Singapore and throughout Asia to improve animal welfare and work toward the eradication of animal abuse. Previously, Amy spent three years in Thailand as Director of the Wildlife Friends of Thailand Rescue Centre, working with wild animals who had been rescued both from the exotic pet trade and from the tourism industry.*

Bringing frozen worms inside the house in winter, moving snails out of the driveway before Dad reversed the car, building shelters for insects in the garden when it rained, looking for lost dogs... I can't remember a time when I didn't have an overwhelming urge to help nonhumans.

Like many children, I adored other animals. My bedroom walls were covered under a mass of animal posters, and every night I had to fight my huge collection of stuffed animal toys to get into bed. My fantasy of being Snow White had nothing to do with Prince Charming, but everything to do with wanting to sit in a forest surrounded by nonhumans. Later on, my dream was to become a farmer, until I learned the awful truth—that my beloved cows and pigs would be made into steaks and sausage.

My favorite childhood book was *Charlotte's Web*, which made me decide at a very young age that I did not want to eat nonhumans. Anyway, I could not understand why we would pet cows and sheep on weekend trips to the petting farm, then go home and eat nonhumans for dinner. And how do people adore their dog then eat a pig without a second thought? On my eleventh birthday I became fully vegetarian. I would have been earlier, but there were so many misconceptions about vegetarian diets that my parents were worried I would not grow properly if I turned vegetarian when I was younger. Taking the next logical step, I no longer eat dairy or eggs. I am a vegan.

Looking back at my childhood in Bournemouth, England, it strikes me that, from a young age, along with all the happy nonhuman animal characters we encounter in children's fairytales, and the stuffed animal toys that we adore, we are surrounded by instances of animal suffering and exploitation on a daily basis—the Sunday roast on the table and meat hanging in the butchers' windows, posters advertising circuses, school trips to the zoo, horseracing on TV, people wearing fur coats, goldfish in small bags given as prizes at the funfair—as if they were toys.

Most of us are never told the horrifying truth behind all these forms of industrialized animal cruelty when we are young, and companies have a very clever way of hiding their disturbing secrets behind closed doors. Although we may well be told by our parents or teachers that it is cruel to hit a dog or neglect a companion animal, most of us are not told about the cruelty involved in modern farmed animal practices, in animal experimentation, in the mass production of pedigree dogs on puppy farms or in the performing animal industry. If we question things that are widely seen as "acceptable" such as eating meat, most of us are told this is a normal way of life, the way things are, a tradition. Tragically, people are usually brought up to believe that nonhumans are commodities, that humans have the right to do to them whatever we like.

Thankfully, many organizations are doing an outstanding job of raising awareness about industrialized animal cruelty and the fact that nonhuman animals are sentient beings. But most young children remain sheltered from the issues for a long time, and it's harder to change attitudes as we age. I passionately advocate instilling a sense of compassion toward all beings in people when they are very young, and I strongly believe that public education, especially of the young, is the fundamentally most important aspect of advancing animal welfare all over the world.

Luckily, my mum taught me from a very young age that nonhumans have feelings, and to respect their feelings. She carefully explained why we didn't go to the circus, or go along with other family members to watch the local hunt, and why we would never visit certain countries until they stopped bullfighting and other "festivals" involving nonhuman torture.

I was also lucky enough to live in a town where every weekend, come rain or shine, a group of dedicated individuals stood in the town center displaying posters and handing out leaflets on animal welfare issues. I still clearly remember the haunting images of animal experiments, blood sports, and slaughterhouses: Cats with electrodes screwed into their brains, agonizing pain carved on their faces; a live fox being torn limb from limb by hounds; a sheep having her throat cut with a look of absolute terror in her eyes. These images are still etched in my mind. If I have to pick out the one main factor that set me on the path to becoming an advocate for nonhumans, I have to say it was the feeling of simply having to do something to help the beings that I saw in those pictures, to stop their suffering. This has taught me to never underestimate the importance of leafleting, of holding public educational exhibitions, to reach out to people who may become animal advocates themselves.

The more I learned about the horrific animal abuse going on in the world, the more I knew I had to do something about it. The images on those leaflets played over and over again in my mind; I could not just sit back and let these things continue without doing something. The sense of injustice bubbled up inside me whenever I saw the hunt in the forest, knowing that an innocent fox was about to face hours of torture, or seeing horses having their bodies being mercilessly broken on the Grand National steeplechase on TV, or seeing terrified, wailing calves being loaded onto the ferry to France heading for slaughter, or the misery of veal crates.

And so began my first steps toward being an advocate for nonhumans. I joined many animal welfare groups, bugged my family for pennies for animal charities, volunteered to help with street collections, and organized petitions against the "Grand" National and blood sports. I even chose "Animal Rights" as my topic for my first presentation in English class.

One of my proudest memories, perhaps the bravest thing I have ever done, was, aged twelve years old, striding up to the exhibition tent of the local hunt at the New Forest show and questioning the huntsmen as to how could they could happily kill innocent wild animals, and with such brutality, as it was just completely beyond my comprehension. I could not just walk past, while they were busy promoting their "sport" to passersby, without at least trying to get inside their heads, to get some idea how they could possibly justify their brutal pastime. Anyway, they simply ignored me or gave me awkward smiles. Looking back, it brings to mind the famous words of Mahatma Gandhi: "First they ignore you, then they laugh at you, then they fight you, then you win." Recently, the campaign against hunting with dogs in the United Kingdom has, at least partially, been won, thanks to the hard work of many dedicated individuals speaking up for persecuted wildlife.

At the University of Sheffield I studied zoology to further my understanding of nonhumans and empower myself as an animal advocate. I chose a course where dissection was not required. I joined a campus animal welfare group and began leafleting and holding public "roadshows" (as exhibitions that raise awareness are called in Singapore).

After university I wanted to help nonhumans where the movement was less developed. I came across the organization Wildlife Friends of Thailand (WFFT), which rescues nonhumans caught up in the exotic pet trade or exploited for the tourist industry. This organization appealed to me because it treated all beings as equally important, including those with disabilities and less "popular" species. Wildlife Friends of Thailand had just been founded by Edwin Wiek, and I joined them at their wildlife rescue center.

Three months as a volunteer at the center turned into three immensely rewarding years of full-time employment. I learned about the vast trade in wild animals, selling them as "pets," and the immense suffering caused by this business. My eyes were also opened to the widespread exploitation of nonhumans for the tourist industry. I was struck by an apparent lack of awareness of nonhuman animal sentience, of industrial animal exploitation. I decided that it was my mission to make a difference for nonhumans in Asia, not necessarily because problems in Asia are worse than in the rest of the world—every country has its fair share of animal abuse issues—but because Asia's animal welfare movement is in its infancy.

I had many incredible experiences in Thailand, both immensely rewarding and emotionally crushing. Sometimes help arrived too late for a rescued gibbon or langur, or babies who arrived too weak to survive, which was always heartbreaking and frustrating. Dealing with death never got any easier, but each time it happened I was yet more determined to bring change.

My best experiences at Wildlife Friends of Thailand were freeing nonhumans in dire situations, especially ones who had been suffering for a long time. The two sun bears, Ompoom and Apec, were just such a case. These two bears had been kept in small, rusty cages at a noisy fish market in the port of Ranong, never seeing the light of day. Every time I went to Ranong I was haunted by the sight of those poor bears, and each time we were there Edwin Wiek tried to persuade the woman keeping the bears to let them come to our rescue center. Finally, after years of negotiation, she was persuaded to let the bears go. They were free of their miserable existence—they felt grass under their feet, and the sun on their backs, for the first time in years. It was incredibly uplifting to witness rescued nonhumans, who had been kept alone their whole lives, socializing with others for the first time. And it was a joy to see previously fixated stereotypic behaviors gradually fade away, behaviors such as self-mutilation and rocking back and forth, developed to cope with years of environmental and social deprivation.

Although each nonhuman is as valuable as the next, like people, there are certain beings, because of their personality, or because of an interaction, who hold a special place in my heart. Mango, Zach, Bailey, and Jack, infant gibbons I hand-reared, will always be precious to me, especially Zach. Zach was incredibly cheeky and had priceless "grumpy old man" facial expressions! The sun bear cubs I hand-reared, Pom, Pinda, and Pepper, were full of life, each with unique personalities. Laurie the slow loris became dear to me after I nursed him through a leg amputation following his capture in a snare. Seeing him recover and return to the wild was priceless. I had a soft spot for Pooh the sun bear, such a happy-go-lucky character despite years of being kept on a short chain with nothing to do but run around in circles. She always seemed to make new bears feel welcome. Then there was Henry the gibbon, a real gentleman who took great care of his fragile female companion, June.

The nonhuman I have shared the closest bond with is a beautiful dog called Eva, rescued from a temple in Thailand. Eva was a sorry sight when she was rescued: nursing, yet a bag of bones, suffering from mange and riddled with tumors. With lots of TLC (and plenty of special treats sneaked to her out of sight of the other dogs!) Eva bounced back, and quickly became my best friend and loyal companion. Eva was the first friendly face I would see every morning and my shadow, rarely leaving my side. She was always there when times were tough; the wrench of leaving Eva was almost unbearable when I left Thailand. But I felt that she was better off in her familiar surroundings at the rescue center, with her many dog companions and the freedom to run freely in the forest. I knew she would always be well looked after, and it would be unfair and selfish of me to remove her from her happy life in Thailand to live in a small flat in Singapore.

So often we read numbers and statistics—how many animals are subject to abuse each year. But from the individual point of view, statistics lose their meaning, and even one being suffering is one too many. Looking at things from an individual point motivates me to keep going—even if I can only help a tiny proportion of the nonhumans who need help, the incredible difference I can make to an individual's life is absolutely worth it.

In this line of work, whether helping animals or people, we reach unique emotional states. Certain experiences touch you and stay with you forever. One of my most profound experiences involved beautiful Pompuang, an elderly female elephant who had spent many sad years begging on the streets of Bangkok. When she arrived at the center she was skeletal, had lost all her teeth, and was extremely weak. We were determined to make sure her last moments on earth were happy ones, roaming the forest and being fed mashed up mangos—her favorite. One day Pompuang collapsed. Knowing the end was near, we moved her to a peaceful spot under a mango tree. I sat with her until the early hours, fanning her and stroking her, talking to her about anything and everything, not wanting her to be alone. I felt privileged to spend those last hours with her, and her deep, soft rumblings and the gentle look in those amazing wise eyes seemed to say that she appreciated the company. When she peacefully passed away, I was glad that at least her last few weeks were spent in the peace and quiet of the sanctuary, and not on the city streets, and that there are people like Edwin Wiek, who make these things possible.

In Southeast Asia, as in any area of the world, cruelty to nonhumans abounds, but such instances are perhaps more visible here. In many countries, especially those where tourism is thriving, the use of nonhumans in entertainment is prolific. In every city you can see medieval-style zoos, packed with tormented, depressed souls in horrific conditions. At any tourist resort you can see petrified baby gibbons being paraded around the streets for tourists. On every corner you can see the degrading nonhuman animal shows, including the appalling boxing orangutans, cycling bears, and football-playing elephants. In every country nonhumans are poached from the wild and either brutally slaughtered for their body parts or end up in the living hell of markets, for meat or the pet trade. The list goes on and on.

In Thailand, one of the worst cases of cruelty I encountered was a little gibbon named Tua Rohd, captured from the wild for the pet trade. When Tua Rohd came to us he was barely recognizable as a gibbon. You could see every bone in his tiny skeletal body, his fur and delicate skin had been burned off by iodine, and his eyes were sunken, pus-filled holes. Despite our best efforts, Tua Rohd only survived a few days with us. When he died in my arms, I was emotionally crushed at this unfairness: He should have been in the wild with his family, not mutilated and dead.

Another shocking case was that of Bouncer, a wild Asiatic black bear cub. His front leg had been caught in a snare and by the time he was handed to us the leg was completely rotten, infested with maggots and ants. I will never forget the panic in his eyes as we handled him when, after his leg was amputated, I had to give him daily antibiotic injections. Happily, Bouncer survived, quickly learned to adapt to life with three legs, and he is now living happily with other rescued bears.

The most important decision I have made in my work with nonhuman animals was the decision to move to Southeast Asia, to be part of an animal welfare movement still in its infancy. I now work for the Animal Concerns Research and Education Society in Singapore (ACRES). ACRES focuses on raising awareness on industrialized animal cruelty (factory farming, animal experimentation, and so on), the plight of captive nonhumans and nonhuman animals used in entertainment, and the illegal wildlife trade. ACRES has run a number of campaigns, in Singapore and other Asian countries, to improve animal welfare and work toward the eradication of animal abuse. Although currently based in Singapore for now, ultimately we plan to expand to other Southeast Asian countries where there are virtually no animal advocacy groups, either establishing groups or providing advice to emerging local groups.

Even in Singapore, by all accounts a developed and forward-thinking country, I am still confronted by nonhuman suffering on a daily basis. Everywhere I turn I see songbirds in small cages, live frogs and turtles crammed into tanks at food stalls and markets, horrific conditions at puppy farms and pet shops, and wild animals exploited in nonhuman shows. Improving animal welfare in Singapore is vitally important to advancing animal welfare in Southeast Asia as a whole, as other countries in the region look up to Singapore and follow Singapore's example.

All over the world women have been pioneers in championing the cause of nonhumans, and Asia is no exception. There are many women here who serve as great role models and whom I personally look up to: Jill Robinson started the Animals Asia Foundation, which is making a huge difference for nonhumans all over Asia; Lek Chailaert, the founder of Elephant Nature Park in Thailand, has bravely overcome difficult obstacles to help the elephants; Karmele Sanchez is working in challenging conditions in Indonesia to help macaques and lorises. These are just a few of the remarkable women doing amazing things to help nonhumans in Asia. At ACRES four of the six full-time staff are women, as are most of our regular, long-term volunteers. It seems women are more willing to make a long-term commitment to follow their passion to help nonhumans.

Sometimes it is very difficult to remain positive as the problems facing nonhumans are so huge. It is hard not to feel disheartened when I see only a handful of people ask for vegetarian food on a plane, when I see on restaurant menus that most dishes are meat-based, or when I see people buying tickets to watch performing dolphins or to visit a zoo. More than anything, it tears me up inside when early in the morning, on the way to work, we drive past trucks with chickens and ducks crammed into crates on their way to slaughter. I am not ashamed to say that every time tears of frustration emerge. I would give everything I could to stop the trucks, to set them free. But I have to take a deep breath, go to work, and maybe, hopefully, there will be an e-mail from someone asking more about being vegetarian or vegan. That gives me hope and keeps me motivated.

It is easy to feel overwhelmed by the problems facing nonhumans, but the truth is that we as individuals really can help, and make a difference. One quote which I live by these days, especially when things seem overwhelming, is the following by Edward Everett Hale: "I am only one, but still I am one. I cannot do everything, but still I can do something; and because I cannot do everything, I will not refuse to do the something I can do."

When it comes to helping nonhumans, it is true that things are not going to change overnight, but that is not an excuse to sit back and do nothing, and it doesn't mean that helping a few nonhuman animals or taking small steps is not important. Today, when someone tells me that, as a result of ACRES outreach programs, they will never use bear bile products, they will never keep a wild animal as a pet, they will not visit establishments with captive dolphins, and most of all when they say they will turn vegetarian, it is a great incentive to keep going. Also, young people give me hope. Every year since ACRES was founded (2001), the number of young people volunteering with us and supporting our work has grown by leaps and bounds. Hopefully they will pass on what they have learned.

It's not easy to change the way of the world or change people's mindsets, but change is possible. When ACRES started in 2001, the animal welfare issues we tackled were unheard of in Singapore, and people thought of animal welfare as something for "extremists" and "bunny huggers." Many said that Singapore was no place for ACRES. But persistence and determination, especially on the part of Louis Ng, the founder of ACRES, paid off. We are now a well-respected organization that has run many successful campaigns. ACRES has made a real difference in the lives of many nonhumans.

It is very difficult and overwhelming knowing where to start with animal advocacy in countries where terms such as "animal welfare" and "vegetarianism," let alone "veganism," are mostly unheard. The concepts of "free range" and "not tested on animals" are completely new. In Chinese-speaking countries it's even worse—the word for "animal" literally translates as "moving object." It is easy for those just learning about nonhuman concerns to wonder where to start when faced with such obstacles. Don't be afraid to start a new organization, or to engage in leafleting or postering.

Don't be afraid to ask for help and advice. The best way to initiate change is to educate, especially the young, to raise awareness either professionally or as a volunteer in our day-to-day lives, and to persist and never give up. Giving the nonhumans a voice is the best gift we can give to them. The nonhumans really need you to speak up for them. If you don't, who will?

Part III

# Potpourri—From Dancing Bears to Undercover Investigation

# Chapter 14

# A Fight for Justice

*Anuradha Sawhney*

**Anuradha Sawhney** *is Mentor Emeritus for the Indian chapter of People for the Ethical Treatment of Animals (PETA, http://www.petaindia.com). After St. Xavier's High School in Bokaro Steel City, India, she attended Sophia College in the city of Mumbai, India, where she graduated with a double major in Sociology and Philosophy, earning top honors in the study of ethics. PETA opened its first Indian office in 2000. Anuradha was the head of PETA India for more than nine years. She continues to work with PETA India rescuing nonhumans abused in the food, clothing, entertainment, and experimentation industries, but is now primarily a mentor.*

> The question is not, "Can they reason?" nor, "Can they talk?" but rather, "Can they suffer?"
>
> —*Jeremy Bentham*

> Ask the experimenters why they experiment on animals, and the answer is: "Because the animals are like us." Ask the experimenters why it is morally okay to experiment on animals, and the answer is: "Because the animals are not like us." Animal experimentation rests on a logical contradiction.
>
> —*Charles R. Magel*

Every day we have countless opportunities—from what we eat to what we wear—to choose to be kind or to be cruel. The two quotes above help inspire and drive me in my work for nonhumans. I hope that my work with PETA India will inspire others to choose compassion.

I have always loved other animals. In primary school I shared my lunch with stray cats and dogs, and birds, and often went hungry myself. I drove my family crazy trying to smuggle dogs home. I would con neighbors and acquaintances into adopting stray and half-breed puppies by saying that these dogs were purebreds. Once I had to change my route to school after lying to a neighbor about a stray puppy I gave him, claiming he was a German Shepherd. The man used to lie in wait for me every day, desperately telling me that the puppy looked nothing like a German Shepherd, and to take him back!

I did most of my schooling from Delhi, and Bokaro Steel City, in India. I studied science with intent to become a veterinary doctor, but gave up the idea when I realized that I would have to kill nonhumans to get a veterinary degree! I switched to arts, and to Sophia College in Mumbai, and graduated with a double degree in sociology and philosophy, where I excelled in moral philosophy.

While working, I would often arrive late to work because I had stopped to help an injured dog in the middle of a road, or a cow hit by a speeding vehicle. I carried an injured calf to a shelter in my small car, and talked friends into picking up an injured donkey at 3 a.m. When I saw a being in need, I would do everything in my power to help him or her, regardless of the time or the place.

But I am not so different from most folks. When I'm not helping nonhumans, I head for bookshops. I love reading books; they are a treasure of knowledge waiting to be explored. I spend hours browsing, or huddled with my favorite books, reading at home. I have a huge collection of books and comics. I love reading Calvin & Hobbes, Tintin, Asterix, and Archie comics, the new generation of female Irish writers, and of course classics like Jane Austen. I have all the Agatha Christie's, Perry Mason's, Irving Wallace's... I can go on forever about my books. But the books I read are almost always cheerful. I see enough sadness in my work, and on the streets of India.

I took a job with a leather-buying house in Delhi. My boss was good to me, but I was always unhappy. When I saw the leather outfits lying around, I knew they were dead animal skins. Then one day my eyes rested on a black and white piece of leather, with hair still clinging to the skin, lying on the office table. Inadvertently, I stroked the hair and apologized to the nonhuman. A passing colleague commented that I was petting a dead horse imported from New Zealand! That was it. I decided to immediately get another job.

I went home and searched on the web, and found that PETA had an office in India. I was living in Delhi then, and PETA is in Mumbai (Bombay). I wrote and asked if I could visit. They agreed. I was traveling to Pune to see my sister, and climbed off the train in Mumbai and found my way to the PETA office. I liked what I saw, so I asked if by any chance, PETA was recruiting. They were! I immediately called my mother in Delhi and asked her to mail my resume. I called PETA India's office each week, badgering them until they decided to hire me (just to be free of my phone calls!).

Sometimes in life, you cross paths with people who inspire you, touch your soul, and leave you changed forever. This happened to me when I met Ingrid Newkirk, the founder of PETA. Ingrid visited Delhi just after I had been accepted for a job in PETA India, and I had the honor of meeting her. I had heard so much about Ingrid, and meeting her was a dream come true. First, she removed candles that were lying on the table in front of us, noting that they may have been made with animal fat. That is Ingrid, through and through, always conscious of where animal exploitation can happen, and careful not to participate. She has helped to shape my perceptions with her compassionate and caring heart. She has transformed many lives and ignited the spark of compassion in many souls. She is an institution in and of herself. Her contribution to the cause is enormous.

I quickly realized that this was the job I had always wanted, but until I joined PETA India I had not known that it was possible to work for nonhumans as a career.

Since the office and operations are based in Mumbai, I relocated. My mother was not very happy that I was moving so far away. My friends all thought (and still think) that I was mad to abandon a well-paying job to work for PETA. My family still makes fun of me, though my mother and sisters have always supported me. When I arrived in Mumbai, I had not even thought where I would stay. When I arrived, a friend was kind enough to let me stay at her place. And that's how my life took a different turn altogether.

The skills that I had learned in my earlier jobs helped me immensely at PETA. My experience to date in office administration, managing accounts, company law, and (very importantly) managing people helped me to help organize PETA India in a professional manner.

PETA India was launched in January 2000. PETA operates under the simple principle that nonhumans are not ours to eat, wear, experiment on, or use for entertainment. PETA operates by educating policymakers, and the public, about animal abuse. PETA promotes the right of all nonhumans to be treated with respect and to enjoy basic rights.

PETA's investigative work, public education, research, animal rescue, legislation, special events, celebrity involvement, and international media coverage have resulted in countless improvements in the quality of life for nonhumans, as well as in saving the lives of millions of nonhuman animals. PETA focuses on four types of cruelty to nonhumans: diet, clothing, entertainment (such as circus and zoos), and experimentation.

I have now been with PETA India for more than seven years. I have been vegan since I joined. I am on call 24-7, and I have no regrets. The main difference in my life is, of course, the erratic work schedule, and the lack of fat sums of money. (I married a little while after joining PETA, and my husband and in-laws cope with my erratic work schedule.) But, at the end of the day, I feel my work is worthwhile on a personal level. It's a matter of choice, and I am very happy that I made this change. This is not just a job, but a calling. I love nonhumans, and now I fight for nonhumans; I make a difference in their lives. Actually, my work is more than a profession; it is a fight for justice. I hardly have a social life, but that is no hardship for me; I am helping nonhumans. As a result of joining PETA I have been able to help many beings, to better their living conditions. PETA India has brought nonhuman issues to the forefront, even affecting public policy.

Nonhumans in India are increasingly raised in factory farms, where they are treated like machines. Chickens spend their brief lives in crowded conditions, many of them so cramped that they can't even turn around or spread a wing. Most do not have any fresh air until they are prodded and crammed onto trucks for a nightmarish ride to the abattoir, often in suffocatingly hot weather, and always without food or water. At the slaughterhouse, if they arrive alive, chickens are hung upside down and their throats are sliced open, too often while they are conscious.

PETA's investigation of India's trade in cattle, goats, sheep, and other nonhumans has uncovered beatings, mutilation, and miserable deaths at the hands of transporters, during transport, and at slaughterhouses. After farmed animals are sold at auction, many are marched for days and are given neither a sip of water nor a bite to eat. When they collapse from exhaustion, handlers twist and break their tails or rub tobacco or hot chili peppers in their eyes to make them keep going. Others are crammed into hideously overcrowded trucks. By the time they reach the slaughterhouse, bones have been broken and some have perished. Live nonhumans stand among the dead. Most of the slaughterhouse workers have never been trained to kill farmed animals. They often work with dull blades, sawing back and forth across a nonhuman's throat.

Nonhumans also suffer horribly for the sake of human entertainment in India. They are beaten or starved until they learn to perform silly tricks; they are confined to small cages and deprived of all that is natural to them; they are forced to run for their lives or fight other nonhumans to the death. Defying the law, Indian *madaris* (animal exploiters) force sloth bears to "dance" for money, as a form of begging. Before they are even a year old, these bear cubs have a rope forced through their nose, and most of their teeth pulled out—without any painkillers. The bear is held down by a group of men while an iron needle, heated in a coal fire, is forced through the squealing nonhuman's nose. No anesthetic is used. A rope is then shoved into the piercing, which usually becomes infected. When the rope is tugged, the bear lifts his or her legs, and "dances."

*Madaris* are known to be very aggressive, and will do anything to prevent "their" bears from being taken. But when we receive a tip on where to find illegal "dancing" bears, PETA India does not hesitate to intervene. Recently we undertook a daring, spur-of-the-moment coup to rescue several bears. Within a couple of hours from the time of notification, the exploiters were in the custody of the police, and six mutilated, tormented bears were on their way to a sanctuary. Now these bears enjoy life with nothing on their noses except the sunshine and breezes to heal their bodies and spirits. PETA India has helped facilitate the rescue of over fifty-three tigers and lions from circuses across India.

An estimated 60 to 70 million nonhumans are used in experiments every year. These beings suffer and die in painful and outdated tests. (Scientists now have more accurate nonanimal alternatives.) Following the discovery of atrocious conditions, thirty-seven abused monkeys and two goats were seized from the National Institute of Virology (NIV) in Pune, India. The nonhumans were caged in filth and searing heat—some for more than a decade. Many were crippled from untreated illness and injuries. Some of the primates were missing fingers or teeth, others were disfigured or paralyzed. Many whirled in endless circles, driven insane by confinement in small, barren cages. Now these unfortunate victims are in a rehabilitation center in the city of Pune, relearning how to live.

Looking back, going vegan was probably the best decision of my life. I wasn't raised vegan. In India, we may not eat much meat, but milk is a part of our culture. I was unaware of the cruelty prevalent in the dairy industry. Through PETA, I learned how the dairy industry treats cows and their calves. Cattle, once revered partners in Hindu culture—part of our spirituality and considered part of our families—now endure dreadful lives and miserable deaths. Visit any Indian *tabela* (a shed where cows and buffaloes are kept for milking purposes), and you will see how cattle exploited by the dairy industry are chained by the neck in narrow stalls, unable to stretch or move. This causes terrible pain and lameness in cows' legs. In some villages, farmers poke sharp sticks into a cow's uterus, or inject a labor-inducing drug called oxytocin. They believe this will increase milk production. Oxytocin causes hormone imbalances and other illnesses in people, and so this drug is illegal. But oxytocin can be purchased in India in cigarette shops. We should not be surprised if oxytocin, along with growth hormones, pesticides, and pus from infections such as mastitis, are passed into cows' milk and consumed by children, and others, who drink milk.

Constant confinement is just one of many abuses that Indian cows face. They are impregnated and milked over and over until their bodies are too worn out to produce milk. Then they are sent to slaughter, or abandoned on the streets of India. I became vegan the day I joined PETA and have never looked back. I am very proud of this decision. If you care about nonhumans, the best way to help them is to stop eating them, and to stop drinking milk.

Vegan food is a treat for taste buds—and it is great for health, too. Leading scientists are now proving that what we eat directly affects the quality of our lives. While a diet rich in animal products contributes to cancer, heart disease, obesity, and many other deadly human ailments, a vegan diet can improve our health. The consumption of meat and dairy products is also linked to diabetes, arthritis, osteoporosis, clogged arteries, asthma, and impotence. Additionally, as deadly animal-borne diseases such as SARS, mad cow disease, and avian flu spread across the globe, adopting a meat-free diet is more important than ever. Studies show that vegans have stronger immune systems, and are far less likely to die of heart disease or cancer. With the right food selections, vegans have clearer skin, lose weight permanently, and even reverse existing heart disease. Why subject nonhumans to suffering and slaughter when we have a better choice? It is hard for me to understand people who love some beings as pets, but consume other nonhumans on their dinner table.

Being compassionate towards nonhumans comes easy because I am a Hindu. Our religion advocates compassion. Ahimsa teaches us not to harm others—any others. If people would only stop to think that other animals are more *like* us than *unlike* us, more of us would extend our empathy to nonhumans. We would speak out when nonhumans are treated unkindly. Many Hindu gods are nonhumans. For example, Hanuman has the physical form of a monkey, and Ganesh has the head of an elephant. Hinduism advocates *ahimsa*, or nonviolence. Mahatma Gandhi showed the political power of *ahimsa*, how *ahimsa* can change our world, by using this principle to force British imperialists to leave India.

I have always believed that spirituality requires compassion; helping those who cannot help themselves forces us to find the courage to speak up. I believe that if I love my work and help another soul, I am living out good karma. I believe that every action in my life was taking me to this point, where I stand today. I have wound through many different avenues to get here, but I am finally doing what I love most, and I feel it would not have been possible without divine intervention. I believe that there is a higher power that is guiding and directing my actions. And it is all these actions, throughout my life, that are helping me to help nonhumans today.

Each nonhuman is special when you get to know him or her. They are loyal, affectionate, inquisitive, playful—and more often than not they are taken for granted, as if they were created specifically for our enjoyment, to cater to our selfish whims. Albert Schweitzer said, "We must fight against the spirit of unconscious cruelty with which we treat other beings. Nonhumans suffer as much as we do. True humanity does not allow us to impose such sufferings on them. It is our duty to make the whole world recognize it. Until we extend our circle of compassion to all living things, humanity will not find peace." Like us, nonhumans have a soul. They feel love, joy, sadness, and other emotions. They feel pain, too.

My heart cries out when I see a nonhuman animal suffering. Abhorrence of injustice drives me. I hate knowing that, just because a nonhuman is unable to stand up for him or herself, human beings take advantage and cause harm. Have you ever looked into the eyes of a bull pulling a loaded cart all day long without rest? Have you looked into the eyes of a horse left to stand in the monsoon rain and tropical sun alike? Have you looked into the eyes of a dog who has been beaten by his human? Their incomprehension—their pain—drives me, makes me work harder in search of justice.

I am thankful that I am doing what I love. I am thankful that I can make a difference for nonhumans. Many people join social causes because it makes *them* feel good. At the end of the day, though, working for nonhumans is not about our own satisfaction, or making ourselves feel good. The needs of exploited nonhumans must come first, and be attended to first; that is the most important fact I've learned through my endeavors with PETA.

# Chapter 15

# Using My Voice

*Kris "Risa" Candour*

**Kris "Risa" Candour** *has been educating the public about nonhuman exploitation and the benefits of vegetarianism since she was sixteen. Her master's thesis is titled "Health Marketing Strategies to Encourage African American New Yorkers to Eat More Fruits and Vegetables" (Milano Graduate School, New School University, 2006), and she wrote "The Black Vegan Woman: Her Strength and Her Duty," for* Sistah Vegan! Food, Identity, Health and Society: Female Vegans of the African Diaspora in the U.S.A, *edited by Amie Louise Harper (Lantern Books, 2008). Risa is a singer and songwriter (www.Myspace.com/SelectAhh), who operates a Reiki natural healing practice for humans and their animal companions (www.PrimeMeridians.com) in Vancouver, Canada.*

Some say that animal activists provide voices for nonhumans, who have no voices. I hold a different philosophy; someone once noted that nonhumans have their own voices, but that humans have been unwilling to hear them. As animal advocates, it is our job to use our voices on behalf of nonhumans to help people listen: listen to the nonhuman animals, listen to the facts, listen to their hearts and consciences.

When I was growing up, I never dreamt of being an advocate, but in the process of "finding myself," I found my voice. As an adolescent, I didn't quite fit in. I was an eccentric nerd who dressed rather formally—I had a fondness for wearing a full suit and tie to school, even though we had no school uniforms. Paradoxically, I embraced the "hippie" label whenever political issues were raised. I was outspoken about my burgeoning political beliefs; I was progressive—I supported peace, not war. Indeed, I was a "hippie" in spirit, listening as much to Bob Dylan or Simon and Garfunkel as I did to the R&B and rap that were popular with my friends. Around the age of eleven, I wrote a poem about the destruction of the environment and society's preference for money over nature. Perhaps I was born somewhat tapped into political and social justice issues.

As an African American raised in a mostly white suburb of Dallas, Texas, I was aware of racism and its subtle manifestations as prejudice. My mother taught me and my little sister to handle any incidents we experienced with refined defiance. Still, we were raised eating meat, and I was older than I care to admit before I realized that eating "chicken" had anything to do with the farmed animals illustrated in children's books. I'd never seen a real chicken before. "Chicken" was an object, a hunk of brown or white "food" on my plate—not "*a* chicken," not a someone. It just didn't occur to me that there was a beating heart, blood, and life attached to that hunk of "food." My food was literally dead, and I never thought about the fact that it was once a living being.

In 1997, at age sixteen, I went vegetarian. I had a vague notion that my "hippie"-kind were often vegetarians. My main motivation, however, was vanity. I was slightly overweight, and I decided to cut meat out of my diet because of its high fat and cholesterol content. It was just a couple of days before the Fourth of July, and I remember that my mother was supportive, buying a box of Gardenburgers for the holiday grilling, for her newly vegetarian daughter.

When school resumed in the fall, I had been a vegetarian for a couple of months. In English class, we were assigned a research paper in which we could research anything we wanted. I thought, "Well, I'm pretty sure that a lot of people are vegetarian who aren't dieting. I'll research why people go vegetarian." I found a few books in the library, then requested information from People for the Ethical Treatment of Animals (PETA). My history teacher, Mr. Burke, gave me his copy of John Robbins' *Diet for a New America*.

In my paper, I outlined the scientifically proven health benefits of vegetarianism; the environmental reasons supporting vegetarianism; and most poignant for me, the horrors of factory farming and the processes of "meat production." I learned about breeding, confinement, mutilation, and slaughter. My inquiry made my temporary diet permanent; I knew that I was never going back to eating nonhumans as I had found that the path that a nonhuman takes to the dinner table is a painful, bloody, moral injustice. I got an A on my paper, and was asked to present the information to the class—my first exercise in vegetarian advocacy. (Over a decade later, I still remember the looks of disbelief from my fellow students as I told them that I would not eat anymore meat!)

Focusing school papers, group assignments, and presentations on animal rights and vegetarianism became a trend that I continued for the next six years. School was a great opportunity to learn how to advocate for nonhumans. I had ready-made audiences of educators and fellow students, and the potential to reach minds. My awareness of the suffering that humans cause nonhumans sparked hope that if I informed people, they would change their behaviors, and fewer beings would suffer.

I became truly active for nonhumans the next year, as a freshman at the University of Texas. Austin was a hotbed of political activism at the time. On any given day, there was usually a protest at the capitol. I joined Students Against Cruelty to Animals (SACA) at UT, the local Austin advocacy group, Action for Animals, and a handful of groups focused on other political causes, such as fighting sweatshops and the death penalty. As a new member of the animal rights *community*, I joined protest after protest—against McDonald's, circuses, fur shops, vivisection, rodeos—we did it all.

Activism—particularly political demonstrations—was a new experience for me. In high school I'd read about protests, but they were not commonplace when and where I grew up. In the midst of these new and exciting experiences, I saw activism as a practical counterpart to idealism: As mores evolve—one changed person and one improvement at a time—eventually slaughterhouses, factory farms, and animal testing facilities could become historical relics memorializing a time in history before most humans respected the rights of other species.

In college, I began to see speaking out against animal exploitation as my moral responsibility. I wanted to do what I could to help nonhumans and change their circumstances, and I decided that the most effective thing that I could do was to use my voice. Sometimes I just connected with others or tried to inform them; sometimes I chanted with my fellow animal activists to draw attention; and sometimes, I yelled! I was so bent on learning how to persuade others to change their behaviors that I chose advertising as my major.

SACA fought for the release of a beagle puppy exploited by researchers at our university. The student newspaper covered SACA's campaign, and several of us went on a tour of the laboratory. I remember the poor dog pacing back and forth, alone in a sterile, cement cell. Eventually, we won his release, and he was adopted by an activist. The dog, Stampy, was well cared for from then on, although he often reverted to the learned behavior of pacing.

When Craig Rosebraugh's "Primate Freedom Tour" came through Texas in 1999, I hopped on board for a while, joining activists from all over the United States to protest against animal laboratories. Animal activism and my social life were nearly one and the same.

Later that year, I attended a talk by Erik Marcus (author of *Vegan: The New Ethics of Eating*), which brought home for me the link between dairy and meat. If one consumes dairy products, she is complicit in the inhumane treatment of male calves, confined and malnourished for veal, and the exploitation of mother cows. I had been vegetarian for more than two years. After that speech, I was vegan.

My greatest concern in going vegan, I think, was fear of my mother's reproach. She was already concerned about my "extreme" act of going vegetarian (although she thought it was "a passing phase"), so, like many a fearful child, I lied. I told my mother that my vegan friend, Jesse, had bet me that I couldn't stay vegan for a month, and that a great reward awaited me if I completed the challenge. My "temporary" veganism disguised my motives, and did not pose a political or moral threat. Then, a month or so later, after I "won the bet!" I told my mom how awesome and healthy I felt as a vegan, and that I was going to stick with the new vegan diet "for a while." *Voila!* Problem solved. Nowadays, my mother and I sometimes enjoy vegan meals together.

In my third year of college, in 2000, I traveled to London for a semester abroad, where I saw the British brand of diehard activism against fur shops and Huntingdon Life Sciences (HLS), an infamous animal experimentation institution that, under pressure from animal activists, has since changed their name to Life Sciences Research. I met many inspirational people whose hard work and dedication I admire. There were elderly protesters standing out in the cold and rain to make a difference. I had never protested alongside people who were older than my grandmother!

My fellow activists in England would relate stories about the hunt saboteurs in the forests—women and men risking their lives to protect hunted foxes. (A hunter would have no problem shooting an activist trying to disrupt his hunt!) Activism in England was a revelation to me. The British police seemed wary of these brave and bold protesters! Quite a reversal from what I had seen at home.

When I returned to the United States, animal rights activists were also campaigning to shut down HLS, where 500 nonhumans are killed every day in laboratory tests. The bravery and boldness that I had witnessed in British activists was manifest in the United States as well. Some activists broke laws, committed crimes of compassion. But the "guilty" were not activists, but rather legislators who passed laws to protect profiteers and corporations that gain from suffering and death. The fault lies with perpetrators of crimes against nonhumans, nature, humans, human decency, and moral responsibility—not with activists.

I remained active for nonhumans during my final semesters of college, sometimes traveling across several states for protests. I watched police presence and repression increase, especially following the events of September 11, 2001. The "freedom of speech" that we activists used in order to speak out for the nonhuman animals became less "free" under the guise of protecting national security. The protests continued though, as activists around the United States remained committed to the cause of resisting animal exploitation, even as the task became more and more difficult.

Less than a week after I had completed my last undergraduate course in Texas, I went to Norfolk, Virginia, for an internship with PETA. I asked to work with Seba Johnson, a former Olympian who was PETA's African American outreach coordinator. She and I brainstormed ideas for materials to reach Black people with messages about vegetarianism and animal rights. PETA was a good introduction into the workings of a professional nonprofit advocacy organization. (It was also fun to meet all of the awesome, committed vegans on PETA's staff!)

After my internship, I moved to New York City, and started graduate school in the fall of 2002 in order to learn how to manage nonprofit organizations. In my first semester, I was awarded a scholarship to attend Liberation Now!, a conference for student animal rights activists. It was inspirational, and a great place to meet other young advocates. It was uplifting to find many other people who care about what I care about, working toward the same goals in different places. At my university, I knew no other animal rights activists. Without a group of animal advocates to join, I sometimes set up a table by myself in the cafeteria, with leaflets and brochures about vegetarianism and factory farming, and my laptop, on which I would show PETA's "Meet Your Meat" DVD. I talked to students who passed by, creating my own personal outreach. You don't need a group, or nonprofit organization, to help nonhumans. Anyone can make a difference for nonhumans. Over the years, I've been able provide support for newbie vegetarians and vegans. What an honor it is to help someone (and the nonhumans) in this way! It's a gem of a privilege every time.

When I have money to spare, I donate to organizations with missions that I support. Once, by chance, I found a bag of real furs in an alley, which I was able to give to an animal rights group for anti-fur outreach. Everyone can do something for nonhumans: A supportive word, a few bucks, a potluck, a leaflet—every little bit counts! "Each one, teach one."

I have also tried to do my part to support fellow animal rights activists. I visited a couple of incarcerated animal rights activists at Rikers Island, New York. Their work in the Stop Huntingdon Animal Cruelty (SHAC) movement cost them their freedom, at least for a time. At Rikers, I came face to face with humility. I met a young female activist who was weary, but hopeful, and a young male activist who said that support from the animal rights community made the loneliness and malnutrition in prison somewhat bearable. Vegan food is scarce in prison. I saw the couple at Rikers not as criminals, but as champions of the law. As Martin Luther King Jr. said, "An individual who breaks a law that conscience tells him is unjust, and who willingly accepts the penalty of imprisonment in order to arouse the conscience of the community over its injustice, is in reality expressing the highest respect for the law." He also said, "The time is always right to do what is right."

Many injustices of the past were once legal, and, although morally right, to counter such practices was illegal. It was illegal to harbor Jews in Germany during the Holocaust; it was illegal to teach an African slave to read in the southern United States, where slavery was legal. (It still is legal in the U.S. prison system, according to the Thirteenth Amendment of the Constitution.) Today, in the United States, attempting to shut down businesses that exploit, brutalize, and kill nonhumans is illegal, as is freeing nonhumans in such peril.

Many imprisoned animal rights activists, especially those branded "domestic terrorists" in the post-9/11 hostility to activists for nonhumans or the environment, exemplify the finer aspects of humanity. They inspire me and other activists because they personify dedication.

Most of my activism before graduate school was a matter of showing up to protests and events organized by others. In graduate school, I became more dedicated. I cofounded Justice for All Species (JAS), with

Tashee Meadows and Aashish Bhimani, two animal activists of color whom I met while visiting Washington, DC. Tashee and Aashish both worked for the Fund for Animals. We used our experience with nonprofit organizations and animal advocacy to establish processes, brainstorm programs, and even acquire a few thousand dollars in grants for JAS. We developed the following mission statement: "Justice for All Species (JAS) is an organization of people of color with the mission of providing resources to communities of color to promote a vegetarian diet and a harmonious relationship with humans, fellow species and the earth we share." JAS helped to fill a gap in the animal rights movement—getting education about the rights and plight of other species to people of color. We found that we were uniquely positioned to articulate connections, to make links between other social movements (especially for people of color) and the animal rights movement.

At the National Hip Hop Political Convention, in a panel discussion on environmental issues affecting people of color, Tashee and I infused into the dialogue the rights of other species, and environmental injustices entailed in the placement of meat purveyors, polluting slaughterhouses and rendering plants in predominantly Black and Latino neighborhoods.

A couple of months later, JAS hosted a discussion on vegetarianism that featured a panel of doctors, and an ethnic vegetarian cooking class with demonstrations for the preparation of Mexican, Ethiopian, and Indian dishes.

In addition to connecting the animal rights movement to other social justice movements, JAS had a special niche within the animal rights movement. As an invited panelist at the 2005 Grassroots Animal Rights Convention, I spoke about mitigating racism in the animal rights movement. In my discussion, I came from a place of being a minority in a minority movement; my talk included the tokenism of people of color in animal rights groups. My talk was well received. I think it is important for us to check in, as a movement, to assess how we're doing and recognize ways that we might improve, especially concerning how we relate to and take care of one another inside the movement.

JAS had a fresh perspective. By the end of the first series of activities, the "Make Your Next Meal Veg!" campaign, we had reached quite a few people, and we had a growing mailing list. We were also burned out. Tashee and Aashish were full-time activists, and I was a graduate student. Our plates were overloaded. In hindsight, we bit off too much for ourselves; we were too ambitious. Although it was short-lived, I am quite proud of the work we did in JAS.

I found work at various nonprofit organizations both before and after I graduated with a master's degree in nonprofit management. I promoted social services in Harlem, combated institutional racism on Long Island, and worked as operations director for Rocky Mountain Animal Defense.

During this time, I found the perfect partner. Our bond was enhanced by our love for nonhumans, a belief in animal rights, and passion for delicious vegan food. Joshua was a vegan chef, trained at a distinguished culinary institute in New York City, the Natural Gourmet Cookery. But a snakebite in Thailand landed him in a Bangkok hospital, where he was administered the wrong drugs, and he passed away. I was 25, he was 23, and we had loved each other just two years.

My life changed tremendously after my partner's death in 2006. Realizing how short life can be, I began to phase out my persona as a professional in the nonprofit sector; I was tired of working in an office, in front of a computer, behind a desk. My right brain took over, and I focused on healing—healing my grief and helping to bring physical well-being and balance into the lives of others. I began developing my intuition and focusing on the arts. I had begun what some folks call "a spiritual journey." I dabbled in yoga and meditation, read spiritual texts, and traveled. I became serious about songwriting and singing, and Reiki.

Reiki is a form of hands-on healing using energy. It is a natural, therapeutic practice that has allowed me to help many people. I've also had the privilege of performing Reiki on nonhuman clients; Reiki works just as well on cats and dogs as it does on humans. I've seen cats bliss-out in delight during a Reiki session.

In addition to practicing Reiki, I am singing—recording and performing around my new home base of Vancouver, Canada. For a while I wasn't sure how my animal rights work would fit into my new, somewhat "new age" passions. Then, a song about nonhumans came to me that paid homage to a protest song by one of my musical influences, Billie Holiday. Her song, "Strange Fruit," protested the lynching of Black people in the South, and was one of the first protest songs to reach bars, clubs, and music venues during the forties and fifties. The song I wrote is also called "Strange Fruit," and protests the suffering of nonhumans drugged, mutilated, confined, and killed for meat and dairy production. "Strange Fruit" allows me to use my voice in contemporary bars, clubs, and music venues, as well as online. As I sing "Strange Fruit" I draw attention to the injustices of factory farming and meat consumption.[1]

An excerpt from my "Strange Fruit":[1]

*You bleed, you scream*
*Strange and bitter fruit they eat*
*A bit of death, wrapped in torture*
*The slaughterhouse is the orchard for*
*Such a strange and bitter fruit they eat*
*This is the truth behind the meat*

When I perform "Strange Fruit," I carry literature on how to go vegetarian. There are myriad ways to reach people with a message about the plight of nonhuman animals; I came of age discovering them and I'm still finding new ways to use my voice to educate people about nonhumans and vegetarianism. But now, I've got music to back me up.

# NOTE

1. © 2008 Select Ahh (Lyrics and Melodic lines by Kris "Risa" Candour; Music by Obediya Jones-Darrell). Visit www.Myspace.com/SelectAhh to hear this song.

## Chapter 16

# Loving Life in Lebanon

*Joelle El-Massih*

**Joelle El-Massih,** *born in Beirut, fled war-torn Lebanon in 1985 when she was just seven. After six years in Chicago and two in Michigan, the war ended, and she returned to Lebanon with her mother and two brothers. When she was just twenty, her mother died, and she gave up dreams of a degree and career in hotel management. She was working several jobs to make ends meet when a few young women asked her to join in creating a dog and cat shelter. Joelle jumped at the chance, and in 2004 they founded the charitable organization, Beirut for the Ethical Treatment of Animals (BETA, http://www.betalebanon.org/).*

> The greatness of a nation and its moral progress can be judged by the way its animals are treated.
> —*Mahatma Gandhi (1869–1948)*

> An eye for eye only ends up making the whole world blind.
> —*Mahatma Gandhi (1869–1948)*

My name is Joelle El-Massih; I am twenty-nine years old, and Lebanese. I have lived in Lebanon for most of my life but my parents decided we had to leave in 1985, when the war was in full swing. I was seven years old; I and my family fled to the United States, where we lived for eight years before returning home in 1993, after the war was over, when things were getting back to normal.

In Lebanon there isn't much respect for people, nonhumans, or the environment; we have been through thirty-five years of harsh war. There is much corruption, and education is not always available. The war has ended, Lebanon has been rebuilt, and now we must change our mentality with regard to nonhumans. If we can change one person's mind then there's hope for changing many others. Turning a blind eye is easy, seeing more clearly is challenging.

I love all beings. I have loved nonhumans ever since I can remember. I've always had pets of various kinds. When I was a kid, we weren't aware of spaying and neutering. I remember one of our cats repeatedly gave birth inside my brothers' closet. My mother would have to throw away the boys' clothes each time and buy new ones. We had kittens running around the house—it was fun.

Some of my neighbors had cats, too, but they were domestic cats. We took in strays. In other homes, when a cat gave birth people would take the kittens away from the mother as soon as they were born, put them in a plastic bag, and throw them out. Whenever I noticed a neighbor throwing away kittens, I would go straight to the garbage, take out the bag, and find a surrogate mother, which would most probably be in our house or in the garden. Many, of course, died. They were too weak to survive such rough treatment, and there were so many I wasn't able to save.

One time my mother took me to the village to watch a festival that our president was attending. In villages of Lebanon it is a ritual to slaughter sheep when there is some sort of festivity. There was a big crowd. All I could see were some people walking towards the president with a sheep, who had a rope tied around her neck. I asked my mother what was going on. When she told me, I let go of her hand and ran through the crowd toward the sheep, yelling and crying for them stop, to spare the sheep. People thought I was crazy. Many became angry and asked my mother to keep me under control. They were only worried about the president, and thought that I was being disrespectful. As a little kid, "president" meant nothing to me, *but that sheep did.* They slaughtered the sheep, and the day was ruined for me.

I respect people, nonhumans, and the environment alike. I've always believed that no individual is better than any other, and that we should respect all living things. No matter what religion, color, or class a person is, we are all the same. Similarly, we have no right to abuse nonhumans. I respect other animals and humans equally. We cannot make people love nonhumans, but we can ask people not to hurt other animals, and to just leave them alone.

I am a Christian Maronite, but I am not a very religious person. I believe there is only one God and not that each religion has their own God. I do not believe that any religion teaches people to abuse or torture nonhumans. Cruelty is learned. Cruelty is what people want to believe and practice. People who abuse nonhumans merely for entertainment are cowards. But these people can change. A dog is man's best friend. We need the love of nonhuman animals in our lives. I believe it makes us better people, more sensitive, and that nonhumans bring us together.

Fear is how kids are raised from a very young age; parents tell their kids, "Don't go near that dog, it will bite," or that the dog will infect them with horrible diseases.

My parents did not teach me to be afraid. On the contrary: My parents kept the door open for all strays. From the time I was a little girl, my mother used to let stray cats and dogs into the house. If they were wounded, she would treat them with whatever medication was available. That is what I grew up with, and that is what I do today.

Three years ago, when I was sitting in a sports bar, a friend told me that there were two girls standing at the door asking for me. I didn't know the two girls, so I said that they must be mistaken. He insisted that they wanted to talk to me. I went outside to meet them, and my life has never been the same since.

These two girls had heard from my ex-boss (in a nearby bar) that I liked nonhumans and was willing to take care of them. They asked if I wanted to work with them to start an animal organization. I was so excited! We are now friends and colleagues, and the founders of a registered charity organization, BETA (Beirut for the Ethical Treatment of Animals).

BETA has nine cofounders, and eight of us are females. We started BETA three years ago, and we are going strong. We have achieved much more than we ever imagined in these three long years. We rescue stray cats and dogs and try to find homes for them. We have one dog shelter and two cat shelters. We have created two committees; we call them "cat people" and they call us "dog people." Of course I help cats if I see one who needs rescuing, and sometimes I board cats at my house before they go to the shelter.

We also work with schools to educate kids about nonhumans. People in Lebanon are not very educated when it comes to nonhuman animals. Kids are the biggest problem—and our biggest hope for change. BETA works closely with the government to implement new laws against animal abuse, illegal pet shops, and the illegal trade in wildlife. Oh, and we don't just rescue dogs and cats; we've rescued horses, sea turtles, birds, hedgehogs, and primates.

At BETA we have thirty-five dedicated volunteers. Some come to the shelters regularly to care for the nonhumans, and some help with fundraising and educational work. We are a poor organization because we don't get much support from Lebanese people, or our government. We try to raise money through mailing list contacts, and through foreign organizations that help nonhumans, but we do not have a regular flow of income. Consequently, on top of rescuing nonhumans and running the dog shelter, we are constantly searching for ways to fund BETA.

I work at BETA full time. (All other cofounders have full-time jobs outside of BETA.) I am responsible for the dog shelter, adoptions, and rescues. Helena Hesayne, an architect, joined BETA one year ago. (She designed our future shelter, which we are raising money to build.) She shares duties with me, and also dedicates most of her time to BETA. Helena has three huskies of her own, and also uses her house to board stray animals. She's single; in Lebanon, no man allows his wife to use his house as a shelter. Myself, I have three dogs and three cats—but I am not married. I live alone so there is no one to tell me that I cannot have so many pets in my house. Helena is very positive, and gives that positive energy to the rest of us when we feel like hope is fading. I enjoy working with her very much; we go on rescues and take care of dogs together.

In the morning, I attend to my own dogs and cats before I head off to the dog shelter. At the shelter, I check on each dog to be sure that no one is sick and that everything is clean. Any sick dogs are taken to the vet, then treated in quarantine at the shelter. We walk the dogs and play with them in their pens. I welcome people who come to adopt a nonhuman and show them around. I explain the characteristics of the dogs and help them choose a suitable companion. If I am informed of an urgent rescue, I go immediately. On a normal day, I work eight or nine hours. On a busy day, I work ten to twelve hours. I also do lots of work from home, on my computer.

Working with nonhumans is what we love to do, but it is difficult and heartbreaking. Rescuing nonhuman animals leaves a pain in my heart that I must live with every day. Mostly it's the pain of guilt. Sometimes we have to turn dogs away. When I can't help an unwanted dog, I feel guilty, and I wonder what will happen to that poor being. We don't have enough money to be able to do all that we would like to do, or all that needs to be done, but hopefully someday we will. Sometimes my work hurts a little, other times it hurts a lot. But we have to be strong and not give up, no matter what. This line of work is tough, and depression sometimes gets the better of me, but we stick together; we help one another to get through the hard times, and we enjoy the good times as much as we can.

Adoptions are one of our biggest challenges. We spay and neuter all of our rescues. We also try to spay and neuter packs of dogs on the streets to lower the population. Unfortunately, we cannot afford to operate on all of the stray dogs in the streets. People in Lebanon like pedigreed dogs and cats. Most of our strays are either three-legged, blind, deaf, or crippled. But they are the sweetest dogs, and we love them unconditionally. Sometimes people from abroad adopt our nonhumans, and this is helpful. We fly with the dog or cat, delivering them to their new home.

To adopt a dog or cat from BETA, people must fill out an adoption form and pay $40. We review the adoption form, and if we feel that this is a good adoptee, we take the dog or cat to their house. If needed, we explain how to take care of their new family member. We follow up with home-checks to be sure things are going smoothly. If we see that the dog is being neglected or abused, we have every right to take him or her back to the shelter and search for a new home.

BETA also promotes vegetarianism. I've been a vegetarian for two years, and I love it. It just feels better. People ask me why I do it—the nonhuman is already dead, so who cares? But I know how they torture, kill, and transport livestock in the most horrible ways. I feel better knowing that I am not eating others who have suffered just for my pleasure. I've managed to convince some of my friends to be vegetarians, too. Now, they thank me for this change.

Once BETA rescued a baboon, and I became very attached to him; I named him Tom, and his name suited him. Tom was kept in a small, filthy cage next to a restaurant, where we watched him year after year, miserable and alone. He was extremely dirty and smelled like sewege. He was kept there merely for human entertainment. But I was not entertained. One day, the restaurant closed so they could do some renovations in the area. Tom was moved behind a garbage bin right next to the main street. He ate from what people threw at him, and was not provided with drinking water. So we stole Tom, and moved him to my friend's villa, placing his cage in the garden. No one lived there, and it was fenced, so it was a perfect place for him. For four months I took care of Tom, bringing him fruits and vegetables every day, and his favorite food, pumpkin seeds.

Baboons are incredible creatures. We developed a close bond. I came to know his preferences and desires, and also those things that he did not like, and what made him really angry. His facial expressions said it all. Sometimes I took friends over to see him, but he did not accept many of them. He used to hold my hand and rub it gently. He was jealous if a man was standing next to me.

Eventually BETA flew Tom to a sanctuary in Wales where he is clean and fluffy, happy and free. He has a lady baboon who was rescued by BETA from Tripoli, and they now have a baby baboon at the sanctuary. My experience with Tom was out of this world.

Recently, a kind woman who was out for a morning jog found a dog tied to a tree in the middle of a forest. He was a mongrel, tan color, with a rough face. She untied him, found a phone, and called BETA. We received her call at 9 a.m., and rushed to help the dog we named Scarface. It looked like someone had tied him there just to abuse him, with no food or water, in the middle of nowhere, leaving him to die a slow and agonizing death. He was badly beaten, and was nothing but skin and bones. He had a very deep, open wound in his neck from pulling desperately to escape. We took him to the vet, treated him, then placed him in a temporary home. Scarface is now at the shelter. He has four other furry friends in his play area, and he is an adorable, sweet dog. Hopefully, one day he will be adopted and will get to live with his own family.

Our most difficult work was during the summer of 2006, during the Israeli/Hezbollah war in Lebanon. The war broke out on July 13; we heard the first bomb. That night Marguerite Shaarawi, one of the cofounders, slept at my house so that we could work together if anything horrible happened. Many people left because of the war. Only four cofounders remained in Lebanon to help with rescues throughout the war. The others had to leave the country or were not able to leave the house because of family pressures and concerns.

As chance would have it, the dog shelter was located opposite the war zone. The dogs were panicking, and so were we! We had to relocate them quickly. Luckily, a caring German woman told us about an abandoned pig farm in a secluded and safe area. We checked out the site and found that it was big enough, but there were only a few walls, and lots of trash. We decided to bring the dogs there anyway, as we had no time to waste. We worked around the clock. A kind family, and dear friends of ours, Viola and John Barret, never left on the ship that was evacuating British citizens. They stayed behind and helped us from beginning to end. Even their son Glen, who came to Lebanon only for a few days, helped out. Working together, we cleaned out the abandoned pig farm in two days, with the help of many volunteers. Helena rounded up some workers from her company to build walls, cages, doors, windows, and bathrooms. Then we returned to the war zone, and with bombing just 400 meters away, transported all 150 dogs to the new shelter in one day. It was scary, but these dogs had already been abandoned at least once. We were responsible for their lives: we needed to bring them to safety.

We received many more rescues during the war. Lots of people fled, and they simply threw their dogs out onto the street. Others left their pets at home, locked up. We could not reach these trapped beings, but we knew how much they would suffer before dying of thirst and hunger. Every time the bombings stopped, Marguerite, Helena, and I would jump into a jeep packed with food and water, and rush into the war zone. We would have to act quickly; we needed to leave before the bombing stared again. It was risky, but the dogs and cats had to be fed.

The war zone was a ghost town. Fearing for their lives, everyone had left. The first time we drove into the war zone Hezbollah confronted us, thinking we were spies. We showed our IDs and our organization papers. These men were furious that we were feeding dogs and cats. Because so many people had fled, there was no food. The dogs and cats could not even find garbage to eat, which is what happens in war zones, and sometimes in normal circumstances, for stray dogs and cats. I have often seen dogs and cats in Lebanon going through garbage in search of scraps of food. We fed and watered the dogs and cats even though the men were angry. We also rescued a dog and two cats from an abandoned pet shop. The horrible owner had saved his own life from all possible harm, and left the nonhumans in his care trapped in the shop with nothing to eat or drink. We named the pet shop dog Grigio; he now lives in Pennsylvania. The two cats also live in the United States, with wonderful families who love and care for them.

During the war, BETA also rescued monkeys from a local zoo. There were only a few attendants left at the zoo, and they asked us for bags of food to help feed strays. It made us happy that they supported our work. They were nice people and we were thankful.

By the time the war was over we had 350 dogs at the shelter—a very full house, with dogs running around everywhere. We were tired and worn-out. We couldn't care for so many dogs; money was running out. Thankfully, donations helped, which we used for food, medications, spay/neuter, and vaccines. An American organization, Best Friends, flew 150 dogs and 150 cats by cargo plane to Utah. We were excited the night the dogs flew out, but when we had to put them in crates for their long journey, we were in tears. We cried for hours. Those dogs came to us in the worst possible condition, and we helped them. We loved them with all of our hearts. They have all been adopted in the United States, in homes with loving people who are giving them the care that they deserve. Still, we miss them very much.

Rescues continue, and we now have 220 dogs. People who do not care about what we are doing criticize us. They accuse us of wasting time on nonhumans. We hope this mentality will change. We try to explain that our work is helpful to our country and our people, and not harmful. Some understand. It takes time and energy, and that is part of our job, to open hearts and minds. If the abuse stops, the suffering stops. But we still have a very long way to go. Many people threw harsh words at us for caring for nonhuman animals while people were dying in a war zone, and many people do not understand why we continue to care for so many stray nonhumans, and our response is always the same: There are 6,000 organizations in Lebanon for humans, and only one for nonhumans.

CHAPTER 17

# Animal Ways

*Gay Bradshaw*

**Gay Bradshaw**, *PhD, is the founder and director of the Kerulos Center (www.kerulos. org) and author of* Elephants on the Edge: What Animals Teach Us About Humanity *(Yale University Press, 2009) and* Being Sanctuary: A Guide to Compassionate Living with Animal Kin *(2011). Her discovery of Post-Traumatic Stress Disorder (PTSD) in free-ranging African elephants established the field of trans-species science and psychology.*

Panama is a Yellow-naped Amazon parrot (*Amazona auropalliata*) nearing his sixties. When he was sold to our family, we were told he was about fifteen to twenty years old. Being wild-caught means that he has spent the majority of his life far away from his homeland, the verdant treetops of southern Mexico and Central America. Instead, Panama has lived thousands of miles north, bereft of his natal flock, in the company of a featherless human tribe. Similar to other wild-caught parrots, he was forcibly taken from his family and pressed into a steel-mesh cage, in the crush of other young birds, for shipment and commercial gain. More than half (some statistics indicate that the percentage is greater than 70 percent) of wild-caught parrots perish before they reach "pet" stores. The shock, terror, and hardship of capture tax every individual's mental and physical resilience. However, remarkably, Panama endured, and it can only be marveled how he survived.

177

I was entering my teens when we met. My mother and I were buying food in a local pet store for our rescued Embden goose, April, when we heard a well-articulated *"por favor"* usher from a brilliant green and yellow parrot, who was looking out from the bars of his cage with great beauty and soul. Within hours, he was riding back to our home outside Berkeley, California. In many ways, we have become two sides of the same coin, sharing much of the same history, twins by proximity, siblings by circumstance, friends through love.

One of the first things people remark when they see us together is how similar we sound and act. As Nobel Prize winner Francois Mauriac noted, this is hardly surprising: "We are molded and re-molded by those who have loved us; and though the love may pass, we are nevertheless their work, for good or for ill" (Mauriac 62). Neuroscience agrees albeit less poetically: Along with genes, the bonds we form and experiences go beyond skin-deep to sculpt brain and mind. Science has come to understand Mauriac's lyrical "molding" as one of the most important processes in growth and development across all species. At the level of the complex web of neurons and synapses, species lines blur.

Panama and I learned much from each other. Shared experiences of playing hide-and-go-seek, cuddling under the covers, gazing out into the dusk side by side, munching almonds, and singing in the shower have become neurobiologically etched into both of us. The eyes that meet, smiles and murmurings exchanged, and fresh scents of feather and skin inhaled in embrace, tune the delicate patterns and processes of our physiological beings, of the chemicals that flow through us. This melding of hearts and minds can be found throughout multispecies households, and reflects a profound, unconscious, interspecies connection.

Talking with each other is not always verbal. In fact, most exchanges appear almost like mind reading. Tom Dorrance, a cowboy of seventy-eight years, called by seasoned horse people the "original" horse whisperer, maintained that "the best thing I try to do is listen to the horse. I listen to how he's operating: What he's understanding or what he doesn't understand; what's bothering him and what isn't bothering him. I try to feel what the horse is feeling and operate from where the horse is" (Dorrance 13). Feeling. It is the felt world of meaning and commitment where we meet.

There was little room for the felt world that Panama and I shared in the career path that I chose. Unfortunately, much of childhood intuition and sensitivity submerge in the process of what philosopher Paul Shepard called the lifelong work of differentiating, which evolves as we mature under the pressure of collective acculturation. Relational nuances and their meaning—the sound of the wind shifting, the sudden cacophony of jays, the pungency of budding sage, and a million details of other animals, plants, air, water, and earth around us—become dulled by daily exposure to anorexic cityscapes and synthetic homes.

From the time I left for college, through my career as an environmental scientist, I straddled two worlds: a personal life of feeling, and the professional, disembodied world of mind. Despite its claims of universality, science is exceptionally exclusive. The epistemic yardstick used to define humanity is largely based on what science has insisted that other animals lack: language, culture, emotions, self-awareness, and a science of their own. This arbitrary, self-proclaimed measure dictates who has power and who does not in the world of humanity. Even now, as a new trans-species psychology emerges, declaring a common model of brain, behavior, and mind for all vertebrates (and scientific evidence is now indicating that we need to include invertebrates), other animals continue to be denied legal and ethical parity with the human animal. To renounce human uniqueness and privilege threatens modern Western culture as we know it. Hence, for most scholars, even those who devote a lifetime to the study of other species, it is much more comfortable and lucrative to maintain an artificial barrier between humanity and the rest of the animal world.

As time went on in my life as a scientist, it became clear that my work was not serving animals. More often than not, science seemed to impede my ability to change situations that endangered wildlife. For instance, despite expounding the fascination and beauty of wildlife, researchers have made a practice of caging and harming nonhumans in the quest for knowledge. While enslaving rats, birds, and other animals is a routine practice in the sciences, imprisonment for the sake of human knowledge exacts a terrible toll on the individuals we study. Almost by definition, these animals will suffer Complex Post-Traumatic Stress Disorder (C-PTSD), a condition shared by human prisoners of war, victims of domestic violence, and concentration camp survivors. In plain terms, C-PTSD holds the symptoms of devastating anguish, including death, that prisoners experience regardless of their species.

The brutality of scientific pursuits is not limited to captives. Many conservation approaches—zoos, translocations, culls (mass killings), and sustainable harvests (another version of mass killing)—have proven to be as damaging to wildlife as the problems they were purported to fix. As a result, elephants, lions, whales, wolves, parrots, and thousands of other animal communities teeter on the edge of extinction, undermined by psychological trauma and loss caused by scientific studies. Despite the veritable wealth of information readily accessible on the internet—and stored in dusty journals—the academic community at large perpetually seeks to mine yet more facts from the natural world in the hope of slowing increasingly widespread, human-induced environmental collapse. Countless conferences and events describe the deplorable plight of tigers, lions, seabirds, and scores of other species, while extinctions proceed relentlessly. Few conservation plans address the causes that underlie today's environmental problems—human overpopulation, consumerism, and the human assumption of privilege over all nonhuman species. Sadly, science has become a Cadillac on blocks—the finest engine, technology, and style with no way to move down the road, no way to help stop planetary destruction.

Yet change has come—radical change. The present social and ecological turmoil gripping us today is a sign of what science philosopher Thomas Kuhn calls a paradigm shift. A paradigm shift, such as that provided by the work of Galileo and Copernicus, catapults society into a completely different realm of thought and perception. Kuhn intentionally evokes an image of strife and struggle when he refers to this process as a scientific revolution. Similar to any other knowledge system, science embodies the values and beliefs of its human creators and users. In other words, knowledge is not arbitrary, but exists in a particular frame of reference. By upholding the belief that animals are intellectually and emotionally inferior to humans, science provides Western culture an ethical rationale for reducing animals to servitude, for using animals as food and clothing, as petri dishes in lieu of humans.

Now, scientific theory and data have demonstrated that other species are on a par with humans in morally relevant ways, and in so doing, have inadvertently demanded a translation of this knowledge into action—action that will transform science. By recognizing commonality among all species, modern humanity has begun to remember our profound kinship with all life. Piece by piece, the millennia-old perceptual and conceptual architecture that justified animal oppression is being dismantled, and the beginnings of a new identity emerge. This personal recognition inspired me to leave mainstream science.

With this realization, I understood that I had become part of the problem. I could not, in good faith, continue on this path, so I shifted my focus: To try and see the world through the eyes of other animals by understanding animal experience from the perspective of traumatology. What I saw was horrifying. The roars of tigers behind zoo bars, the swaying of elephants in concrete exhibits, and screaming parrots in pet store cages were not just unhappy animals, but rather souls in anguish from human-imposed suffering. The brokenhearted lions who howled in grief at the loss of a companion who was killed by park rangers symbolized a much more widespread breakdown in wildlife societies. Trans-species psychology and traumatology, the study of animal mental and emotional experience—this was science, but science with open eyes and an honest heart.

Traumatology is considered radical even in the area of human studies because the field is intrinsically political. As pioneer traumatologist Judith Herman notes, psychological trauma is an "affliction of the powerless" (Herman 27). Traumatology is different from many other scientific studies because it probes beyond the suffering individual to identify underlying causes, and in so doing, begins to question basic assumptions: What are the institutions and ideologies that cause brain-altering stress and misery? What are the beliefs and social customs that encourage someone to capture a sentient being who has a family, and life of his or her own, and subject this individual to torture and pain?

The study of animal trauma, of animals as victims of violence, compels a fundamental re-examination of contemporary human ethics and assumptions. Even language. I now see "culls" as mass killings and genocide, "translocation" as deportation, "vivisection" and "captivity" as torture and imprisonment, and "parks" as ghettos for wildlife refugees. In this shift, I have entered a trans-species world where conventional separations between species no longer hold. The boundary between science and animal rights dissolves in trans-species psychology.

Although trauma studies voice what both my heart and my mind know, the journey has not been without burdens. This has been a path, as a colleague once remarked wryly, fraught with the loneliness of the long-distance thinker. Not only the isolation of my work, but the work itself is difficult: I watch, listen to, and write about animals in crisis and trauma, with little to no hope of helping them beyond providing a few individuals with homes. Mostly, I can only document their testimonies. I listened to the trials and sufferings of Jeannie, a chimpanzee who survived years at a biomedical laboratory, where she was forced to be the subject for intensive and invasive research, including repeated vaginal washes; multiple cervical, liver punch, wedge, and lymph node biopsies; and intentional infection with HIV and hepatitis viruses. In total, she experienced over 200 "knockdowns" (i.e., anesthetization with a dart gun). I read about the traumas of Molly, a wild-caught Moluccan cockatoo. When his human guardians moved to Hawaii without him, abandoning him, Molly eventually committed suicide by picking at his breast until he bled to death. These, and countless other stories of hard-hearted human behaviors and nonhuman victims, comprise the focus of my work.

Nonhuman animals need us to bring change, to carry animal voices to the ears of a reluctant humanity. These horrors will never disappear if we ignore them, or pretend they don't exist, or simply refuse to know what goes on in our laboratories. For me, working in the realms of trans-species studies, in what psychologist Jerome Bernstein calls "the borderland," has turned the silence in which animal genocides normally take place into a deafening roar (Bernstein). Obscuring human brutality that is fundamental to Western culture—Thanksgiving celebrations, rodeos, barbeques, invisible windows, fast-moving cars, human sprawl, frog leaping contests, circuses—wordlessly corrodes the soul, and devastates other individuals and communities. Modern life makes it easy to be shocked at a program about elephant slaughter, "fryer" chickens in cramped cages, or cats and frogs vivisected in school biology classes, and yet, at the same time, promotes a lifestyle that contributes to these very practices. Modern Western life dulls our natural capacity for empathy and care.

The animal rights movement is about coming to our senses, about understanding the subtle connections that link the horror of dolphin hunts with the sensation of Sea World and a seafood dinner. With new knowledge, we are asked to move beyond outdated understandings to action. We are asked to relearn what many have known since time began: All beings are connected; all beings feel. The trans-species scientific paradigm is making a simple point: Whatever we imagined made us different from all other creatures is a fantasy.

Do I think that parrots, elephants, and other animals will have a chance to survive? Not unless we each make radical changes in the way we live. Now. The time for excuses is well over. It is time for change based on new understandings. Why not live according to what we now know to be true?

## References

Bernstein, Jerome. *Living in the Borderland: The Pathological and the Sacred in Our Understanding of Consciousness.* Philadelphia: Brunner-Routledge, 2005.
Bradshaw, Gay. *Elephants on the Edge: What Animals Teach Us About Humanity.* New Haven: Yale University Press, 2009.
———. "We, Matata: Bicultural Living Amongst Apes." *Spring* 83 (2010): 162–182.
Bradshaw, Gay, et al. "Building an Inner Sanctuary: Trauma-induced Symptoms in Nonhuman Great Apes. *Journal of Trauma and Dissociation* 9.1 (2008): 9–34.
Bradshaw, Gay, et al. "Developmental Context Effects on Bicultural Post-Trauma Self Repair in Chimpanzees. *Developmental Psychology* 45 (2009): 1376–1388.

Bradshaw, Gay, and Allen N. Schore. "How Elephants are Opening Doors: Developmental Neuroethology, Attachment, and Social Context." *Ethology* 113 (2007): 426–436.

Bradshaw, Gay, and Barbara L. Finlay. "Natural Symmetry." *Nature* (2005): 435:149.

Bradshaw, Gay, and Mary Watkins. "Trans-species Psychology: Theory and Praxis." *Psyche & Nature* 75 (2006): 69–94.

Bradshaw, Gay, and R. M. Sapolsky. "Mirror, Mirror." *American Scientist* 94.6 (2006): 487–489.

Dorrance, Tom, and Milly Hunt Porter. *True Unity: Willing Communication Between Horse and Human.* Bruneau, ID: Give-It-A-Go Enterprises, 1987.

Herman, Judith. *Trauma and Recovery: The Aftermath of Violence—from Domestic Abuse to Political Terror.* New York: Basic Books, 1992.

Kuhn, Thomas. *The Structure of Scientific Revolutions.* Chicago: University of Chicago Press, 1962.

Mauriac, Francois. *The Desert of Love.* Paris: Metheun, 1984.

## Chapter 18

# From the Files of Agent Nerd

*Michele Rokke*

**Michele Rokke** *evolved from an "animal lover" in a rural Minnesota town to an undercover investigator for People for the Ethical Treatment of Animals (PETA) and other animal advocacy organizations, and finally became an activist at large. Her work has exposed cruel and unethical practices in factory farming, the animal entertainment industry, Pregnant Mares' Urine (PMU) farms, biomedical research, and contract research (product testing) laboratories. Always an animal advocate, she has recently worked as a veterinary technician for local spay/neuter programs, and is currently rehabilitating two rescued dogs (and repairing systems that let these dogs down) in Santa Fe, New Mexico, where she lives with her husband and four canine companions.*

I was born in the summer of 1966. Vietnam, communism, and spy scandals filled the news. Martin Luther King Jr. and others bravely led civil rights marches. The Supreme Court ruled that police must Mirandize suspects and the Freedom of Information Act was signed into law. The Beatles played their final concert while the status of "protest" singers like Bob Dylan was on the rise. The National Organization for Women was founded and women of the United States of America were on the horizon of symbolically burning their bras to move forward their own liberation—even now, I would have to purchase a bra in order to participate.

Perhaps because of the altruistic fervor and the camaraderie of that period of war demonstrations and empowerment and civil rights, I felt I was born well past the time I should have been. I felt I belonged to that generation who said, "No. This is not how things are going to be." It isn't that I wanted to be a rebel. In fact, I am just the opposite, preferring anonymity and quiet to fame and confrontation. But, I felt allied with those people two decades my senior who challenged the status quo. I knew I belonged in a revolution, a movement for social change—something that was good and unselfish and proactive.

I was just a small child when I had my first epiphany about my behavior and the way it affects nonhuman animals. I didn't know it at the time, but what happened, that little, almost nonevent, has always bothered me.

One night—maybe I was sick or worried about the ghosts in the closet in my bedroom—my parents put me to bed in their room. I was playing with our family poodle, Snooky, just a year younger than myself—she with more conviction than I. I remember both of us under the crisp sheets, the light and sounds from the living room down the hall bleeding into the room, the puppy jumping on me and pulling my hand with her mouth. Probably just to get attention rather than to voice an actual threat, I called for help. My mother came in, surely onto my insincere cries, and grabbed the puppy by the collar, immediately taking her from the room in silence. I was left alone. No words of consolation. No special friend. No playmate. Worst of all, the perfunctory way my mother, a kind woman, had grabbed the dog made me worry that my plea for attention had caused unintended consequences for my best and most innocent friend. I worried about putting the blame on my puppy and cried for real over my selfish actions.

Snooky was why I *was*. Though I swore at the time I would always remember her, today I don't recall as much as I hoped—sans family legend—much as I have trouble recalling my grandmother who died when I was ten.

However, I will never forget Snooky. We were inseparable. She was the sage, hidden beneath charcoal-colored curls, tolerating a typical family, within which she was lowest in the hierarchy. I spent hours serenading her with Olivia Newton John's "I Honestly Love You" on my portable green and white battery-operated record player. She, stretched out on the end of my twin bed, or, curled in the orange beanbag chair next to it, looking less than interested, even embarrassed, as I pledged always to take care of her.

My undying love for this special childhood friend helped shape me. Having a real connection with a little dog that included concern, love, and friendship for seventeen formative years imprinted my soul with compassion.

We were a normal family of four (five including Snooky, which I always do mentally) living in a small, rural Minnesota town, surrounded by cornfields, dairy farms, and the occasional hog farm. My parents provided us with a Norman Rockwell life. We were those photos freeze-framed on the *Saturday Evening Post* depicting a happy, untroubled family skating on a lake with a dog pulling playfully on someone's scarf.

Both of my parents worked. My Dad hunted and fished. My sister and I fished, too. I was the one who was never afraid to jam the wriggling worm onto the barbed fishhook, over and over again, though my Dad was the one who had to pull the sharp hook from the lips of the unsuspecting sunfish living under the dock. Sometimes we fed the "sunnies" oatmeal and bread (wayward ants weren't safe during these times, either), marveling at their individuality as they smacked at the unexpected morsels we tossed in, only to throw in sharp hooks with "bait" attached later the same evening.

In those days, I had periodic outbursts when I witnessed cruel behavior, like seeing a neighbor smack his new "hunting dog" puppy around during a "training" session and wanting to run across the street and hit him back. My mother stopped me, but I had trouble understanding why it was okay to do nothing while the puppy's head reeled with each blow.

A few years later, I was sent to my room when a notorious Green Peace ad, vividly depicting the bloody slaughter of baby seals in Canada, aired on TV. After my older sister tried to look away and quickly change the channel, I remember fighting with her, saying "Just because you don't see it, doesn't mean it's not happening." I was summarily sent to my room as punishment, but Snooky went with me, so I didn't mind.

Those were good years. I didn't know much about the scope and depth of nonhuman suffering; I didn't recognize the depth of my own naiveté. My ignorance came to a screeching halt when I was twelve.

My cousin, Louise Hoven, came home from Hollywood for Christmas. She was pursuing an acting career with great success, landing walk-on roles in popular television shows like *Baretta* and *Starsky & Hutch*, scoring a regular role on *General Hospital* during the infamous Luke and Laura years, as well as a sitcom that ran for a whole season before being cancelled. I'll never forget how Louise, during Christmas dinner, talked about vegetarianism and tofu and the "poor little animals." That's when everything started to fall into place.

My folks quickly got a subscription to *Vegetarian Times* (a progressive action, at that time, for parents of a twelve-year-old vegetarian in a farming community). My habits and choices changed as information slowly found me about how I was impacting nonhumans. I refused to dissect a live frog in high school biology and learned to channel anger into action.

In my early twenties, my love of nonhuman animals led to volunteer work at a local humane society that was no-kill. I was rabidly opposed to euthanasia, though I could think of no alternative for the millions of existing homeless nonhumans.

Even volunteer hours were not satisfying my need to help nonhuman animals, although I was spending more time on nonhuman issues than at my job as a hairstylist. Eventually, I found my way to People for the Ethical Treatment of Animals (PETA) as an intern and then an employee. I was hired as an "undercover investigator" and left everything I knew within a few days of being called by Mary Beth Sweetland, then director of PETA's research and investigations department.

I worked for PETA for four years as an investigator, abandoning a lucrative career and friends and family without a second thought and little explanation for my sudden departure. I felt lucky to find my path. Agent Nerd (that's what I used to call myself) was born.

I spent all of my free time thinking about ways to conceal the tiny pinhole-lens camera and comparably giant recorder, essential to my new craft. Back then, special cameras could be easily fitted into something about the size of a matchbook, but the images had to be sent somewhere to be recorded. Everything had to be powered, typically by heavy batteries, leaving me with pounds of equipment to conceal. I used to think it would be so easy if I had a voluptuous body and once tried to stuff an enormous bra, loaded with equipment packed in a lot of socks. Little did I, a flat-chested woman, know that big boobs, fake or not, attract attention. At first I worried people were sneaking peeks at the tiny hole I cut in the cleavage area of my black shirt but then decided I'd done a pretty good job turning all that gear into something natural looking. I had never had so many people, men and women, check me out as I did the day I tried this Agent Nerd invention. I would have been better off burning that bra.

Not long after, as I passed a rendering plant, I saw a frightened pig jump from a pile of carcasses on the loading dock and impulsively decided to do a "jog by." I pulled the car over and hastily threw on a fanny pack, equipped with covert camera gear, and "casually" jogged (at top speed) across the parking lot. By the time I got there, an employee was standing over the now dead pig, pointing at me with a bloody knife. My "jog by" had dislodged wires in my gear and smoke was rolling from the pack strapped to my waist. Agent Nerd strikes again.

As a field investigator, I lived on the road, in my car, in my tent, in awful cheap motels, and in crummy apartments—more than one of which the landlords wouldn't even show me after dark, fearing the location and possible crime. I liked the anonymity and the work itself. I liked that I was able to contain my emotions when it mattered and document what I saw, knowing the result of the work was cumulative and systemic, helping to improve the lives of nonhuman animals years after I had come and gone.

I had to go into the work knowing I couldn't save them all. Realistically, I probably wouldn't be able to save any of the nonhumans I met. I was working to save those destined to come after; it was the big picture that mattered. I tried to set aside my own emotions and self, mastering robotic responses in the midst of chaos, while staying true to my new precept of emotional detachment, no matter the cost. Those who knew me before, and have known me since, will probably contend the work took its toll.

I have untold scenes of suffering freeze-framed in my mind. I feel the misery those nonhuman animals endured as intensely now as I did then, and I am always glad I was there to bear witness. There is no such thing as a "worst case of cruelty"—they are all the worst. Whatever suffering any individual is going through at any time is painful and degrading and deprives a sentient being of quality of life. Then, until we act to effect real change, another moment passes and there is still more, and worse, cruelty.

While ignorance is thought to be bliss, knowledge of nonhuman suffering inevitably leads to catharsis—for activists and "pre-activists." Although we are exposed to cruelty in countless ways, there seems to be "that one" incident—a specific cathartic moment when our innocence is lost and we are morally forced into activism, into action. I have learned that action and activism are empowering.

I have never felt more powerless than during a "practice" procedure I witnessed in an animal laboratory. To this day, I cannot in any way rationalize or accept or assimilate what I saw being done to a little beagle on an ordinary day in that laboratory. It is wrong on every level and then starts all over again.

A new experiment mandated vaginal insertion of a test substance in beagle dogs. At the laboratory, none of the entry-level employees who conduct these so-called scientific procedures had performed this procedure before, nor had they been trained in it by someone who had. When I walked down the hallway, I saw five or six employees, mostly men—some women, holding a small female beagle on a cart, poking and prodding and snickering and exclaiming inappropriately about the dog's genitalia. The dog had pulled her head down into her body as far as she could and was staring vacantly at a lost spot at the bottom of the wall as they held her down and raped her in preparation for a fatal rape that would take weeks, probably months, to finalize. After suffering all manner of abuse, the dog would eventually have her throat slit, with choice bits of her body held back for potential review if legal claims should require the standard CYA (cover your ass) defense common in the animal testing industry. The rape of that beagle is what animal testing looks like; there is nothing scientific about it.

Based on my time in animal labs, I can attest unequivocally that animal testing is a fraudulent system, designed to garner profits, rather than structured as true science. The goal of product testing in the laboratory is to gain return business (contracts) from companies that have demonstrated to the government they have paid to have a sizeable cache of data, however meaningless, produced using nonhuman tests. This allows their product to be rubber-stamped and sent to market for use in, by, or on unsuspecting humans, regardless of safety or efficacy and regardless of nonhuman suffering.

I've watched lab workers falsify data, and I've seen the haphazard application of cruel nonhuman tests consumers have been duped into trusting. Behind laboratory doors, employees often declared, "Just because something works in an animal doesn't mean it will work in a human being." This is a sad reality proven time and time again as medicines and products are pulled from the market, or relabeled, leaving untold numbers of dead or damaged gullible consumers in their wake. Vioxx (a medication for arthritis recalled in 2004 after it was found to increase the risk of heart attack and stroke in human beings) and Fen-Phen (a diet drug linked to heart-valve abnormalities) are just two examples out of thousands of drugs recalled, or relabeled, after consumer use. Conversely, products such as aspirin and penicillin (proved safe for use in humans through use in humans) would never have made it to the market if nonhuman tests had been relied upon.

The first time a human being uses any product or drug is the first time anyone knows that product's impact, no matter how many nonhuman animals suffered and died beforehand. Anyone truly caring about their partner, child, parent, sibling, or loved one will demand safe and accurate non–animal based research instead of the scam of current nonhuman-based tests. Nonhuman research is a multi-million dollar pit of slop science, continuously cycling within, endangering human beings. The animal research industry is composed of a complex web of businesses and corporations that profit by breeding, selling, housing, torturing, and disposing of nonhumans during the course of these bogus experiments.

Regardless of the emotional distance I tried to maintain, certain nonhumans I met in my undercover days touched me deeply. Though each being is unique, we adopt that one dog or cat who speaks to us from the cage at the shelter. While we wish only good things for all of the rest in the shelter, or in my case the laboratory, barn, shed, circus, farm ... there is always that one, or those two ... or three ...

Buddy, a primate I took care of in my laboratory days, still brings the weight of remorse. While I was there I had fantasies about taking him out of the torture chamber. He was such a wise old soul. He didn't belong there; none of them did, and especially not my Buddy. When he looked into my eyes and reached out to groom my hair or my eyebrows during a day that was hellish for both of us there was a sickening realization of how stuck we both were.

Of course I couldn't take Buddy out. I was an observer. I couldn't risk compromising all the good that could be accomplished by documenting and distributing the cold hard truth of animal research, even to save my own little soul buddy. One day in May, the door on his empty cage hung open and I knew he was gone. His throat slit, his body emptied of blood and skinned. The world had another mouthwash.

Before I met Buddy, I once sat for hours, in the middle of nowhere, with a little cinnamon-colored steer, downed on a transport truck at a feedlot, his body discarded in the bone-pile, which wasn't a bone-pile as much as a sizzling puddle of lye dissolving flesh and bone while the little steer moaned in agony and terror. All these years later, I can't forget him. After the moon has risen there is a certain light that comes into the sky, bringing with it the sound of his misery echoing in my head.

A few years later, there was a little terrier (think Toto in the *Wizard of Oz*), snug in my arms, his nose pressed firmly into my neck at a puppy mill somewhere in the Midwest. He hadn't turned out to be a productive breeder and was slated for auction, which surely meant miserable confinement and neglect at another breeding farm, or painful, invasive procedures under the label of medical research, or the horror of being ripped apart as bait to train fighting dogs, or being slaughtered for human consumption ... the list of potential fates lengthy and awful. He needed so badly to leave there with me; it was as if he willed himself invisible in my arms. I didn't buy him from the owners and I didn't go back for him. Leaving him behind is one of my few, true regrets, and I agonize still about his eventual fate.

Aside from my personal doubts about individual animals who tested my strength and marked my heart, in the work itself, I admit I have made errors and hold those errors as closely as the nonhuman friends I lost along the way.

I can see clearly a veterinarian and an entry-level technician falsifying data and laughing about an animal's suffering as they stay one step ahead of a visiting United States Department of Agriculture (USDA) inspector. Just down the hall a room full of beagles are dismembered as the dog next in line quakes uncontrollably, seconds from death and positioned on a table just inches from the bloody carcasses of his cellmates, hearing the buzz of a saw rip through a skull; seeing a heap of bloody tri-colored skin pushed impatiently from a bloody table; smelling the terror permeating the room. These memories are closely held, not because they are worse than others, but because I had failed to properly connect a battery to my well-hidden video equipment that morning, forever locking the images solely in my own head.

Other errors are blissfully more comical and even ridiculous; even the worst experiences had their lighter side.

After leaving one laboratory, the story of intrinsic nonhuman abuse and unethical practices broke. Activist friends and I were able to have some laughs of our own wondering how many employees arrived at the staff Halloween party dressed as the odd PETA investigator, with her oversized sweater, ubiquitous coffee cup, ridiculous floppy hat, and inevitable tote bag—all props contrived to host essential gear rather than chosen for comfort, and certainly not for style. The ability to discard one's ego is absolutely part of the unwritten job description for covert work. How else could Agent Nerd laugh at nicknames like "Ms. Tote" and "Floppy Toppy," or endure outright ridicule over the strange outfits that helped me to catch evidence of abuse, time and time again.

During the war in Lebanon in 2006, PETA asked me to help rescue dogs, cats, and other "pets" abandoned by their humans, who were frantically escaping the war zone. Unbelievably, just as in the Gulf Coast during the hurricanes the year before, evacuees were not allowed to leave with their companion animals. One morning in Beirut, after an especially volatile spell of bombing shook the hotel throughout the night, I was out on the streets and had my first overwhelming sense of fear in the war zone. A chilling look from a woman and an equally chilling sense of déjà vu ominously warning me not to cross the next intersection sent me scurrying back to the hotel.

From the balcony I heard random chanting on a bullhorn and was certain the bad vibe I felt on the street would lead to something awful—dramatic broadcast news stories of old fueling my fear fantasy. A beat-up blue pickup passed under the window and the chanting grew louder, sending my imagination spiraling. After a short time hiding in my room, I swallowed my fear and picked up my backpack, loaded with cat and dog food. In this state of crisis, I figured this might be my last chance to leave food for abandoned nonhumans.

I was dozens of blocks down the street when the same blue truck careened around the corner just in front of me, the chanting from the speaker on the truck earsplitting. Frozen with fear, in my bright PETA T-shirt and overstuffed backpack, I couldn't read the Arabic lettering on the white sign, but could clearly see bright drawings of tomatoes, zucchini, and peppers. The truck held vendors selling vegetables.

I spent many post-PETA years working for Animal Protection of New Mexico on everything from cruelty cases, to law enforcement training, to legislative work. I worked with administrations across the state to offer police officers groundbreaking training on New Mexico's felony animal cruelty law. My office quickly became a resource for risk managers, state police officers, livestock inspectors, mayors, and other government decision makers. The lack of infrastructure in animal control departments was a glaring disconnect that led to legislation creating an Animal Sheltering Services Board (ASSB). The ASSB provides critical oversight and training for animal shelter staff to ensure nonhumans are humanely treated in the animal control system, as well as establishing a state sterilization fund to help control the overpopulation of companion animals. The collaborative nature of our work helped create a separate program to protect nonhumans and their guardians victimized by domestic violence.

We often speak of breaking the cycle of abuse in reference to the link between animal cruelty and family violence. Our society has more cycles of abuse than just this one, which is now, finally, widely acknowledged by professionals. Our history is structured on cycles of abuse that allow for rationalization and for gratuitous behavior to be justified; to be subsequently dismissed as habit, no matter the suffering, because it has been named and long-held. Animal testing is one example; intensively confining certain nonhumans, subjecting them to all manner of cruelty under the label of "standard industry practice" before eating their flesh is another.

Human beings accept, without dissent, the most heinous practices as "status quo." Without asking for more information, we let industries and governments spoon-feed us just the information we want to hear. Because it is easier and we are more selfish than altruistic, we have become a weak and thoughtless society. We are self-indulgent to the point of excusing behavior rather than questioning it. The challenge is admitting that we are part of the continuum of abuse when we close our eyes to it, shut down, fail to demand accountability, fail to accept the responsibility of change.

Just as my sister wanted to look away from the slaughter of baby seals, for years I wanted to look away from the euthanasia of homeless nonhumans. More than twenty years ago, I was stridently opposed to euthanasia, and have since had to assimilate some hard realities into my idealism, and accept *that* painful responsibility of change. I admire compassionate realists who have the courage to perform, allow, and accept euthanasia when anything else would compromise quality of life and bring suffering. Once, I could not look at euthanasia, now I cannot, in good conscience, look away.

Euthanasia has become one of three divisive issues causing heartache and slowing progress within the animal rights movement. The other two painful and emotive issues are direct action and animal welfare versus abolition. Conflicts like these turn altruistic struggles into egocentric battles, destroying consensus.

It takes many actions on many levels to truly make historic change. There will never be one single person or action that resolves the myriad of issues harming our animal friends. We are all important in the fight—each voice, each action. If we become apathetic or denigrate the work of our colleagues, instead of proactively carrying on our own work, our nonhuman friends will never escape abuse.

I believe in animal liberation and support nonviolent action, as well as safe direct action to achieve that goal. After years of witnessing cruel practices entrenched in a system that is institutionalized and designed to desensitize participating humans, I am more committed than ever to end animal suffering. Current laws have been crafted to penalize free speech and work to protect abusers rather than to protect sentient beings; these laws must be challenged. In order to change the status quo, the fight must be undertaken on every level. I applaud those brave folks who work outside of the box—risking time inside of one, in pursuit of animal liberation.

The people I most respect work in their communities, daily, to improve the lives of nonhumans. I admire those who tirelessly attend demonstrations and model compassion through a vegan lifestyle, who consistently make time to get involved in federal, state, and local processes to effect change and who take ownership of animal suffering in whatever form it appears—they are the real heroes of this movement.

Now I realize that I belong to the appropriate generation, challenging *this* status quo, advocating for animal liberation. I know I am a woman who belongs to *this* generation making change. Animal activists are setting aside comfort and personal ambition to create a status quo that does no harm, nor allows harm to other sentient beings living among us. When faced with animal suffering, I am driven from within to say "No. That is not how things are going to be." I am an animal liberationist and I was born at the right time.

# Index

Ace Farms, 57–58, 60
American Anti-Vivisection Society (AAVS), 23
American Society for the Prevention of Cruelty to Animals (ASPCA), 65
Animal Acres, 62–69
Animal Concerns Research and Education Society in Singapore (ACRES), 145–146
Animal Liberation Victoria (ALV), 48
Animal Protection of New Mexico, 193
Animal Sheltering Services Board (ASSB), 193
ASPCA. *See* American Society for the Prevention of Cruelty to Animals

Beirut for the Ethical Treatment of Animals (BETA), 171–175
*Beloved* (Morrison), 39
Best Friends, 175
Boone, Allen, 93
"Broilers": living conditions, 13–14; stimulated growth, 13
Brontë, Emily, 38
Buckeye Egg Corporation, 55–56
Buckeye Egg Farm, 64–65
Buddhism, 115
Burns, Vicki, 41

"cage free," 17–19
"cage layer fatigue," 11–12

Cameroon, 120
Cattle: number injured, 16; number killed each hour, 15. *See also* Cows
Chickens: aviaries, 53; "cage layer fatigue," 11–12; debeaking, 11; "free range," 17; in Ohio, 56–59; living conditions, 11; methods of slaughter, 15; number killed per hour, 15; ovulation rates, 11–12; percent exploited yearly, 10; rescue, 65–67; yearly egg production, 11. *See also* "Laying" hens; "broilers"
China, 52
Christian Vegetarian Association, 90
Cobbe, Francis, 22–23
Coe, Sue, 40
Complex Post-Traumatic Stress Disorder (C-PTSD), 179
*Cosco Buson*, 113. *See also* San Francisco Bay Bridge
Cows: dairy, 6; exploitation, 87–88; forced impregnation, 8; genetic manipulation, 7; in India, 155–156; mutilation, 7; veal, 6. *See also* Cattle
CRO (contract research organization), 189, 192

*Dead Meat* (Coe), 40
dogs, 119
*Diet for a New America* (Robbins), 40
"The Dungeons of Alpine Poultry" (television) 50

electricity, 15
Emerson, Ralph Waldo, 38
euthanasia, 194

Factory farming: "broilers," 13–14; cattle, number slaughtered, 15–16; cows, 6–9; hens, 48–50; Humane Slaughter Act violations, 14–15; number exploited, 10–13; pigs, number slaughtered, 9; pneumonia, 10; sows, 9–10; transport of animals, 14–15
Farm Sanctuary, 26, 61–62
feminism: 1–6; 19–25
fertilizer, 12
fish, 97–98
"Fit for Life" (Diamond), 110
Friends of the Earth Malaysia (FOEM), 27, 117–121. *See also* Sahabat Alam Malaysia (SAM)
"free range," 17–19

goats, 67–68
Goodall, Jane, 77, 126
groupers, 96–97. *See* Red groupers

hens, 15, 17–18, 48–50. *See also* Chickens
hierarchies: feminism and, 5; gender exploitation and, 5; patriarchy, 3–6
*Hinch at Seven* (television), 50
Hinduism, 156
Holiday, Billie, 166
Horses: mares used for Premarin, 2; number of slaughtered foals, 2
Humane Farming Association (HFA), 26, 75–77
Humane Slaughter Act (HSA): Christine Stevens, 77; enforcement investigation, 74–75;
percentage of exempt birds, 14;
hunting, 2-3
Huntington Life Sciences (HLS), 162–163. *See also* Life Sciences Research

International Primate Protection League (IPPL), 133
Ireland, 99

Justice for All Species (JAS), 164–165

kaparot, 59
Kenya, 120
Kerulos Center, 177
King, Martin Luther, Jr., 164
*Kinship with All Life* (Boone), 93
Kuhn, Thomas, 180

Lancaster Stockyard, 61
Life Sciences Research, 162

*madaris*, 155
Malacca, 120
*Malay Mail* (newspaper), 118
male dominance. *See* Patriarchy
Manipulation: genetic, 7; biological, 11
Marcus, Erik, 162
Marine Mammal Center, 110–113
margays, 136
Mauriac, Francois, 178
McGreal, Shirley, 133
*Meet Your Meat* (PETA), 163–164
Melville, Herman, 39
menopause, 2
Mercy for Animals, 7
*Moby Dick* (Melville), 39
Moltmann, Jurgen, 93
monkeys, 118. *See also* Talkin' Monkeys Project and primates
Moore, Paula, 100
Morrison, Toni, 39

National Hip Hop Political Convention, 165
National Institute of Virology, 155
"natural," 17
Nigeria, 120

objectification, 3–6
Open Rescue, 45–47, 50, 53–54
"organic," 16–17
oxycotin, 156

Patriarchy: culture, 2; feminism and, 5; hunting and animal exploitation,

2–3; indifference, 20. *See also* Hierarchies
Peaceable Kingdom, 27
Penang Society for the Prevention of Cruelty to Animals (RSPCA), 117
People for the Ethical Treatment of Animals (PETA), 100–103, 153–156, 163–164, 188, 192
Pierson, Christine, 135–136
Pigs: HFA investigation, 76–77; living conditions, 51–52; number slaughtered, 9; overcrowding, 10; percentage factory farmed, 9; pneumonia rates, 10; transgenic, 10. *See* Sows
Premarin (Prempro): foals slaughtered (statistics), 2; manufacture of, 2
Primate Freedom Tour, 29
primates, 126–130. *See also* Talkin' Monkeys Project
Primates for Primates, 134

Quit-Stalling campaign, 41

rBGH (recombinant bovine growth hormone), 8
rBST (recombinant bovine somatotropin), 8
red groupers, 96–97
Regan, Tom, 79
Reiki, 166
reproduction, 2–21
Royal Indian Circus, 119

Safari World, 121
Sahabat Alam Malaysia (SAM), 117–121
San Francisco Bay Bridge, 113–114
"Say Goodbye" (documentary), 72
School of Biological Sciences at Queen's University, 99
Schweitzer, Albert, 78, 157
Sea animals: numbers consumed, 95; numbers killed, 95

seals, 111–113
sexism, 3–6
slaughterhouse: *See* Factory farming
social justice, 21–24
Society for the Protection of Animals Liable to Vivisection (SPALV), 23
Sows: living conditions, 9; parable, 78. *See also* Pigs
Stevens, Christine, 77. *See* Humane Slaughter Act
Stop Huntingdon Animal Cruelty (SHAC), 164
"Strange Fruit" (Holiday), 166–167
Strongheart, 93–94
Students Against Cruelty to Animals (SACA), 161–162

Taiping Four, 120
Talkin' Monkeys Project, Inc., 129–130
Trade Record Analysis for Flora and Fauna in Commerce (TRAFFIC), 119
transport of animals, 14–15
traumatology, 180–181
turkeys, 15

Veal Farm, 80
*Vegan: The New Ethics of Eating* (Marcus), 162
*Vivisection of America* (Cobbe), 22

Ward Egg Ranch, 12
White, Caroline, 23
Wildlife Friends of Thailand (WFFT), 142
Winnipeg Humane Society (WHS), 41
*Wuthering Heights* (Brontë), 38
Wyeth-Ayerst Laboratories, Inc., 2. *See also* Premarin

Xenotransplantation, 135

Yom Kippur, 59

# About the Editor

Lisa Kemmerer, PhD, is a philosopher-activist, artist, and lover of wild places, who has hiked, biked, kayaked, backpacked, and traveled widely. She is the author of *In Search of Consistency: Ethics and Animals* (Brill 2006) and *Religion and Animals: Rightful Relations* (Oxford 2011), and she has edited several other anthologies, including *Sister Species: Women, Animals, and Social Justice* (University of Illinois Press 2011). Kemmerer is currently Associate Professor of Philosophy and Religions at Montana State University–Billings.